WORLD WAR II
A GLOBAL PERSPECTIVE

Donald L. Layton
Indiana State University

KENDALL/HUNT PUBLISHING COMPANY
4050 Westmark Drive   Dubuque, Iowa 52002

For Martha

Copyright © 1995, 1998 by Kendall/Hunt Publishing Company

ISBN 0-7872-1942-8

All rights reserved. No part of this publication may be reproduced, stored in a retrieval system, or transmitted, in any form or by any means, electronic, mechanical, photocopying, recording, or otherwise, without the prior written permission of the copyright owner.

Printed in the United States of America
10 9 8 7 6 5 4 3 2 1

Contents

Introduction	v
Chapter I The Rise of Fascism	1
Chapter II Steps Leading to War in Europe	7
Chapter III The German Invasion of Poland and the Phong War	13
Chapter IV Blitzkrieg on the Western Front	19
Chapter V The Battle of Britain	29
Chapter VI The German Invasion of the Soviet Union	37
Chapter VII The Mediterranean Conflict	49
Chapter VIII The Italian Campaign	59
Chapter IX The Second Front	69
Chapter X Victory in Europe	79
Chapter XI Disintegration	87
Chapter XII The War in Europe: Conclusion	95
Chapter XIII The Rise of Japanese Militarism	103
Chapter XIV Pearl Harbor	109
Chapter XV Japan's 100 Days of Glory	117
Chapter XVI The Turning Points	125
Chapter XVII America on the Offensive	131
Chapter XVIII America on the Offensive II: 1944–45	137
Chapter XIX The Fall of Japan	145
Exercises	151

Introduction

World War II began on December 11, 1941. On that day, four days after the Japanese attack on the American fleet at Pearl Harbor, Nazi Germany declared war on the United States. This act fused an Asian conflict, begun by the Japanese invasion of Manchuria in 1931, and an European one, initiated by the Nazi strike against Poland in September, 1939.

It is possible (though not likely) that the two conflicts might never have been joined, had not Hitler made his declaration of war against the United States. Despite some six months of a hot but undeclared war with the Germans in the Atlantic, President Roosevelt's war message to Congress following Pearl Harbor did not request a U.S. declaration of war against Germany, only one against Japan. Indeed, many Americans felt, as did the *Chicago Tribune,* that the U.S. now had its conflict with Japan in the Pacific, while the European conflict was the sole concern of the Europeans. Whatever merit that contention may have had, vanished four days later. Apparently believing that the United States was internally corrupt and dominated by a hated clique of Jewish bankers, Hitler perceived that German entrance into the war against the United States would spark a fascist revolution here. All that the Nazi intervention managed to accomplish, however, was to throw the weight of the United States' economy and its military might into the war against Nazi Germany. Perhaps even more fantastic that Hitler's view of America was the fact that after Germany and Japan became wartime allies, there was virtually no military cooperation between the two—no coordination of military strategy, no joint planning, no economic cooperation, no mutual military assistance; nothing other than normal diplomatic exchanges between the two.

The following pages are an attempt to illuminate the causes, the nature, and the significance of World War II. As a world conflict it lasted only four years, not long as history goes, but it produced the biggest armies, the longest battle lines, and the most devastating weapons of any war. It inflicted more suffering, destroyed more, and cost more than any other war in history. It killed perhaps as many as 50 million people, including many millions who were never in uniform. Although it was not so clear at the time as it is now, World War II was a vast, earth-shaking revolution, the effects of which are still going on. What began with artillery fire in Manchuria and dive-bombing in Poland, ended with a nuclear explosion over Japan. We have been living under that cloud ever since.

This book is by no means the whole story of that war. No single volume could possibly provide that. The aim here is to cover the essential history of this greatest of human tragedies, and to basically recreate somewhat of a feeling of what it meant in terms of the people who were swept up by it. It is easy to be overwhelmed by the enormity of the statistics involved—over six million Jews willfully murdered; the city of Leningrad reduced to rubble with more casualties than the United States has suffered in all of its wars put together; 20 million Russians—one out of every ten—perishing. The figures are so enormous that they tend to become meaningless abstractions to us. But those who died were real people, not abstractions. They were individuals who laughed, had families, and were loved and missed by someone. The words of a grieving wife, placed on her British husband's tombstone in Holland, perhaps summed it up best of all:

To all the world but one
But to me, all the world

The major thesis which pervades this work is that, from the Allied point of view, World War II was the closest thing to a just war that has been fought. Indeed, few wars have had such a clear cut purpose.

Quite simply, we fought to destroy a monstrous evil which threatened all civilization. Although it may be difficult for today's college students to believe, there was a time when it was possible to wear the country's uniform with pride, shoulder a rifle, and righteously shoot to kill. And that time was World War II. Unlike the origins of World War I, which were so complicated and entangled that it is almost impossible to assign blame for causing that tragedy, the origins of the twentieth century's second great conflict can be traced to the policies of two groups: The Japanese militarists in Asia; and the Nazi fanatics in Europe.

This book is divided into two main sections: The first will deal with the European war; the second with the Asian war. Each of these sections will trace the origin, the course, and the results of the two conflicts. The coverage in these sections will be basically chronological, although attention will be given to certain topical matters, e.g., strategic bombing, wartime diplomacy, naval warfare, and the role of military intelligence. An epilogue will take a retrospective look at the war, and particularly its consequences for, and effects on, the world in which we now live.

Finally, in an age increasingly dominated by "peace studies" and by a desire to both forget and do away with war, I am reminded of Herman Wouk's admonition in the introduction to his novel, *War and Remembrance*: "The beginning of the end of war, lies in remembering what it is like." Hopefully, this work will provide that remembrance.

CAPTURED GERMAN PAINTING, U.S. ARMY

Chapter I

The Rise of Fascism

❖   ❖   ❖

The French writer Jacques Bainville, as early as 1919, described with rather unerring accuracy, the events leading from World War I up to the outbreak of the Second World War. In retrospect, this was a rather disconcerting prediction because it suggests that World War II was implicit in the outcome of World War I and that little could have been done to prevent the second of the two conflicts. The fact is, that as far as Europe is concerned, World War I did create a world in which international stability was impossible and another war virtually unavoidable. John Maynard Keynes realized that fact when he said that the tragedy of World War I was that the treaty which concluded it was "neither a peace of iron nor a peace of reconciliation." It was not strong enough to hold the Germans down forever, nor mild enough to reconcile them to their new condition.

In later years it became common for historians to lament the fact that the West, after Adolph Hitler came to power, never stood up to his encroachments and aggressions until it was too late to do anything about them. Less often considered, however, is the question of what made Hitler possible in the first place. What conditions prevailed in Germany which put the German people in such a frame of mind that they ultimately accepted someone of Hitler's ilk? It is this question which takes us back to the Great War and its outcome.

The armistice, which ended the fighting in that conflict, really foreshadowed the peace treaty that was to come some seven months later, "a victor's peace imposed on a vanquished foe." When Mathias Erzburger, a civilian and member of the German Reichstag (Parliament), sought out Marshal Foch, the Supreme Allied Commander, and an armistice, he hoped he would be able to negotiate with Foch. Instead, Foch's aide simply read off an already prepared list of conditions, which the Germans had to accept. It was a victor's settlement imposed on a vanquished foe. Among other things Germany was forced to evacuate all territories invaded by her, as well as Alsace Lorraine (acquired by Germany in the Franco-Prussian War of 1870–71); evacuate the left bank of the Rhine River—which would then be occupied by the victors—and surrender military equipment and railroad stock, warships and submarines.

The Treaty of Versailles, subsequently signed on June 28, 1919 just outside of Paris, was similarly imposed on the German people, who called it a *Diktat*, a dictated peace. Even democracy was forced on Germany. The new democratic government, the Weimar Republic, did not result from a popular revolt against autocracy, but was imposed on Germany by the victorious Allied powers.

The terms of the Treaty were harsh enough to "brand in the minds of the German people, a desire for revenge," as Hitler was to later phrase it in his book, *Mein Kampf*. Territorially, the Treaty ceded land to Belgium, Denmark, France, Czechoslovakia, and the newly restored Poland—the latter territory effectively cut off Germany proper from East Prussia and made the German city of Danzig a free city under the jurisdiction of the League of Nations.

Under the military clauses, Germany was to reduce her army to 100,000 men, and the General Staff was to be dissolved. She was not to maintain a navy in excess of six battleships of 10,000 tons each, six light cruisers, twelve destroyers and twelve torpedo boats. She was neither to manufacture nor to possess submarines, military aircraft, heavy artillery, tanks, and poison gas. There were to be no fortifications nor armed forces on the Left Bank of the Rhine River or within 50 kilometers of the Right Bank. Also, the Saar industrial basin was to go to France for fifteen years.

The most grating of all provisions of the Treaty, however, was the so called guilt clause by which Germany was forced to accept the responsibility for "causing all the loss and damages...as a consequence of the war...." Although the final amount was unspecified in the Treaty, Germany was compelled to pay the equivalent of 20,000,000,000 gold marks by May 1, 1921, at which time she would receive the final bill. In addition, she was to deliver coal and timber to France, livestock to Belgium, and ships to Britain. Not only was it beyond Germany's capacity to meet these financial reparations, the guilt clause was also a radical distortion of the origins of the war. Germany certainly was not solely to blame for causing the First World War. Her responsibility was, in fact, quite minimal when compared to that of Austria-Hungary, Serbia, Russia, and certainly no more than that of France. The point is, however, that this guilt clause was to rankle the German minds for years to come and to create a fertile ground for the nationalist pleased Adolph Hitler.

Also attached to the Versailles Treaty was a provision establishing the League of Nations, an international association of countries designed to maintain peace among the nations of the world. Germany, however, was not permitted to join the League—whose main purpose seemed to be in the minds of most Germans—to maintain the territorial settlements imposed on Germany by the Versailles agreement.*

The immediate sequel to the Versailles Treaty was economic and social chaos for Germany. Deprived of the economic resources of the Saar Basin, Alsace-Lorraine and Silesia; saddled with exorbitant war debts, Germany nearly collapsed under the weight of the world's worst inflationary spirals. The mark which stood at 4.2 to the dollar in 1914 and 8.9 in 1919, had depreciated to 4 trillion to the dollar by the end of 1923. Milk sold for 25,000,000,000 marks a quart and prices were generally so high that Germans shopped with wheelbarrows loaded with currency. Money was being turned out so fast that only one side of the bill was being printed on, and there was an expiration date in the lower corner of the bill.

Circumstances such as these produced radical, extremist groups of all types—communists, anarchists, monarchists. One such group was the German Workers Party, a fervent nationalist and patriotic party which aimed to compete with the Socialists and Communists for support among the masses in Munich, capital of Bavaria. Worried about the possible subversive nature of this organization, the political department of the district army assigned an army reservist, Adolph Hitler, to check on it.

The thirty year-old Hitler was an Austrian, son of a minor customs' official and a servant girl. He left the provincial town of Linz when he was sixteen and headed for the more cosmopolitan city of Vienna, where he applied for admission to the Academy of Fine Arts. Rejected because his sketches were "without sufficient merit," he was ultimately reduced to doing odd jobs, an occasional water color, and advertising posters. Already a nonsmoker and a vegetarian, Hitler was able to live cheaply.**

In 1913, Hitler moved to Munich where he became an ardent supporter of his newly adopted country. The next year, Hitler enlisted in an infantry regiment, served at the front and earned the Iron Cross, both Second and First Class. He suffered a leg wound and near the end of the war was gassed. His survival convinced him that he had been spared for some special mission in his life.

Hitler found the vehicle for that mission in the party which he was sent to observe. Intrigued by its aims and goals, he accepted an invitation to attend a meeting of the Party's executive committee, and two days later joined the small group (he was its 55th member). Revealing a gift, both for propaganda and organization, Hitler soon became the leader (*Der Fuhrer*) of the Party, whose name he changed to National Socialist German Workers Party (*Nationalsozialistische Deutsche Arbeiterspartei*)—Nazi for short. He also issued a manifesto demanding abolition of the Versailles Treaty and denial of German

---

* The League was weakened by a number of factors: 1. disagreement among members over the League's actual purpose; 2. lack of means to enforce decisions; 3. failure of the United States to join the League.

**A fellow down-and-outer happily recalled these days in print after Hitler had come to power. Hitler had him tracked down and murdered, always preferring to remember these Vienna days as the saddest period of his life.

citizenship to Jews, and finally, he adopted a party symbol, the swastika, and introduced "heil" as the standard greeting between party members.*

Chaotic conditions in Germany, including the fantastic runaway inflation and French occupation of the Ruhr industrial region (bought about by German default on her reparations payments), enabled the party to grow in the early 1920's, and even to acquire an army of brown-shirted storm troopers (S.A.) as its military force. In such conditions, Hitler decided that the party could, with a bold stroke, take over the state of Bavaria—an act which would propel him into a position of national prominence. The specific occasion he chose was a meeting of Bavarian civil servants and state officials in a Munich beer hall. The conference had just gotten underway when Hitler, Hermann Goering, and a bodyguard of Storm Troopers burst into the room.** Shouting that the national revolution had begun and that the police and army barracks were already occupied, Hitler announced the formation of a provisional government. Although it was all a bluff—there was no provisional government, and the barracks had not been occupied—Hitler hoped that officials, troops, and police would flock to his support. None did. A subsequent march through the city of Munich with some 2000 Storm Troopers and sympathizers the next morning sought to elicit mass support and topple the government of Bavaria. Instead, the Munich police halted the march, and an exchange of gunfire ensued, killing three policemen and sixteen marchers.

Hitler escaped but was arrested the next day and forced to stand trial for treason. The trial made him a national figure, as he used it as a forum to influence public opinion and to make it seem as if his accusers were the ones guilty of treason. "There can be no question of treason," he said, "that aims to undo the betrayal of a country." The court actually sympathized with Hitler and his followers. General Eric von Ludendorff, the World War I hero, and one of the marchers, was acquitted. Hitler was found guilty, although it was generally understood that he would never serve out his full five year sentence. In fact, he served only nine months, during which time he lived as an honored guest, with ample food, rest, and exercise in the garden. He was allowed to receive visitors, to read and write, and to get well along with the writing of *Mein Kampf*.***

A turgid presentation of his political and social beliefs, which later became the bible of the Nazi party, *Mein Kampf* was a remarkable book because it put forth ideas and policies which later, in spite of the greatest difficulties and obstacles, Hitler was able to carry out in practice. Spelled out at the very beginning of the book were Hitler's fundamental aims: Unification of Germany and Austria; need for living space (*lebensraum*) for the German people, particularly to the East in Russia; superiority of the Aryan race and inferiority of Jews.

Released from prison in December, 1924, Hitler began the task of rebuilding the Nazi Party, which had deteriorated badly during his absence. Seemingly convinced that in a stabilized Germany, armed coups were futile, he decided to give the party a new look. The reconstituted party would now function as a regular political party and attempt to win seats in the German Reichstag.

The struggle to win votes proved a difficult task in the years between 1924 and 1929. Buoyed by short term loans from the United States, the German economy recovered dramatically during these years. Industry began to show profits and pay wages; unemployment declined; there was food, and in 1925, the Munich Carnival was held for the first time since 1915. The order of the day was recovery, peace and international conciliation. Hitler and the Nazis initially had ridden a wave of national despair, but as that wave receded, so too did the appeal of their radical program. Hitler spent most of this period in the comfort of a mountain villa above the village of Berchtesgaden, near the Austrian border, occasionally writing articles for the Party newspaper (*Volkischer Beobachter*), but basically living a quiet, pleasant, homey life.

---

*According to Germanic myth, the swastika was the instrument that had stirred up the primal ooze at earth's creation.

**A former World War I flying ace, Goering was also a wealthy landowner, and he loaned the struggling party substantial sums of money.

***Hitler's own title for the book was *Four and a Half Years of Struggle Against Lies, Stupidity and Cowardice*, but the editor shortened it to *My Struggle* (*Mein Kampf*).

Despite difficulties and years of party doldrums, the Nazi party slowly grew and solidified its organization. At the end of 1925 its recorded membership was 27,000; by the end of 1929 that figure had increased to 178,000. In the elections of May, 1928, Goering, Dr. Joseph Goebbels, and eleven others were elected to the Reichstag on the Nazi list.* Still, the Party pulled only 810,000 total votes, compared to over four million by the German National Party of Conservatives and nine million by the Social Democratic Party.

The onset of the depression in 1929 improved the fortunes of the Party. In the summer of 1929, its membership had been 120,000; by the end of 1929 it was 178,000; and by March, 1930, it had grown to 210,000. It was at this time that the Nazi Party became a major factor in national politics, playing upon the serious social dislocations of the depression, the most obvious of which was unemployment. In Germany this figure rose from 1,320,000 in September, 1930 to over five million some three years later.** These people grasped for any promise of an active program to replace the confusion of the leaders of the Weimar government, looking more and more to the extremes, both the Left and the Right. As membership in the Communist Party rose, many Germans, workers and middle class bourgeoisie alike, saw in Hitler and the Nazis a bulwark against Communism. The result was a rapid increase in size and electoral strength for the Nazi Party. By the end of 1930 it boasted a membership of over 400,000 and a vote of over six million in the September, 1930 elections. Nazi strength in the Reichstag reached 107 in that same year.

The Nazis made these gains by attacking the parties and policies which could produce nothing better than economic chaos and unemployment; they attacked the Versailles Treaty as not only an insult to Germany, but a prime source of its economic ills. In 1932 Hitler opposed von Hindenburg for the presidency of the Weimar Republic, basically a titular position. He lost his bid to unseat the aging World War I hero but he managed to make himself and his ideas known all over Germany.*** The July, 1932 parliamentary elections, however, made the Nazis the biggest party in the Reichstag, although not a majority. Hitler requested the Chancellorship but was refused by Hindenburg. A second election in 1932 saw a small decline in Nazi party support, but still left it as the single largest party in the Reichstag. Faced with weak, ineffectual leaders, President Hindenburg, whose earlier refusals to name Hitler Chancellor were based on his belief that the Nazis wanted power only to serve their own ends, now relented and asked Hitler to form a new government.

Thus, on January 30, 1933, Hindenburg formally appointed Adolph Hitler, Chancellor of Germany. Shunning his earlier inclinations towards violent revolution, Hitler and the Nazis had risen to power through the constitutional process of the Weimar Republic. Hitler did not seize office, it was conferred upon him.

Adolph Hitler was not the only European leader to rise to power as a direct result of the legacies of World War I. In Italy, Benito Mussolini, a former socialist, who broke with the party over its opposition to World War I, was another. Mussolini joined the Italian army in 1915 and fought on the Alpine front, rising to the rank of sergeant. Even thought Italy had been on the victor's side in World War I, she came out of that conflict seriously divided and dissilusioned. Lured into the conflict on the Allied side by promises of territorial gains at the expense of the Austro-Hungarian Empire, Italy had been denied the fruits of victory at the peace table. In addition, she was beset with serious economic dislocations. The war had cost 138 billion lire, double the country's total expenditures between 1861 and 1913. This in turn generated inflation, unemployment, strikes, pillaging of food shops and street battles among the conflicting extremist groups.

---

* Goebbels was a little Rhinelander with a crippled foot, who had studied philosophy and literature at six different universities.

**By 1933 this figure peaked at six million.

***Hitler, at the suggestion of Goebbels, used the airplane to travel all over Germany, using the slogan, "Hitler over Germany."

It was among the demobilized soldiers that the most serious discontent arose. Mussolini joined one of these disgruntled groups and outlined his plan to organize a combat group—*fascio di combattimento*—to uphold the material claims of the veterans, to oppose the imperialism of "any countries damaging to Italy," and to fight all those who did not support candidates favorable to the veterans. Mussolini's first attempt to get elected to the Italian Parliament in 1919 was not very successful—he received only 4,000 votes to 80,000 for his Socialist rival. Utilizing strong-arm tactics and force, the Fascists grew in strength and within one year of Mussolini's electoral defeat, boasted some 2200 local fasci and 320,000 enrolled members. By May, 1921, 35 Fascists—including Mussolini—were in the Italian Parliament, but local fascist leaders threatened to march on Rome and overthrow the government if King Victor Emmanuel III did not turn over the reigns of government to Mussolini. On October 30, 1921, the king complied and Mussolini became the youngest Premier in Italy's history.

The two European dictators who were later to plunge that continent into war thus came to power legally, within the framework of their respective constitutions. They both came to power promising to restore the greatness of their countries—Hitler promising to bring all Germans into a new, enlarged German state, the 3rd Reich; and Mussolini vowing to restore the glory and grandeur of the Roman Empire. It was their pursuit of these goals which led Europe into the conflagration of the Second World War.

Chapter II

Steps Leading to War in Europe

❖   ❖   ❖

Though very different personalities, Adolph Hitler and Benito Mussolini were quite similar in the methods they used to set themselves above their people. Although it took Mussolini some four years to consolidate his position while Hitler achieved the same result in only two, their techniques were nearly identical: violent suppression of the opposition; promises of restoring past prestige and creating new glories; suppression of minority groups; and manipulation of established churches.

The purpose of this chapter, however, is not to detail their rise to power but rather, to elucidate the steps taken by these two leaders after they had consolidated their power, steps that led to the outbreak of war in Europe. In some cases, these actions actually brought prestige and popularity to the two rulers and thus strengthened their respective positions. But the chief concern of this chapter is not Hitler's and Mussolini's centralization of political power, but rather their policies of conquest and expansion that led Europe into armed conflict.

The first such step was taken by Italy in 1935. Prior to that time, there had been no war involving major European powers since the Polish and Russian conflict had ended in 1922. But that peace was shattered in October, 1935, when Italian troops invaded the African country of Ethiopia, seeking revenge for an 1896 Italian defeat there (it was then called Abbysenia). By an overwhelming vote, the League of Nations Assembly branded Italy an aggressor—the first such step in the League's short history. The Covenant of the League next required members to take punitive measures—in the form of economic sanctions—against the designated aggressor, Italy. As one cynic observed, however, these sanctions, *i.e.* items which could not be exported to Italy, were "not lacking in a sense of humor." They included such "important" items as camels, mules, donkeys, and aluminum—a metal which Italy itself produced in sufficient quantity to be exported. Some truly important items, for example, rubber, nickel, and tin were included on the list of items not to be exported to Italy, but no embargo was imposed on such fundamental materials of war as coal, iron, steel, or oil, a resource which Italy totally lacked. Most importantly, the League recommendations did not include closing the Suez Canal, Italy's principle access to Ethiopia, a move that probably would have ended the Italian venture in Africa.

As it was, Mussolini's armies continued the conquest of Ethiopia without interference. No one was willing to go to war over Ethiopia. No nation sent troops or ships to assist her. In May, 1936, the Ethiopian capital, Addis Ababa, fell to the Italians, although Haile Selassie, the Ethiopian Emperor, had left the country three days earlier in the country's one airplane. On June 30, Selassie appeared before a special session of the League Assembly in Geneva, Switzerland, and the words he spoke there returned to haunt League members many times in the coming years. What was involved, he said, was international morality and the confidence which a small state could attach to promises that their independence and integrity would be respected and ensured. "It is us today." he said, "It will be you tomorrow."

Meanwhile, Hitler initiated his program for restoring German prestige and power. In March, 1935, he announced that he was reintroducing compulsory military service and forming a new German air force. Up to this point, German rearmament had been accomplished by ruse and subterfuge, in order to get around the limits imposed by the Versailles Treaty. Even from the end of World War I, Germany had been rearming clandestinely under the leadership of General Hans von Seckt, the basis for which was an agreement signed with the Soviet Union in 1922. Committed to industrialization and modernization, Soviet leaders needed engineers and technicians. Germany provided them to the Soviet Union in exchange for training facilities and armaments plants in the Soviet Union. But now, Hitler brought rearmament out in the open.*

Hitler did not wait long before utilizing his new armed force. In March 1936, one year after openly beginning to rearm, he sent German troops into the Rhineland. The Versailles Treaty had required that 9,450 square miles of the Rhineland west of the Rhine, and a 30 mile-wide zone east of the River, be permanently demilitarized to form a buffer between Germany and France. By violating that Treaty provision, Hitler was, in effect, tearing up the Versailles agreement. The German troops were, in fact, a token force, equipped only with rifles, carbines, and machine guns, while the Luftwaffe planes that flew overhead lacked guns and ammunition. Indeed, Hitler's generals had warned him that Germany was not militarily prepared to fight the West and if the French resisted, Germany should immediately pull back. Even Hitler later admitted, "Had France moved in, we would have had to withdraw with our tails between our legs."

But no French troops or planes appeared. Instead, France protested to the League of Nations. In turn, the League pronounced Germany guilty of violating the Locarno Pact of 1925, a mutual-security treaty with the French in which Germany pledged to keep the Rhineland demilitarized. But no action was taken to force Germany to withdraw and German troops were once again poised on the French frontier. Hitler was now emboldened to believe that Germany could gain her living space (*Lebensraum*) without interference. German imperialism and the League's and Western nations' failure to resist it sealed the future fates of Austria, Czechoslovakia, and Poland.

Before he moved again, however, Hitler provided combat experience and training for his troops and tested his new military equipment. The occasion was the Spanish Civil War, which broke out in the summer of 1936. In that year the Spanish military led by Francisco Franco rose in rebellion against the Spanish Republic, thus initiating a conflict which was to drag on for some 33 months and provided in the process a dress rehearsal for new German and Italian weaponry and tactics. Both Nazi Germany and Fascist Italy sent men and material to Franco; Italy ultimately supplying 763 aircraft, at least 50,000 troops, and large numbers of cannon and small arms. Germany supplied transport planes, fighter planes, and support forces that composed the so-called Condor Legion, an air and ground force made up entirely of Germans. Eventually, some 6000 Germans manned not only planes, but tanks and antiaircraft units as well. These forces aided Franco's successful bid to overthrow the legally constituted government of Spain, and developed new air tactics—dive-bombing and the combined use of incendiary and high-explosive bombs. Pilots of the Condor Legion were later to lead the Luftwaffe attacks on Poland, France, and England.

Some assistance to the Spanish Republic came from the Soviet Union, intent upon undermining the Spanish democracy and converting it instead into a Communist dictatorship. Western countries, however, stood aloof from direct involvement in the conflict although they did allow "volunteer" brigades to assist the Republic. Again, acts of aggression went unanswered and the German and Italian units returned home in June, 1939, to triumphal welcomes.

Hitler's next aggressive act involved his native Austria. On the first page of *Mein Kampf*, he had set forth his objective of absorbing Austria into a Greater Germany, a goal prohibited by the peace treaties that ended the First World War. Hitler, however, demanded an Austrian-German union, and he utilized a strong native Nazi movement to bring pressure to bear on the Austrian government. Austria, they argued, was German both ethnically and linguistically, and they demanded *Anschluss*—a union with Germany. The chief obstacle to their and Hitler's realization of this goal was the Austrian Chancellor, Engelbert Dolfuss. Not quite five feet tall, Dolfuss behaved as a virtual dictator, outlawing the

---

*Already as early as October, 1933, Hitler had taken his country out of the League of Nations and the Geneva Disarmament Conference, claiming that Germany was not given equality with other nations.

Austrian Nazi Party and declaring that a death sentence awaited any Nazi caught possessing explosives. In July, 1934, Dolfuss was assassinated by Nazis who burst into a cabinet meeting dressed in the uniform of Austria's army and police, but the Nazi bid for power failed, and the new Chancellor, Kurt von Schuschnigg, continued to oppose *Anschluss*.

For four years, Hitler bided his time, in part because Mussolini was also opposed to *Anschluss*.* But in February, 1938, with Italian approval finally secured, Hitler moved. He invited Chancellor Schuschnigg to visit his beautiful mountain retreat at Berchtesgaden, but not "...to discuss the view and the weather." Instead, Hitler directed a two hour tirade against Schuschnigg, demanding that the Austrian Nazi Party be legalized, and that Arthur Seyss-Inquart, a pro-Nazi Viennese lawyer, be made Minister of the Interior, in command of the country's security force. He also demanded that the cabinet ministries of defense and finance be given to Nazis. Browbeaten, Schuschnigg signed Hitler's ultimatum.

Upon his return to Vienna, however, Schuschnigg proved recalcitrant. He reaffirmed Austria's independence and scheduled a national plebiscite to determine whether Austrians wanted a "free, independent, social, Christian, and united Austria." The Nazi response was to demand that Schuschnigg postpone the plebiscite or suffer a German invasion. Schuschnigg's agreement to postpone the vote came too late. On March 12, 1938, German troops crossed into Austria. They met virtually no resistance and Hitler returned in triumph to Vienna, site of his earlier failures. England and France protested the Nazi move, but once again did nothing. The world moved another step closer to war.

Encouraged by his unopposed successes, Hitler returned next to Czechoslovakia, the only state in Central or Eastern Europe where parliamentary democracy had been successful after World War I. This was not enough, however, to keep the country from ultimately being smashed by outside forces working on its minorities, the most sensitive of which was a group of 3 ½ million Germans, the so-called Sudeten Germans. Placed in the newly created Czech state after World War I because they inhabited an area (Bohemia and Moravia) that provided the new state with natural defensive barriers, these Germans felt superior to the Slavs and resisted the new republic at every turn, even when the Czech government in Prague made concessions to them. Sudeten extremists turned to Hitler early, and even the moderates in the Sudetenland were more or less pan-German in their views. From 1933 on, Nazi agitation, supported by Hitler with men and money, became increasingly serious and widespread in Czechoslovakia. Early in 1938, having secured Austria, Hitler decided to push the Czech affair next. His Sudeten agent, Konrad Henlein, made demands on the Prague government for what amounted to complete Sudeten autonomy.

The Czechs turned to France, with whom they had a formal alliance, and to England. It now seems clear in retrospect, that the English and French had already decided not to defend the territorial integrity of Czechoslovakia. Although it is doubtful that Hitler was aware of this at the time, he obviously counted on what he termed "the moral weakness" of the West allowing him to proceed unhindered. On September 12, 1938, he made a violent speech at Nuremburg, insisting on self-determination for the Sudeten Germans—a signal for widespread disorders in Czechoslovakia. The Czech government proclaimed martial law, and the affair became a full-fledged European crisis. British Prime Minister Neville Chamberlain made two preliminary visits to Hitler in an effort to moderate German demands. With the aid of Mussolini, he finally persuaded Hitler to call a full conference of the four great western powers. The four leaders—Hitler, Mussolini, Chamberlain, and Edouard Daladier of France—met at Munich on September 29, 1938. The Soviet Union, like France, had an alliance with Czechoslovakia, but was not invited; nor were the Czechs whose fate was being decided.

Munich proved to be a sweeping victory for Hitler. Instead of autonomy within the Czech state—Hitler's original demand—the Sudeten areas were turned over to Germany and incorporated into the

---

*Mussolini coveted Austrian territory in the so-called Southern Tyrol in the Dalmatian Alps.

Reich. Nevertheless, Chamberlain, the champion of this so-called appeasement policy—basically buying off your enemy by giving him what he wants—returned home to England as a hero who had prevented war. Hitler, he said, was now satisfied and had no more territorial claims in Europe.

Hitler was far from satisfied, however, and it did not take him long to make his next move. In the Spring, 1939, even before the final demarcation lines set at Munich had actually been drawn, he summoned Emil Hacha, the Czech President, to Germany and told him the fate of the Czech people must be placed trustingly in the hands of the Fuhrer. Hitler reportedly turned, left the room, and Hacha promptly fainted. He was revived and at four o'clock in the morning on March 15, 1939, he signed Czechoslovakia over to Nazi control. The German army marched into Czechoslovakia, meeting no real resistance from a country deprived of its natural frontiers and abandoned by its friends and allies.

It was clear now—even to Chamberlain—that Hitler was not going to settle down and work to preserve the European balance of power. It is not so clear whether Hitler believed he could continue his aggressions without bringing on a general war. He made no secret of his belief that the British and French were spineless and unable to summon the courage needed to resist Germany. Yet there is some evidence that Hitler did expect at least a localized war over his next victim.

Inexorably, that victim was Poland. The Polish Corridor, cut largely out of former German territory after World War I, was an affront to Germany's great power psychology.* So, too, was the separation from Germany of the Free City of Danzig, on the edge of the Polish Corridor, a city that was thoroughly German in language and tradition. Poland's likelihood as the next Czechoslovakia was so obvious that England and France both signed mutual assistance pacts with her in April, 1939. The two Western Countries pledged to come to Poland's assistance if Germany attacked her. Chamberlain was now particularly determined that there would be no more Munichs.

The crucial issue for Germany at this time was not so much what England and France would do, but rather the attitude of the Soviet Union. Hitler seemed to be obsessed with the fear of a two-front war. He knew that an attack on Poland could mean war with England and France in the West. What he wished to avoid was the Soviet Union coming to Poland's aid and tying down German armies in the East. As events developed, Hitler was able to seize Poland without bringing Soviet intervention against Germany. Indeed, he even arranged a pact with Stalin that led to the two countries carving up Polish territory between them.

There were several reasons for this development. For their part, the Western powers, particularly Great Britain, were decidedly anti-Communist, perhaps even more so than was Nazi Germany. The delegation that they belatedly sent to Moscow to discuss a mutual assistance pact with the Soviets was a low-level delegation, at the same time inept and half-hearted in its efforts. In addition, the Soviet price for an agreement was one that the West could not afford. The Soviet Union wanted the right to send troops into Poland and the Baltic Republics of Latvia, Lithuania, and Estonia. If she were to fight Germany, she wanted to do so on Polish rather than on Russian soil. And because of strong German influences in the Baltic states, the Soviets wished to deny the use of these areas to Germany for an attack against the Soviet Union. England and France would not—indeed could not—grant these demands. Contemplating leading their countries into war over the issue of the violation of the territorial integrity of a small nation, Poland, they could not give that country's territory to the Russians along with the small Baltic states. That would not only have been unedifying but ludicrous.

Additionally, the Western states did not trust Soviet ambitions in Poland, nor did the Poles look favorably upon Soviet troops based on Polish soil. A Polish maxim popular at the time, reflected this belief: "With the Germans we risk our freedom, with the Russians our souls." It was quite clear that Poles would not welcome Russian troops, even as a bulwark against the Germans.

---

*Poland, which had not existed as an independent country since the end of the 18th century, was recreated at the Paris Peace Conferences after World War I. She was given access to the Baltic Sea via the port of Danzig, reached via the land bridge known as the Polish Corridor.

For their part, the Russians were hurt by their exclusion from the negotiations over the Czechoslovakian crisis, an exclusion they blamed primarily on the French and the British. Based upon the failures of the western powers to stand up to German violations of the Versailles Treaty, the Russians had come to believe that the West would not fight. They had apparently reached the conclusion that it was a broken reed and if the Soviets themselves did not come to terms with Hitler, he would attack them. There is also evidence that Stalin believed the West was not standing up to Hitler because they hoped to encourage him to continue his expansion to the East at Russia's expense, while they remained out of the conflict.

Despite his longtime hatred of Communism ("Jewish Bolshevism"), Hitler needed Russian cooperation for his attack on Poland. He sent his Foreign Minister, Joachim von Ribbentrop, to Moscow to see the Soviet leader, Stalin, and his Foreign Minister, Viachaslav Molotov. On the same afternoon of his arrival, the three of them hammered out a mutual non-aggression pact, which freed Hitler to invade Poland without fear of Russian involvement. It also allowed Stalin to move into Finland, Latvia, Estonia, Rumania's Bessarabian province, and the Eastern half of Poland as well. Only the non-aggression part of the agreement was publically announced; the rest was part of a secret protocol. That night, Stalin drank to the health of the German Fuhrer.

The Soviet Union formally ratified the Pact on August 31, 1939. On September 1, exactly as Hitler had planned all along, German soldiers poured across the Polish border. Two days later, after Germany had ignored their demands to pull its troops out of Poland, the French and the British declared war on Germany. The prelude to war had ended. The European phase of World War II had begun.

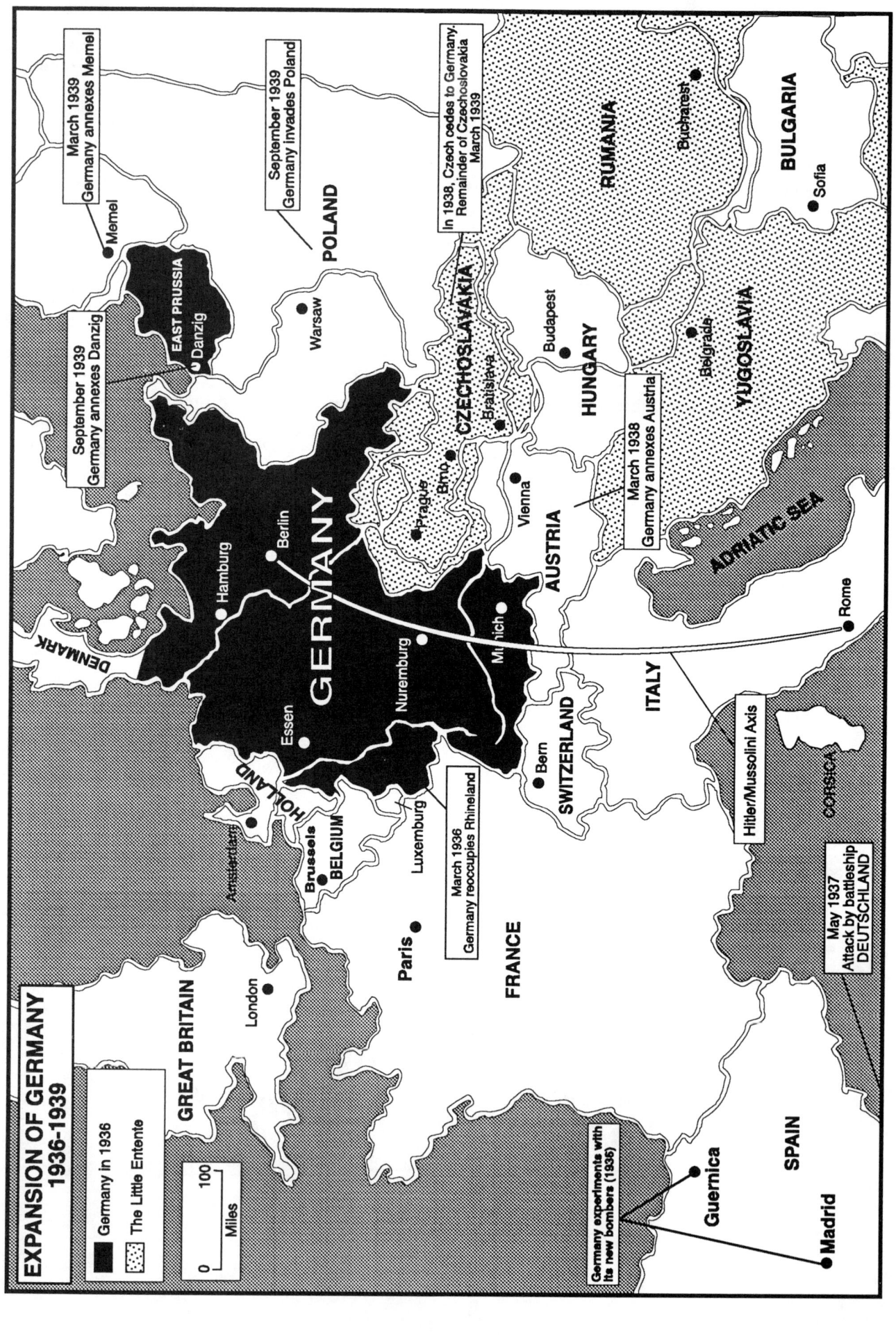

Chapter III

The German Invasion of Poland and the Phony War

❖   ❖   ❖

On August 31, 1939, a Polish-speaking voice interrupted the radio announcer in the German border town of Gleiwitz with shouts that Poland was attacking Germany. With the sound of gun shots echoing in the background, he called for all Poles to join the attack. The next morning foreign journalists were escorted to Gleiwitz and shown thirteen corpses dressed in Polish military uniforms lying scattered on the ground around the radio station. At 10 A.M. that same day, September 1, 1939, Adolph Hitler delivered a speech to the Reichstag citing the events at Gleiwitz as an instance of Polish aggression on German soil, and he announced that he had thrown all the armed might of Germany against Poland.*

In fact, the whole Gleiwitz scenario had been orchestrated by Hitler to provide the pretext for the German attack. The "Polish soldiers" were actually convicted criminals taken from a concentration camp at Oranienburg in Eastern Germany. Dressed in Polish uniforms, they were given fatal injections of a drug and then shot. Their bodies were arranged in front of the station to make it appear as if they had been invading Germany. The German attack made use of a new, revolutionary military strategy, known as Blitzkrieg. Refined by General Heinz Guderian from theories earlier advanced by General J.F.C. Fuller in England and Colonel Charles de Gaulle in France (they were both ignored in their own countries), Blitzkrieg called for lightning war waged by the combined tank-infantry force—the Panzer Division—backed by a kind of aerial heavy artillery in the form of dive bombers. The Panzer division was a small army in its own right, combining speed and strength; it moved forward under the protection of the Air Force, which preceded it, bombing the opponents' positions, and attacking enemy tanks and delaying any reinforcements. Paratroopers could also be dropped behind the enemy lines to capture and hold any important points.

Once a penetration of enemy lines was achieved, the panzer divisions dashed ahead, attempting to disperse any hostile forces they encountered. At all levels, the emphasis was on boldness, speed, shock action, and firepower. The enemy was to be given no time to recover or to shift reserves to block the gap. Finally, a well-prepared, flexible, cross-country logistical system kept a steady flow of fuel, ammunition, and food moving up to the front. This was warfare as it had been waged by Alexander the Great, Ghengis Khan, and Napoleon, modified only to make use of the latest military and technological developments.

The German plan was to unleash Blitzkrieg from Prussia in the East and from Germany proper and Silesia in the West. Altogether, the Germans had some one-and-a-quarter million men (organized in 60 divisions, including five mobile army corps) to throw against an 800,000 man Polish force with only one mechanized cavalry brigade. In support, Germany had 2000 aircraft against a 600-plane Polish airforce, only about one-half of which could be considered modern.

Polish military commanders really had only two choices for countering a German attack. The first and most logical choice was to pull the Polish troops back across the Vistula River, forcing the German attackers to cross the wide, flood-prone stream. This meant, however, abandoning the capital city of Warsaw as well as the richest part of the country, which the Polish command deemed to be

---
*The German attack had begun almost 6 hours earlier in the pre-dawn darkness.

unacceptable. The alternative strategy was to make a stand along the frontier, some 1750 miles in length, in hopes of halting the invaders in their tracks. The country's geography hampered this plan, however. The immense Polish plain did not lend itself to fortification but did offer great possibilities for the movement of motorized units, such as those possessed by the Germans.

What the Poles decided upon was a compromise between the two options: they would fight initially on the frontiers, then fall back to prepared positions, holding on long enough for the British and French to attack Germany from the west. There was, however, a two-fold problem with this strategy: It counted on a British and French attack on Germany's western frontiers, which never came; and secondly, utilizing the Blitzkrieg strategy, German forces moved so quickly that they were able to cut off and annihilate the Polish forces before they had an opportunity to pull back.

The first shots of the war were actually fired at Danzig in the Polish Corridor, which cut off East Prussia from the rest of Germany. Made an international city under the administration of the League of Nations following World War I, Danzig was in reality a German city, and an old Hanseatic League port. A German training ship, the *Schleswig-Holstein*, was in the Danzig harbor, and began firing. German planes soon filled the sky over all of Poland, hitting the Polish air force on the ground, destroying bridges, barracks, and generally ravaging the factories and cities of the country.

The Polish military was no match for the German onslaught. German armor penetrated and shattered the Polish front in the first two or three days of battle, allowing the Poles no opportunity to form a new one. Polish forces fought valiantly and proved resourceful and courageous. They blocked Nazi tanks with barricades of trolley cars, and they charged German panzers on horseback, but these were the futile acts of an outmanned army. The Polish airforce collapsed early on as well. In two days it was crippled and in two weeks extinguished, primarily as a result of air combat and the overrunning of airfields by the advancing German army.

On September 17, in accordance with the secret protocol of the Nazi-Soviet Pact, Russian forces moved into Eastern Poland (what the Russians called Western Belo-Russia and the Western Ukraine), meeting virtually no resistance. The Red Army's intervention ended the last hopes of the Polish High Command for prolonged resistance against its opponents, since the Russians occupied the Eastern sections of Poland beyond the Vistula River.

The only remaining stake in the struggle was the city of Warsaw. German infantry surrounded the Polish capital by September 14, at which time they delivered a demand to the Poles for unconditional surrender. But instead of giving up, the people of Warsaw began to fortify the city. When the German tanks jumped off for the attack, instead of blitzing through the city, they were stopped dead, and German infantrymen were pinned down by snipers. Even Warsaw radio entered the fray, transmitting portions of a polonaise by Frederic Chopin every 30 seconds, to tell the world that the capital was still in Polish hands.

Finally, food ran out and on September 28, 1939, the polonaise was replaced by a funeral dirge. The same day, Warsaw surrendered after two weeks of heroic resistance. Other pockets of resistance continued to fight for several more days: Gdynia in the north held out until October 2, while the last organized Polish fighting force, southeast of Warsaw, surrendered on October 6.

German casualties were not light in Poland: 13,981 killed and 30,322 wounded. In addition, the Luftwaffe lost 734 men and 285 aircraft (over 100 bombers). Polish losses in killed and wounded totaled some 266,000, most incurred in the first two weeks of fighting. Additionally, the Poles lost 450,000 prisoners to the Germans and 200,000 to the Russians. Russian dead in the conflict numbered only 734.

About 100,000 Polish soldiers, only a fraction of the forces which started out, managed to escape both the Germans and the Russians and make it to Rumania and ultimately to the West. They later formed Free Polish units that fought with the French and the British. Many of the Polish prisoners taken by the Russians died while in captivity, but when the Germans attacked the Soviet Union two years later, a number of those who had survived, including General Wladyslaw Anders, were allowed to leave and fight the Germans again in North Africa and Italy.

During the campaign, German armies had largely overrun the demarcation line previously agreed upon with the Soviet Union. This led to a new agreement between the two powers in accordance with which Lithuania, originally allocated to Germany, was put into the Soviet sphere along with oil fields of Southeastern Poland. In return, all of central Poland, including the entire province of Lublin, were conceded to Germany. The new partition line now ran along the Bug, San, and Naarew Rivers. Germany formally annexed the western provinces, inhabited by many ethnic Germans, into the Reich. The parts of Poland that the Germans did not annex were made a German fief called the Government General. This was to serve as a reserve of manpower for the Reich, providing it with cheap labor. In short, it was a giant labor camp and the Poles living there, were nothing but slaves.

Jewish intellectuals, the clergy, or anyone whom the Germans thought might lead a future resistance movement were expelled from German annexed territories. Jews generally were forced into ghettoes within the Government General. Although the order for the "Final Solution"—the elimination of all the Jews—did not come for two more years, the martyrdom for Polish Jews was already beginning.

In the meantime, it was "all quiet on the Western Front." Although England and France declared war on Germany September 3, 1939, their forces remained inert. The two countries went to war over the German invasion of Poland, but did absolutely nothing to aid Poland, despite the fact that Germany had stripped down her forces in the west to skeleton size. Facing a French army with 70 divisions, were only 33 German divisions, 25 of which were undermanned and second rate. But more importantly, the Germans had no tanks, no aircraft, and only a three day supply of ammunition to face 3000 French and British tanks and an enemy with complete air superiority. And yet the West did nothing. The British sent 29 planes to bomb German shipping in the Kiel Canal (losing seven of them), but until Winston Churchill became Prime Minister in May, 1940, the RAF dropped only leaflets on German soil. There was a small French offensive in the Saar basin in September, which made some initial headway, but ultimately found itself back at its starting point. It cost the French army exactly 27 killed, 22 wounded, and 28 missing. In addition, they lost nine fighter planes and 18 reconnaissance aircraft. Although the French gave many reasons for their failure to act decisively, the fact is that French military strategy was almost completely one of defense—taking cover behind the magnificent fortress of the Maginot Line.

In the First World War, the French army had suffered disastrous losses as they marched out on the offensive. Because of those losses and the near defeat at the hands of the Germans in that conflict, the French were determined to make their land impregnable from another German attack. Beginning in 1930, they built an 87 mile long string of underground forts facing Germany, at an ultimate cost of $200 million. Finished in 1937, these bastions were named after the man who was Defense Minister at the time construction was begun—Andre Maginot. The Maginot Line, as it was called, was a masterpiece of static defense—with tank traps, barbed wire and pill boxes at its forward edge. Then came rows of guns embedded in concrete some 10 feet thick, further protected by machine guns and anti-tank weapons. Located at 3–5 mile intervals were immense fortresses buried as much as 100 feet beneath the ground, each holding up to 1200 men. When the war began, the French marched into these forts and waited to repel the expected German invasion. They were to have a long wait.

The Phony War

The seven-month period extending from October, 1939, until May, 1940 (from the defeat of Poland to the German invasion of France), has been called the Phony War, because although a state of war existed, there was virtually no fighting.* The propaganda war continued along the French-German

---
*The Phony War was called *sitzkrieg* in German and *la d'role de querre* in French.

frontier and nearly every night British planes dropped leaflets over Germany, explaining that the war was not a good idea and the Germans should call the whole thing off. One result of this attitude was a rather widespread hope, both in France and England, for peace. Chamberlain repeated several times that England was not waging war against the German people, and he is reported to have said that "what I am hoping for is not a military victory—I doubt very much if it is possible—but the collapse of the German homefront." For their part, the Germans mounted a propaganda campaign that attempted to exploit French soldiers' disgruntlement at leaving home and family. Leaflets and loudspeakers, blasting from across the Rhine, told them that they were fighting for England and that while they were at the "front," English men were in their villages keeping company with their wives and sweethearts. As French sentries watched their German counterparts across the lines, there seemed little point in shooting. "After all," said one, "they aren't bad types, and if we fire, they will fire back."

There were two exceptions to the period of the Phony War: The war at sea; and the Russo-Finnish Winter War. The latter of these two resulted from demands issued by the Soviet Union to the Finns in October, 1939. Stalin's basic motive seems to have been a desire to provide better protection to the Soviet Union's second largest city, Leningrad. To achieve this he meant to control that part of Finnish territory commanding access to the city. Stalin also wanted to control access to Leningrad via the Gulf of Finland. Consequently, Soviet demands included Finnish cessation of her islands in the Gulf of Finland; Finnish withdrawal of her frontier in the Karelian Isthmus between the Baltic and Lake Ladoga; lease of an air-naval base on the Hango Peninsula to the Soviet Union for a period of 30 years; and a pact between the two countries for the mutual defense of the Gulf of Finland. In return, the Soviets offered an adjustment, albeit a considerable one, of the Russo-Finnish frontier in northern Karelia.

The Finns rejected the demands and after a month of fruitless discussion, Soviet land, sea, and air forces took the offensive against Finland without any declaration of war. Despite overwhelming Soviet superiority—300,000 troops vs. 120,000 Finnish troops; 800 aircraft vs. 100 for Finland—the war dragged out for three months. Bad winter weather tended to neutralize the Soviet manpower and technical superiority, while the terrain favored the Finns. The vast forests offered ample cover and allowed small detachments of Finnish troops to launch ambushes on the few roads in the area. Finnish soldiers, used to the forest, skilled on skis, and natural fighters, proved to be masters of irregular warfare. The narrowness of the peninsula also prevented the deployment of large numbers of troops, another factor that worked to the disadvantage of the Russians.

By the end of 1939, the Red Army had suffered a series of resounding and humiliating defeats. Under the command of Marshall Mannerheim, a former guard officer in the Imperial Russian army, the Finns even went over to the offensive and virtually wiped out a whole Soviet division north of Lake Ladoga.* By February, however, the greater resources and numbers of the Russians began to overwhelm the Finns and by March 2, Russian forces were at Vyborg. Mannerheim soon became convinced that it was no longer possible to continue fighting and on March 12, 1940, the Peace Treaty was signed with Finland accepting all Russian demands.

The other exception to the Phony War was the war at sea. Actually, when the war began in 1939 the German navy was ill-prepared—even the later renowned U-Boat fleet was inadequate.** Nevertheless, the Germans did utilize a number of surface raiders to prey upon British shipping. One such ship was the pocket battleship, *Graf Spee*. Designed to get around the regulations of the Versailles Treaty, it was fast, light, heavily gunned, and armored. It could out-gun anything that was faster than it and it was faster than anything that could out-gun it. When hostilities began, it dashed for the southern Atlantic where it proceeded to sink some nine cargo vessels off the coast of South America. However, the *Graf Spee* was surprised by three British cruisers, *Exeter*, *Achilles*, and *Ajax* in December, 1939.

---

*Finland was part of the Russian Empire from 1814 until 1917.

**Germany possessed about 50 submarines in 1939, only 29 of which were sea worthy. From September to December, 1939, the Germans sank only 421,156 tons of allied and neutral shipping.

After extended fighting, the *Graf Spee* blew itself up, and three days later its captain, Hans Langsdorff, killed himself.

For the most part, the German navy was too weak to engage in any direct confrontation with the British Royal Navy, waging instead a type of seaborne guerilla war. The first German success came two weeks after the beginning of the war when the submarine, the UK-29, sank the elderly British aircraft carrier, *Courageous*. One month later, the Commander of U-47, Gunther Prien, managed to sneak into Scapa Flow, the vast anchorage of the British fleet, and sink the 29,500-ton *Royal Oak*.

Despite these and other setbacks, by the end of 1939, the Royal Navy and the French Navy had succeeded in safeguarding their sea lanes. Germany, however, was rapidly adding to its U-Boat fleet and by the end of 1942, this undersea force came close to doing what Goering's Luftwaffe was to fail to achieve in the summer and fall of 1940—namely to force Great Britain to surrender.

Perhaps more serious to the Allies than the submarines and surface raiders in the period of the Phony War were magnetic mines dropped in Allied sea lanes, particularly in the estuary of the Thames River. Detonated by the metallic mass of ships passing over them, such exploding mines usually resulted in complete destruction. Between November and December, 1939, fifty-nine Allied and neutral ships were sunk in this manner. Eventually, one of the magnetic mines which had landed in a mud flat was discovered at low tide, and it was examined by the British. The examination led to a process called "degaussing," which involved running a cable around the ship and passing an electric current through it. This neutralized the ship's magnetic field. So successful was this procedure, that by March, 1940, magnetic mines were no longer a serious threat to Allied ships.

Courtesy of Corbis-Bettman. Reprinted by permission.

Chapter IV
Blitzkrieg on the Western Front

❖ ❖ ❖

Even during the Phony War period, Hitler never wavered from his resolve to take the offensive against England and France as soon as possible. The first plan for such an attack, produced by the German General Staff in October, 1939, called for a straight thrust westward through Holland and northern Belgium to the English Channel. Some German generals objected to this scheme since its primary aim was not to knock out the French army as they had the Polish army, but rather to capture the Channel ports. This plan, therefore, raised the possibility of a long and static war. This concerned Hitler, but he accepted the plan as drafted. The severe winter weather of 1939–40, however, caused continual postponements throughout November, December, and into early January.

In mid-January, an unforeseen mishap occurred that caused the Germans to reconsider their strategy. Two Luftwaffe officers, one carrying a copy of sections of the secret operational plan for the German invasion of Holland and Belgium, became lost in bad weather on a flight from Munster to Cologne in Germany. Running low on fuel, the pilot was forced to crash-land in a field near what he thought was the Rhine River, but which in reality was the Meuse River in Belgium. The entire German invasion plan thus fell into the hands of one of its intended victims, Belgium. For a time, Hitler contemplated going ahead with the plan anyway, but bad weather forced another major postponement of the attack, this time until Spring.

In the meantime, a new proposal, formulated by General Eric von Manstein, the articulate Chief of Staff to General Gerd von Rundstedt, was forwarded to Hitler. This scenario called for diversionary attacks on the Low Countries, with the aim of drawing Allied armies north, out of France. The main German strike then would fall further south in the area of the Ardennes forest of Belgium and Luxembourg, an area generally believed impenetrable. The attacking Germans would drive through France directly to the sea, catch the bulk of the Allied armies in a gigantic trap, and end the war quickly. In addition, whereas the original plan had called for sending a single armored corps against the enemy, Manstein now proposed striking with the full weight of Army Group A in the area of the Ardennes. With the original plan now in Allied hands, Hitler was won over to Manstein's proposal, scheduling the attack for May, 1940.

Before putting Case Yellow—as Manstein's plan was called—into effect, Hitler turned his attention to the North, toward Scandinavia. The Allies were also interested in this area, because almost half of the iron ore that Germany needed to make steel for its armament industry came from Sweden, and 80 percent of that iron ore was shipped by rail to the ice-free port of Narvik, Norway. Sailing in neutral Norwegian waters, German ships could evade the British and safely carry the iron ore to Germany. Winston Churchill, England's First Lord of the Admiralty at the time, was convinced that by cutting the ore traffic from Narvik, the Allies could severely cripple the German war industry, and he proposed that the British fleet mine the Norwegian coastal waters and send an expeditionary force into Norway to stop the rail shipments.

As it turned out, Germany was one step ahead of her enemies. Admiral Eric Raeder, the German naval commander, was quite aware of the strategic importance of Norway's coast, not only as a route for German ships carrying iron ore but also as a base for surface raiders and submarines. He was also alert to the dangers inherent for Germany if British troops should occupy Norway and establish air and naval bases there.

A catalyst for German action came in an event involving the Nazi supply ship and tanker, the *Altmark*. The *Altmark* had spent the early war period picking up British sailors whose ships had been sunk in sea battles against the Germans. With about 300 such prisoners on board, she had slipped into Norwegian territorial waters on her way back to Germany. The British government protested the *Altmark's* presence to the Norwegians, who searched the ship but failed to discover the Allied prisoners. The British then acted on their own and intercepted the *Altmark* in an icy Norwegian fjord. A boarding party from the destroyer *Cossack* found and freed the British prisoners, who were given a hero's welcome back in England. Hitler saw this action as a warning of an impending British occupation of Norway and decided to strike first.

The German plan—*Wesserubung*—called not only for the invasion of Norway but for Denmark as well. Denmark was overrun in a period of some four hours by a combination of land troops moving across the Jutland frontier, paratroopers, and commandos landed by ships. On April 19, the Danish cabinet, under protest, accepted a German ultimatum to place its neutrality under German protection, although at least in appearance Denmark would still be running her own affairs.

Coincidentally, German and British troops began landing in Norway almost simultaneously. The German forces, who caught the British completely by surprise, were not very considerable: Seven cruisers, fourteen destroyers, and about 10,000 men. But the decisive factors were the German paratroopers who seized important airfields where additional troops could be landed. The Luftwaffe now also had bases from which to terrorize the Norwegians and to resist Allied counterattacks.

Allied landing parties in Norway were severely hampered by poor planning and inadequate preparations. Troops were landed without skis or snowshoes in areas still snow-covered, and even worse, a contingent of British troops landed equipped with snow shoes but no weapons. In some cases, Allied troops even lacked proper maps. Although they landed at several points along the Norwegian coast, the Allies achieved enduring success only in the far north at Narvik, too far from German airbases to allow air support and supply for the German troops. Two battalions of French Foreign Legion troops and two Polish battalions seized Narvik at the end of May, but when conditions in France soon became so serious in the first part of June, the French and Polish troops were withdrawn.

There were other isolated successes against the Germans, both by the Norwegians and the Allies. The German heavy cruiser, *Blucher*, was sunk by the guns at Oscarborg, with a loss of over 1000 men. The German cruiser, *Koningsburg*, was crippled off the coast of Bergen, and a Norwegian destroyer sank a German munitions ship. The British also took a heavy toll on German shipping. They sank the cruiser, *Karlsruhe*; Royal Air Force (RAF) planes finished off the *Koningsburg*; and British planes heavily damaged the battleship, *Lutzow*, in a torpedo attack. All in all, Germany lost more than half of its navy in the Norwegian campaign: Three cruisers, 10 destroyers, 6 U-Boats, and 11 smaller vessels. In addition, the British damaged five German cruisers. The loss of these ships was later to prove a decisive factor in delaying and eventually canceling Operation Sea Lion, the proposed invasion of Great Britain. German losses were partially offset by the sinking of the British aircraft carrier *Glorious* with two squadrons of aircraft aboard.

Most of the members of the Norwegian government, including King Haakon VIII, managed to flee the country, taking with them the bullion of the Bank of Norway. The new Norwegian Prime Minister was Vidkukm Quisling, whose last name was to become synonymous with the word traitor. Quisling, founder of the National Union Party, a Nazi-oriented group, gained little or no support from the Norwegian people, and the Nazis soon shelved their would-be puppet ruler. They did appoint him Commissioner for Demobilization, a pure sinecure.*

---

*The Norwegians generally loathed Quisling, and after the war he was tried and executed for treason.

Once again, Hitler had achieved complete success in bringing another area of Europe under German control. The Scandinavian campaign lasted less than two months and cost the Germans only about 5000 killed, wounded, and missing. The Germans had surprised and humiliated the French and British, who had exhibited faulty coordination, makeshift plans and inadequate equipment. In Britain, the result of the Allied abortive Norwegian operation was to topple the Chamberlain government and bring Winston Churchill to power on May 10, 1940, the very day that German forces struck along the Belgian, Dutch, and French borders.

Hitler had at his disposal on this day some five million men mobilized, three and one-half million of whom were under arms. These composed 157 frontline divisions, including twelve armored, seven motorized, and three S.S. divisions (motorized). Thirty-seven of the infantry divisions were used as garrisons in occupied territory, fighting in Norway, or in training. There were also ten divisions on the frontier with the Soviet Union (these were mostly reserve troops). On the Western front itself, the Germans had massed 114 divisions. Against the Germans, the French had mobilized 5,700,00 men, of whom some 2,400,000 were engaged in the defense of the northwest frontier. The British had only 1,500,000 men mobilized in May, 1940. There were also 22 Belgian and 9 Dutch divisions that could be thrown against the Germans.

Armored vehicle numbers were nearly the same on both sides, and their quality was roughly equivalent.* The big difference, of course, was the use made of these vehicles. As noted above, the Germans had revolutionized tank warfare through their concept of Blitzkrieg. Several German tank divisions would be grouped into an armored corps and concentrated on a narrow front; they were supported by motorized divisions and equipped with all the combat resources necessary to hold on to essential positions until the arrival of the infantry. The French (and the British) simply had not conceived of tank warfare in these terms. They thought of the tank as a defensive weapon (a mobile blockhouse) and the French tanks were not even equipped with radios. As the French historian, Henri Michel, has noted, "So, in tank warfare, men and ideas from 1914–1918 were fighting against opponents thinking in terms of 1940."

The major discrepancy between the two sides was in airpower. The French had only about 1000 planes, including 600 fighters and 100 bombers. The British had 1500 aircraft but only 350 of them were based in France. On the German side, the Luftwaffe could call on 4000 combat aircraft, more than 3600 of which were on the frontiers of France and the Low Countries. This force included 1500 bombers, 1000 fighters, and 340 Stukas (dive bombers). One other advantage lay with the Germans—namely surprise and initiative.

On the morning of May 10, German forces struck simultaneously at Holland, Belgium, and France. In reality, the first two were diversions while the main thrust, under the command of General von Rundstedt, was aimed at France through the Ardennes Forest. The attack on Holland was perhaps a bit more than a diversion since the Germans appear to have feared its use as a base for RAF planes. As a result, the 400,000-man Dutch army, short of officers, equipment, and training, had to fight a well-coordinated German infantry and airborne attack. By May 13, Dutch defenses were crumbling and Queen Wilhelmina and her ministers embarked for England on a pair of British destroyers. Holland continued to fight on, however.

Only at Rotterdam did the German attack on Holland stall. Losing patience, Hitler ordered Rotterdam bombed into submission if the Dutch refused to surrender. Although the Dutch commander accepted the German ultimatum, apparently faulty communications kept this information from reaching the German bombers, which had already taken off. The result was that on May 14, a massive air attack hit the city, leveling the stock exchange, the town hall, the post office, two railway stations, and the main business street. Some 25,000 houses were destroyed and nearly 1000 people killed.** The next day,

---

*Actually, the Germans with 2270 tanks were numerically weaker than the French and British, who together had about 3200 tanks.

**In retaliation, British bombers based in France bombed the important industrial cities in Germany's industrial district on May, 15.

May 15, at 9:30 A.M., the Dutch commander, General Winkelman, ordered fighting to cease on all fronts, except in Zeeland. For all practical purposes Holland, was not out of the conflict.

Nazi oppression began quickly in the Netherlands. On May 18, Artur von Seyss-Inquart became Reich Commissar for Holland. A Viennese, Seyss-Inquart had aided in the Nazi takeover of Austria, and later was made deputy to Hans Frank, Governor-General of Poland. Starting slowly, Seyss-Inquart ultimately forced the nation into subjection, although a Dutch resistance movement soon grew and responded to the high-handed Nazi policies. When the Nazis began to ship out Jews to concentration camps, the Dutch people went on strike. Although this was suppressed, the Dutch actively aided Jews throughout the war.*

German forces also attacked Belgium on May 10. After mobilization, the Belgian army comprised some 900,000 men, but only one heavy artillery division, no tanks, few anti-aircraft batteries, and only one squadron of fighter planes. The Belgian army put its faith in a series of ultra-modern fortresses, which guarded the wide, level gateway into Belgium from Germany. The most formidable of these was Fort Eben Emael at the juncture of the Meuse River and the Albert Canal, north of Liege. The fort had a garrison of 1500 men protected by thousands of tons of earth and concrete and was fortified with electrically operated artillery—two 120 mm. guns and sixteen 75 mm. guns. It rose some 130 feet above the Albert Canal and had concrete defense works that covered an area of 1000 yards by 750 yards.

The Germans, however, had constructed a model of Eben Emael in Czechoslovakia and rehearsed their assault on this mighty fortress. In the actual attack, they landed gliders with about 300 soldiers on the west bank of the canal and moved so quickly that they captured two of the three bridges intact. One group of nine gliders landed directly on the fort itself, and a force of 80 men was soon storming it. Using flame throwers and demolition charges, the German troops disabled the fortress within an hour's time, although the garrison did not formally surrender until noon on the following day, May 11.

When the German attack came, the Allied armies in northern France moved, according to plan, into Belgium in order to form a continuous front with the Belgian army along the Dyle and Meuse Rivers. With the Maginot Line protecting the French-German frontier from a German attack, the Allies were now ready to confront the aggressors on Belgian soil. This was precisely what the Germans had hoped would occur. As Hitler later said,

> *When the news came through that the enemy was moving forward along the whole front, I could have wept for joy; they had fallen into the trap. It was vital that they believed we were sticking to...(the) old plan, and they had believed it.*

The Allies were completely unaware that the Germans were preparing to outflank the Allied-Belgian armies by attacking in the south, through the supposedly impenetrable Ardennes Forest. Located in southern Belgium, the rolling heavy wooden terrain was thought impassable to tanks, and consequently the French had placed only light motorized forces in the area to backup the few Belgian defenders. Yet it was precisely in this 50-mile gap between the main French-Belgian force to the north and the Maginot Line to the south that the main German blow on the western front was delivered.

Catching the Allied forces completely off guard, the Germans negotiated the rough Ardennes terrain and by May 12 were already at the Meuse River near the French city of Sedan, farther and faster even than Guderian had thought possible. French guns covering the river were neutralized by German dive bombers and low level attack bombers.** In less that a day's time the guns were silenced and German assault boats were crossing the river by the afternoon of May 13. North of Sedan, the 7th German Panzer Division, commanded by Erwin Rommel, found an intact bridge across the Meuse and proceeded unopposed across the river. The battle for France was underway.

---

*It was in Amsterdam that teenager Ann Frank hid with her family for two years and wrote her famous diary before she was discovered and sent to a concentration camp where she died.

**At the point of assault, two German panzer divisions were facing one French light cavalry division—i.e., one horse and one motorized brigade. These forces were blown to pieces by the Luftwaffe attack before they were even in position.

Despite the overwhelming success of their attack, German forces were in a difficult and somewhat tenuous position on May 14. Although a bridgehead had been achieved on the left bank of the Meuse, only the infantry had crossed the river in force, while most of the armor was still on the right bank. On the 14th, Allied planes attempted to bomb the bridges that the Germans had thrown up across the river, but only managed to damage three (and they were quickly rebuilt). The Allies paid dearly for this meager achievement, losing 33 of 65 planes sent on the mission. French attempts to launch a counterattack against the German forces also floundered, although several favorable opportunities presented themselves.

By May 15, the French front lines were broken and the road to the North Sea was open. The 19th Panzer Corps under Guderian's command broke into the French countryside and sliced westward, spreading terror in the French rear. Some French units were seized with panic and stampeded, as a result of fatigue, jarred nerves, and demoralization caused by the enemy's overwhelming air superiority. The French 4th Armored Division, under then Colonel Charles de Gaulle, attempted to hit the southern flank of Guderian's forces on the 16th, and although hard fighting ensued, de Gaulle, soon threatened on his own flanks, had to pull back.

By the 20th, Guderian had taken Amiens and was threatening Abbeville on the coast. The northern group of Allied armies—French, British, and Belgian—was now cut off from the rest of the French armies. German troops had now gone farther in 10 days than German armies had been able to get in four years during World War I. On the night of the 20th, German tanks, under Rommel's command, reached the sea at Noyelles, near Abbeville. Rommel's 7th Panzer Division earned the nickname of the Ghost Division because of its sudden and unexpected appearances. It surprised barracks full of French soldiers, overran retreating French detachments and terrified unsuspecting civilians. At one point, patting Rommel's arm, a villager asked him if he was English. "No, Madam," he replied. "I am German." "Oh, the Barbarians!" she screamed, fleeing back to her home.

Allied armies in the north, including the entire Belgian army, and all but one division of the British Expeditionary Force and the two best French armies, now found themselves hammered by General Feodor von Bock's forces in Belgium and threatened on their flank by the German troops which had broken through at Sedan. Unless these Allied forces could break out quickly and link up with the rest of the French armies south of the Somme River, they would be annihilated in the German trap.

The commander of the French Army, General Maurice Gamlein, now 68 years old and secluded in his isolated headquarters at Vincennes (it had no radio or telephone communications with the outside), drew up a plan by which the troops in the south would strike north to aid Allied troops there to break out and cut off the German forces. Properly executed, the plan might have given the Allies a chance to form a new front in Northern France along the Aisne and Somme Rivers. But that is pure conjecture because before anything could be done, the French Prime Minister, Paul Reynaud, replaced Gamlein with General Maxime Weygand.

A World War I hero, Weygand was 73 years old, and having most recently served in Syria, knew little or nothing about the front in Northern France. He initially discarded Gamlein's plan, but after three days of conferences with Allied commanders drew up one which was almost identical. The delay doomed whatever chances for success existed, because by now Allied armies were reeling and the generals were in a state of shock. When the attack came it did surprise the Germans, and put a bad scare into Rommel, whose forces bore the biggest brunt of the attack. Still, the Allies were stopped, losing more than 40 tanks, compared to 12 for the Germans, and the main German advance continued on unchecked.

The fighting in the Low Countries came to an abrupt end of May 28 when King Leopold of Belgium—acting as Commander-in-Chief of the Belgian Army—surrendered to the Germans.* This was an unilateral decision which was communicated to the French one hour after it had been sent to the Germans.

---

*Leopold ignored the pleas of his own Cabinet when he surrendered. Refusing to go into exile, he was kept as a prisoner by the Nazis during the war. After the war was over, his countrymen didn't want him back.

By May 28, Allied troops north of the Somme had been compressed into a pocket of less than 60 square miles around the French port of Dunkirk. Already on May 26 the British Admiralty had given the signal for the evacuation of Allied troops—Operation Dynamo—even before the British Cabinet had authorized the evacuation. It was not thought that more than a small percentage of the British Expeditionary Force could be evacuated since the British Admiralty believed they would have but two days to carry out the operation. What the British did not know was that General von Rundstedt had ordered his panzers to stop their advance, a halt order confirmed by Hitler. A number of reasons have been advanced as explanations for such an order. The British military historian, Captain Liddle Hart has argued that Hitler let the British army escape from Dunkirk on purpose, hoping to make a separate peace with England after the defeat of France. A more likely explanation for the halt was the terrain around Dunkirk. Up to this time, German tanks had been moving through ideal tank country where fields as well as roads could bear the weight of the German panzers. But around Dunkirk the land became marshy, and the city itself is built entirely on land reclaimed from the sea and is surrounded by canals, ditches, and dykes. Crossing the broad River Aa, halfway between Calais and Dunkirk, presented another problem to the German tanks. Finally, German tanks had been moving so rapidly and unrelentingly up this point that nearly half of them were out of service, mostly through wear and tear. They needed to stop and refurbish before pushing on.

Hitler's confirmation of the halt order was accompanied by a statement that the Air Force should be left to finish off the bottled-up of French and British troops at Dunkirk. Field Marshal Goering, the Luftwaffe Commander, agreed, although the general in command of air operations in France, General Albert Kesselring, was not so sure. At any rate, the German army halted for two days—May 24–26—on the Aa River line.

When the halt order was countermanned on May 26, the new advance followed a different strategy. The panzers were not the lead force, the infantry was; and this made for a lengthier battle. In addition, Army Group B, which was now to join with Army Group A, was slowed by the task of organizing the Belgian Army surrender and failed to adequately coordinate its operations with Army Group A.

The delays and confusion in the German attack gave the British more time than they thought possible to effect the evacuation. Luftwaffe raids, initially stalled by bad flying weather, got underway with a heavy attack on May 29, and the attacks increased over the next three days. By June 2, they were so heavy that daylight evacuations had to be suspended. Most of the Luftwaffe damage was inflicted at sea where they sank six destroyers, eight personnel ships and over 200 small craft. Still, by May 30, 126,000 troops had been evacuated, far more than any anyone had originally hoped for, or thought possible. The operation was finally broken off on June 4, as the Germans pressed in on the beleaguered rear guard protecting the beaches. In all, some 338,000 British and Allied troops had been safely landed in England by the array of private yachts, fishing boats, lifeboats, and regular navy ships which came to the rescue.* It was an amazing accomplishment compared with earlier expectations.

There is no doubt, however, that Dunkirk was a major Allied defeat. Although the bulk of the British Expeditionary Force was safe in England and ready to fight another day, the bulk of their weapons lay strewn along the French and Belgian beaches. So short of weapons was the British Army that the only fully equipped division in Great Britain was Canadian. British troops trained with broom sticks for lack of rifles. A quick German thrust across the Channel soon after Dunkirk would probably have knocked England out of the conflict. Fortunately for the British, Hitler had no such plan in mind for the time being. (See Chapter V).

After Dunkirk, it was simply a matter of time before the French Army would have to surrender. The German offensive was launched on June 5 and although it still met resistance for several days, by June 7 it had broken the French defensive line and had crossed the Seine River by June 9, the same day that

---

*In France another 190,000 men were later evacuated from Normandy and Bordeaux. An attempt to withdraw the British 51st Division from St. Valery failed, however.

the French Government fled Paris for Tours. On June 10, Italy declared war on France, although it was another 10 days before Italian troops moved to the offensive in the French Riviera, and then without much success. The French Cabinet was by this time already debating capitulation, but prolonged that decision for a time when it moved further south to Bordeaux.

On June 14 the Germans entered Paris, which had been declared an open city by the French some three days earlier. Premier Reynaud resigned on June 16 and the new cabinet formed by Marshal Petain transmitted an armistice request to Hitler. German terms were delivered to the French on the 20th in the same railway car in the Compiegne Forest where German representatives had signed the armistice of 1918, and went into effect on June 25, 1940. Under these terms Germany would occupy only the territories which their armies had already conquered, plus the rest of the Atlantic coast stretching down to the Spanish border. About two-thirds of France was to be occupied and governed by the German Army. The southern part of France was not to be occupied by the Germans, as it was allegedly a free and independent government. Marshal Petain, who headed this new government in Vichy, some 175 miles south of Paris, adopted a policy of collaboration with the Germans, and always governed in a manner calculated to satisfy them.* On the question of the powerful French fleet, the armistice provided that all French warships were to be disarmed in their home ports, and the Germans and Italians guaranteed not to make use of them in any subsequent hostilities. Not trusting the Germans, the British Admiralty launched Operation Catapult on July 3rd, an attempt to secure every French warship afloat. In many areas the British were able to do this peacefully. This was not the case, however, with the main French naval force in the Mediterranean. A British squadron came upon this force near Mers-el-Kebir in Algeria, and after some confusing attempts at negotiation, fighting broke out between the two fleets, with the French losing four large warships and 1267 lives. The bitterness which the French felt over this event, was to poison French-English relations for many years to come. In their mind, the English had exploited their darkest hour, to further humiliate and humble her. It also perhaps made French collaboration with the Germans easier.

The defeat of France was the high point of the German Army. They had defeated the French as easily as they had Poland, and while no one was surprised by Poland's demise, France's fall was a great shock to the whole world. The French Army was one of the world's great armies and France herself, the bulwark of Western civilization. As one book has noted, "...the fall of France opened an abyss of uncertainty for the whole continent and shook the imagination as perhaps nothing had shaken it since the victory of the Turks at Mohacs in 1526."

---

*When Allied troops invaded North Africa in November, 1942, German troops occupied the Vichy territories.

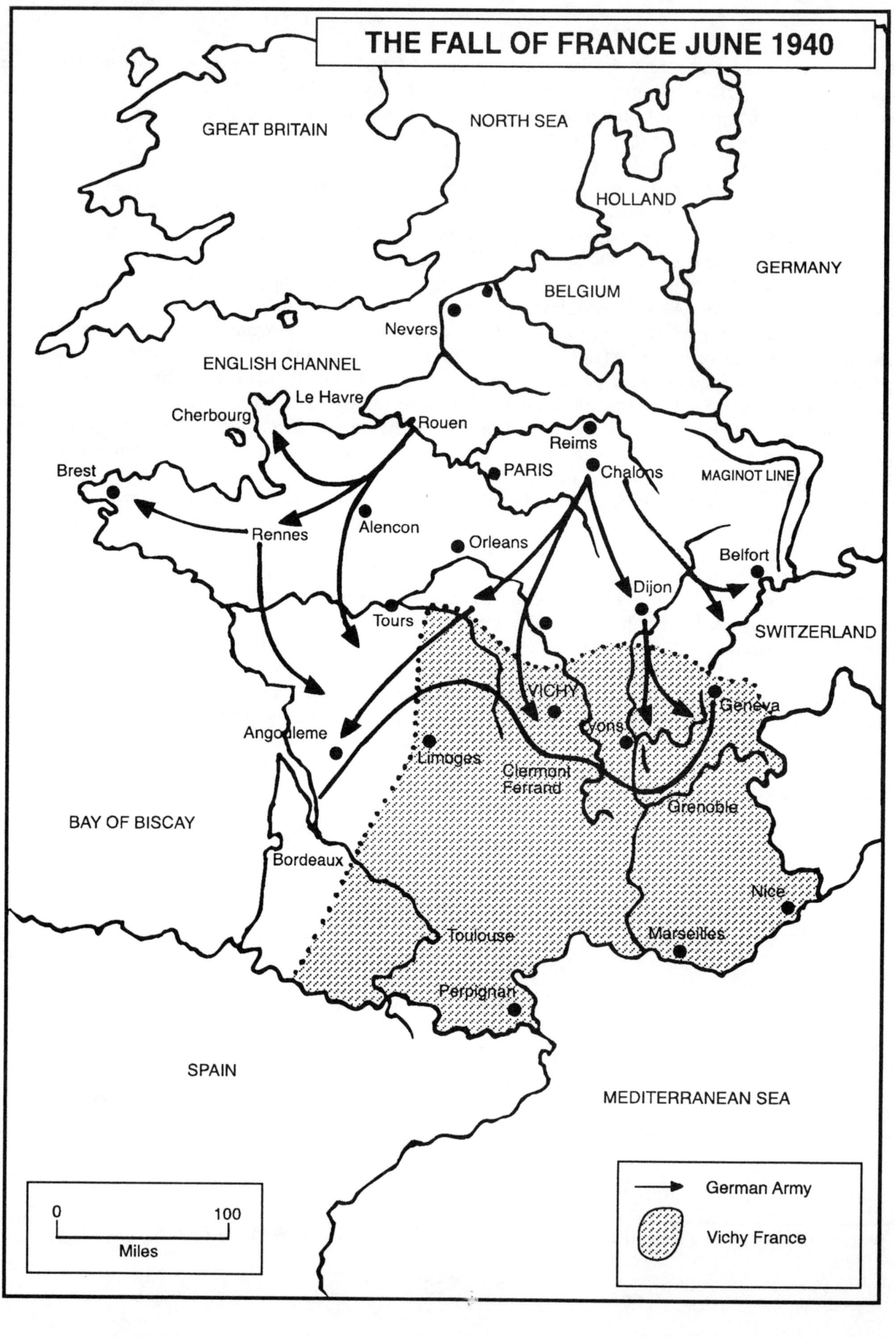

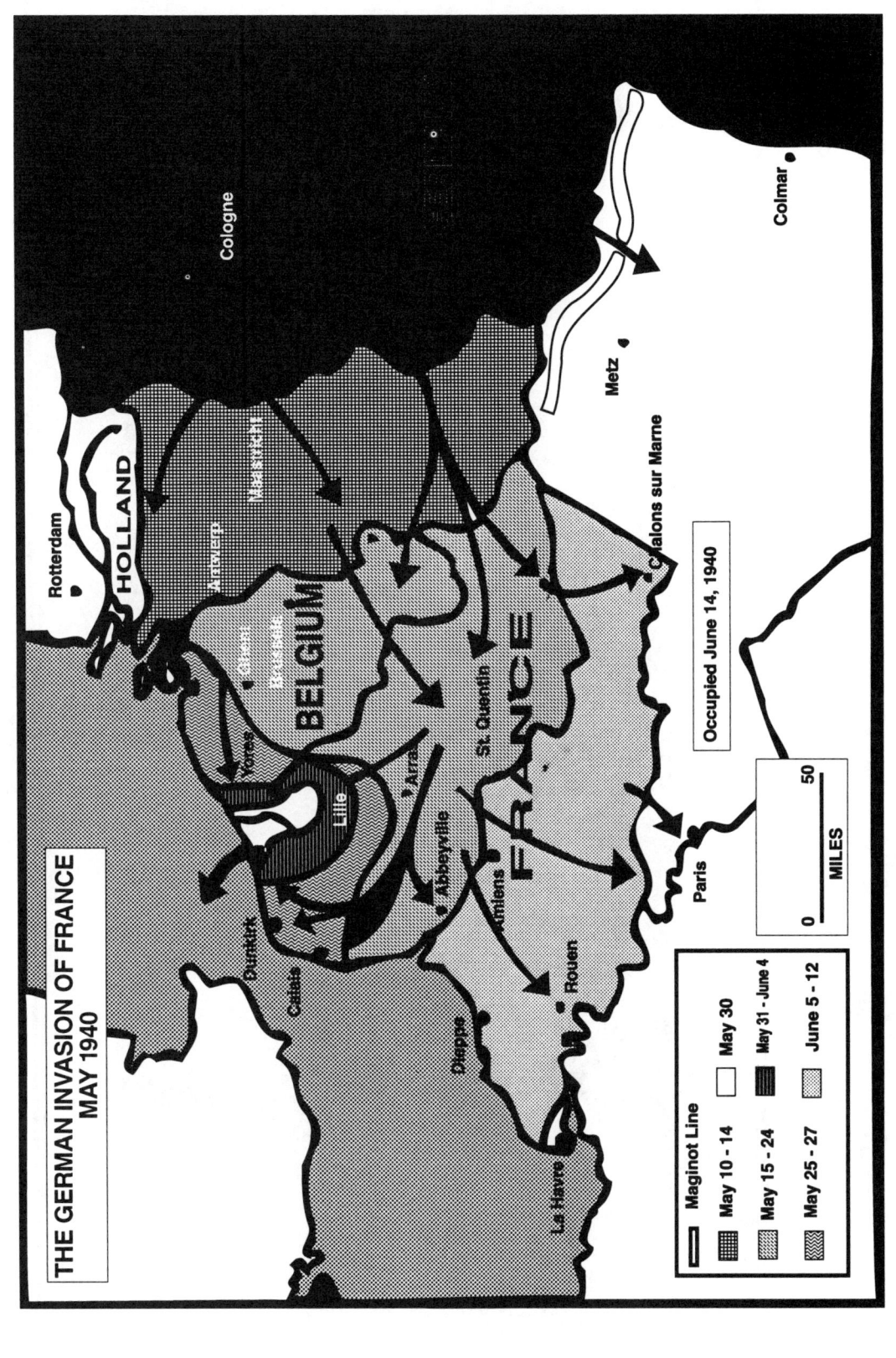

Courtesy of Corbis-Bettman. Reprinted by permission

Chapter V

The Battle of Britain

❖   ❖   ❖

After the German-French Armistice was signed on June 22, 1940, Hitler reportedly remarked to General Alfred Jodl, "The British have lost the war, but they don't know it; one must give them time, and they will come around." This comment reflected Hitler's assumption that once her continental ally, France, was defeated, England too would make peace. Indeed, the Germans had no plans at all for continuing the war with the British, nor did they develop any, even when it became obvious that France was collapsing. German generals were given to understand that the war was over. Leaves were granted to many servicemen, and as many as 35 divisions were demobilized by the end of June, 1940.

For a number of reasons, Hitler not only expected but desired peace with Great Britain. In the first place, he considered the British Commonwealth an institution worth preserving, insomuch as it provided Aryan racial control over British territories around the globe. Secondly, Hitler seems to have nurtured the hope that the British, now led by the strong anti-Communist Churchill, would join Germany in an attempt to destroy Communist Russia. Militarily, Hitler realized that continued war against Great Britain was not the kind of conflict for which the German army or airforce had been designed. He and his generals liked campaigns with easily discernible goals, which could be quickly achieved. The whole concept of "blitzkrieg" was based on such a belief. Continued conflict with Great Britain, however, would involve Germany in a worldwide undertaking with the British Commonwealth of Nations, ranging from Canada to North Africa to India. Such a far-flung type of warfare hardly offered the prospect of a lightning victory. Even an invasion of Great Britain itself was not something for which the German military was designed or trained.

Great Britain's continued belligerence came not only as a surprise to Hitler, it also greatly irritated him. She was a thorn in the German side, a possible base for launching attacks against Nazi-dominated Europe, and a center for anti-Nazi governments in exile. And if other countries, for example the United States, entered the war, Great Britain could become the launching site for a massive invasion of the continent. When no British proposals for an armistice reached Hitler in the month following France's defeat, he adopted a more belligerent attitude toward the British, threatening them in a July 19 address to the Reichstag with unending suffering and misery unless they made peace. He did, at least in his own mind, leave the door open for conciliation with the British when he declared, "At this hour I feel it is my duty to appeal in good faith, for reason and wise counsel on the part of Great Britain...."

Not everyone in Great Britain was deaf to this appeal and some influential Britons felt that the time had come to make peace with Germany. The British Prime Minister was definitely not one of them, however. Churchill considered Hitler to be the devil incarnate and the war, quite simply, to be one between good and evil, civilization and barbarism. As early as June 18, 1940, Churchill had remarked that what General Weygand had called the Battle of France was over. "I expect," he went on, "that the Battle of Britain is about to begin. Upon this battle depends the survival of Christian civilization." At a general staff meeting in his underground headquarters, he reportedly pointed at a wooden chair at the head of a conference table and commented:

This is the room from which I will direct the war. And if the invasion takes place, this is where I'll sit—in that chair. And I'll sit there until either the Germans are driven back or they carry me out dead.

When Hitler received no positive response to his peace proposals, he initiated planning for Operation Lion (later expanded to Sea Lion)—the code name for a projected German invasion of Great Britain. The hastily conceived plan called for September 15 as the date for the attack. According to Hitler's top-secret directive to Germany's military leaders.

Since England, despite her hopeless military situation, still shows no sign of willingness to come to terms, I have decided to prepare and if necessary carry out, a landing operation against her. The aim of this operation is to eliminate the English motherland as a base for carrying on the war against Germany, and, if necessary, to occupy the country completely.

Sea Lion was an ambitious plan, calling for landing up to 250,000 German soldiers along a 200-mile front in southern England. Most of the troops would be transported across the Channel by ships, in everything from converted river barges to tugs and motorboats, although airborne landings were also planned. Once the beachheads were established, German forces would push inland and cut off London from the rest of the country. The German secret police (the Gestapo) would then move in and arrest some 2000 leading British personalities, from Winston Churchill to writers such as Aldous Huxley and Virginia Woolf, and actor, Noel Coward. All able-bodied Englishmen between the ages of 17 and 45 were to be interned and eventually transferred to the continent.

The most notable skeptic of the invasion plan within the German high command was Grand Admiral Eric Raeder, Commander-in-Chief of the German navy, who regarded a naval invasion as virtually impossible. Losses in Norway had been so heavy that the German navy was nearly nonexistent. Raeder did go through the motions of assembling river barges and ships in order to please the generals and Hitler, but he never took the invasion plans seriously.

Even Hitler realized that before an amphibious invasion could be launched, it would be necessary to neutralize the Royal Air Force (RAF) and destroy Britain's air defenses, tasks that Goering enthusiastically accepted. Believing that the bomber would always get through, Goering envisioned fleets of bombers and fighters devastating England from the air, pulverizing her to the brink of surrender. Hitler showed his support for this type of thinking by promoting three Luftwaffe generals to the rank of Field Marshall and granting a special citation for Goering:

For his mighty contribution to victory, I hereby appoint the creator of the Luftwaffe to the rank of Reich Marshall of the Greater German Reich, and award him the Grand Cross of the Iron Cross.

A few days later, Goering announced to Hitler, "that the RAF will be destroyed in time for Operation Sea Lion to be launched by September 15, when our German soldiers will land on British soil." Thus was laid the groundwork for what has been labeled the Battle of Britain, the German attempt to destroy the RAF and allow a generally unopposed invasion of Great Britain to take place.

At its outset, the Battle of Britain seemed a David vs. Goliath confrontation between the weakly defended British Isles and the world's greatest airforce, which had completely destroyed the Polish airforce, reduced the city of Rotterdam to rubble and ruled the skies over France. On paper the Luftwaffe greatly outnumbered the RAF, with some 4500 frontline aircraft to 2900 for the British. But these figures, as well as the German superiority they seemed to indicate, were misleading. A large portion of the Luftwaffe was made-up of transport planes and liaison aircraft, which played no part at all in the Battle. Germany also had fighter squadrons stationed in Poland, in southern Germany, and in Austria, beyond range for participating in attacks on Great Britain. It was also significant that by 1940 the British were producing more fighter aircraft than the Germans. One hundred and forty Bf (Messerschmitt) 109's, the main single-seated German fighter, were being turned out each month, while the two main British fighters, the Hurricanes and the Spitfire, were coming out at the rate of 500 each month.

Actually, the figure for the total number of British planes also was inflated because it included aircraft from Bomber Command, which played only an indirect and tangential role in the Battle of Britain, and RAF transport and liaison aircraft. On July 20, 1940, when the Battle of Britain began, RAF Fighter Command had 531 serviceable fighters (out of a total of 609) and another 289 fighters in reserve.

The British did have a definite advantage in both the design and quality of their airforce compared to the Germans. The Luftwaffe simply had not been designed for the task assigned to it by its Commander. It was an airforce, as noted earlier, primarily intended for close support of ground troops and Guderian's concept of blitzkrieg, not for long-range bombing missions. A plan for a four-engined bomber died with its advocate in 1936, leaving the Luftwaffe with two-engine light and medium bombers, particularly vulnerable to fighter attacks and thus in need of their own fighter escorts.

German fighters, however, were not well-equipped to handle this task. The main fighters in the German arsenal at the time of the Battle of Britain were the Bf 109 and Bf 110. The current model of the 109, the 109E (called the Emil after Emil Messerschmitt) had a faster rate of climb and a higher ceiling than comparable British fighters, and at least theoretically, could turn more sharply than British fighters. The 109's chief drawback was its limited range, a 410-mile maximum cruising range, which meant about 80 minutes flying time. Since it took 30 minutes to attain sufficient altitude over France to reach the English coast and then 30 minutes to get back to base, only 20 minutes were left for operations over England. London was at the outer limits for German fighters. Many 109s were knocked out of the sky not by British planes but by lack of fuel.

The Bf 110 was a long-range, two-engine fighter, especially designed for the role of escort. Its pilots were handpicked from Bf 109 units and formed into elite "Destroyer" units, considered the Luftwaffe's best. The 110 was well-armed with a battery of four 7.92 mm machine guns and two 20 mm cannons and a rear-firing machine gun for a second crewman. At 336 miles-per-hour, it was nearly as fast as the Spitfire, and faster than the Hurricane (about 325 mph). But the 110 also had certain deficiencies as an escort aircraft. Its turning circle was very wide, a distinct disadvantage in air-to-air combat, and its acceleration was poor. Its size made it both easy to recognize and easy to hit. As a result, it proved to be a disappointment in the ensuing conflict, although it did restore some of its prestige by serving as a very effective night fighter later in the war.

The bombers for which these planes were to provide escort duty included the Dornier (Do) 17 and the Do 215; the Heinkel (He) 111; the Junkers (Ju) 88A and the Ju 87 B. The Do 17Z, the "Flying Pencil," was the oldest operational type bomber in use in 1940 and made up about one-fourth of the bomber and reconnaissance units facing the British. It was slow and its bomb load was limited. The Do 215 was really a reconnaissance aircraft that was also slow and lacking in any protective armor. The He 111 was the most numerous of the Luftwaffe bombers. Although it could carry almost double the bomb load of the Do 17Z, it was the slowest of all German bombers. It did have a great deal of protective armor and extra machine guns as compensation, but it proved inadequate in the Battle of Britain, and by September, 1940, was relegated to night bombing. The best bomber in the German service was the Ju 88A, although it was just coming into service at the time of the Battle of Britain. Its bomb load was somewhat less than that of the He 111, but it was considerably faster and had a 1500-mile range. Its effectiveness was somewhat reduced when it was given a dive-bombing role; undue stress caused airframe problems. Finally, the Ju 87 was a single engine dive bomber that in the German plan was to provide precision bombing that would be cheap "in money, materials, and manpower." But the plane's bomb load was very small (1100 pounds vs. 2200 pounds for the Do 17Z and 4400 pounds for the He 111). The Ju 87's range was short (200 miles), it was slow (at 232 mph the slowest plane on either side), and once committed to its dive was highly vulnerable to British fighter planes and anti-aircraft fire. The "B" model (the "Bertha") had even suffered severe casualties during the fighting in Poland, and after almost daily massacres at the hands of the British, the Ju 87 was withdrawn from the Battle of Britain. Despite these weaknesses, the Luftwaffe was still an awesome force. Its past successes and its belief that the RAF had been seriously (perhaps fatally) weakened by the French campaign, leaving only a feeble air defense for Britain itself, greatly enhanced the Luftwaffe's morale.

The Royal Air Force had three main types of fighters to challenge the Germans: the Hurricane, the Spitfire, and the Defiant. The Hurricane was the mainstay of the RAF. In September, 1940, nearly half of Britain's 61 fighter squadrons were equipped with them, while only 20 squadrons were equipped with Spitfires. The Hurricane was a stable airplane, dependable, and had an impressive gun platform. Early models carried 8 machine guns, with four more being added to later models. By 1940 some were also equipped with four 20 mm cannons. The Hurricane's weaknesses included its speed, slower than the 109, and its ceiling, 1000 feet lower than the 109. The Spitfire, which was gradually replacing the Hurricane, was much faster (370 mph vs. 325 mph) and also faster that the 109. Also, the Spitfire was able to turn inside the 109 and get behind it in a dogfight. Theoretically, this should not have been the case since the 109's turning radius was 750 feet compared to 880 feet for the Spitfire. But because of the weaknesses in the wing construction of the 109 (its landing gear, for example, had to be placed on the fuselage instead of the wing for this reason), most German pilots were unwilling to test the theoretical limits of the 109's turning circle. Thus in practice, the Spitfire was able to "get inside" the 109. The Spitfire carried eight .303 caliber machine guns, from which a three-second burst could bring down a German bomber. The Spitfire's engine, however, lacked fuel injection (which the 109 possessed) and often in steep dives its engine would conk out, often with fatal results.

The third British fighter was the two-seated Defiant, which possessed an armored turret with four machine guns in the rear. Since the Defiant resembled a Hurricane, German fighters would often attack it from the back side, usually a mistake because of the rear gun. But once German pilots learned to identify the Defiant, it proved highly vulnerable. It was slow, lacked agility, and proved generally ineffectual during daylight operations.

British bombers did play a role in the Battle of Britain, although a peripheral one. Bombing attacks on the Ruhr, Germany's industrial heartland and on Channel ports where German ships were gathering for Sea Lion, did help divert some German air units from offensive to air-defense functions. But these attacks were really sideshows. The main task in the Summer of 1940 was the defense of the British Isles and this fell to British fighter planes.

Fighter Command was to be ably assisted, however, by the world's first and for a long time, most extensive and sophisticated radar network (the British referred to radar as RDF—Radio Direction Finding). RDF was a method for detecting the position of distant objects by the reflection of radio rays. The fear of air power, particularly the bomber, was so great after World War I that military planners looked for ways to defeat it. Death rays to kill aircrews, and radio transmissions to stop the planes' engines were tried, obviously without success. But from 1934 onwards radar, at least a means of detecting the bombers, was put into use, and by the Spring of 1939, Great Britain had a chain of 51 radar stations in operation along her eastern and southern coasts. The bases for the system were 340 ft. high long-range antennae that could pick up planes as far as 150 miles away at altitudes up to 30,000 feet. When it became known that low-flying aircraft could sneak under the beams from these towers, low-level antennae were added.

When enemy planes were spotted by radar units, their approximate number, distance, and altitude were phoned to a Filter Room at Bentley Prior, headquarters for Fighter Command. Here, reports from radar stations were compared, judged and interpreted. The filtered reports were then plotted on the Filter Room map table with counters, red for the enemy and black for friendly aircraft. Numerals showed estimated altitude and strength; arrows indicated direction. Each formation was given its own reference number. Members of the Women's Auxiliary Air Force (WAAF) plotted the movements of friend and foe as staff officers watched from the Filter Room balcony. Details of all movements were passed on to Operation Rooms at Sector, Group, and Fighter Command Headquarters. At each site the map was identical. The Staff Officers on the balcony had the use of a board fitted with colored lights that showed what squadrons were available in 30 minutes, which were at readiness (5 minutes) or at cockpit readiness (2 minutes) and which were already in the air.

Since British radar stations faced toward the ocean, as soon as the attackers crossed the coast, radar was useless, and the Operations' Rooms were forced to rely on volunteer civilian spotters to plot the movement of enemy planes.* British pilots were guided entirely by the voice of the Controller, who was watching the plotting map.

The importance of this countrywide network is obvious. British fighters could be kept on the ground until needed, thus conserving fuel since it was not necessary to fly standing patrols to guard against German attacks. It was also possible for British fighters to be "scrambled" early enough to gain sufficient altitude to be waiting in the sun to engage the German planes. British pilots could also be directed to points of the heaviest and most serious raids. For most of the fighting, the radar control system proved quite reliable, with the colored markers on the plotting table no more than four minutes or 15 miles behind events. No wonder that many Fighter Command pilots were later to credit radar and the early warning system with winning the Battle of Britain.

Although the Germans had also developed radar (which they used mostly to detect ships) they seem never to have appreciated its value to the British. Attacks were launched against radar stations in August and several were put out of operation for varying periods of time, but these raids were not pursued in any systematic fashion.

In detailing the actual course of events of the Battle of Britain, it is useful to divide the conflict into three phases, which are helpful for analyzing changes in the strategy and nature of the Battle:

PHASE ONE: The phase began in July, 1940, and consisted of a month of attacks on British Channel convoys and port cities.

PHASE TWO: This phase lasted from August 12 to September 6, 1940, and was the major German assault. Its targets were the RAF fighter airfields in Southeast England.

PHASE THREE: Beginning on September 7, German attacks were turned mainly toward London, first by daylight and then by night. Although this phase lasted until Spring, 1941, German invasion was no longer a threat after September 15, 1940, which marks the end of the Battle of Britain.

The first phase of the Battle was characterized by a German attempt to force RAF fighters to cover shipping in the English Channel by attacking British convoys; there were additional attacks on British port cities along the Channel. The Germans hoped to wear down Fighter Command by forcing it to offer continual protection to the convoys and to shoot down its planes over water, where both plane and pilot would likely be lost. Sir Hugh Dowding, head of Fighter Command, however, wisely decided to provide only minimal air support to the convoys, although as shipping losses mounted he came under increasing pressure to give more support and protection for the Channel convoys. This he reluctantly did although rerouting of convoys and nighttime sailing helped to cut down naval losses.

When the attacks on convoys and coastal cities did not bring about the destruction of the RAF, Goering decided to concentrate Luftwaffe attacks on inland airbases, in order to destroy aircraft on the ground, if possible, and to draw British fighters into action, where they hopefully could be shot down. The launching day for this grand offensive, which characterized the 2nd phase of the Battle, was christened Aldertag—Eagle Day—and opened on August 13 with attacks on forward RAF airfields and radar stations. By the end of the day, only 13 RAF fighter planes (the Germans calculated 70) had been destroyed,

---
*There were, of course, no radar sets of any kind in the British fighters.

compared with 45 German aircraft, both fighters and bombers. Nevertheless, the Germans pressed on with their attacks and by the end of the month of August, Fighter Command was in serious trouble. Its rate of loss was more than it could afford on its limited strength, and it was failing to deter the German attackers. Most of the airfields in southern England were seriously damaged and some were out of operation altogether. During the month of August, Fighter Command lost twice as many fighters as the Germans (338 to 117), and by the beginning of September, it seemed that the Germans were close to achieving their goal—the destruction of Britain's fighter strength and its bases in southern England. Fighter Command's Number 11 Group, covering London and southeast England, had six of its seven main control airfields seriously damaged and five of its forward stations put out of action.

On September 3, 1940, Goering notified Hitler of his decision to switch the bombing offensive away from the airfields to London and on the afternoon of September 16, an air armada of about one thousand aircraft attacked the British capital. This was a fateful decision and without a doubt the turning point in the Battle of Britain.

Why, when Fighter Command was on the verge of destruction, did Goering switch his targets to London and to English cities, thus allowing Fighter Command to recoup its losses, train new pilots, and bring new aircraft into service? One of the factors seems to have been a British raid on Berlin on August 25. This was, in turn, a retaliation for a mistaken bombing of London on August 24 by a lost German aircraft, which jettisoned its bomb load on London. The British bombing so infuriated both Hitler and Goering (who had once boasted no British bombs would fall on Berlin), they decided on a policy of retribution. Another factor inducing Goering to press the attacks on London may have been related to German overcounting of British fighter losses. It is possible that Goering, believing that Fighter Command was virtually annihilated, decided to begin the onslaught on civilian morale in the cities. One of the unfortunate results of this new Nazi policy was to begin the indiscriminate bombing of cities and the killing of innocent civilians, without doubt one of the worst features of the war.

To many Englishmen, the heavy bombing of September 7 appeared to be the prelude to invasion. The numbers of invasion barges that had been assembling for some time in the Channel seemed to confirm British fears. On the night of September 7, the alert for Operation Cromwell—invasion imminent—was sounded. The Home Guard was made ready and some church bells, which were to signal the invasion, were actually rung. On September 11, Churchill broadcast an invasion warning and on September 15, the Germans made one last great effort to destroy the RAF. Although the British lost 26 aircraft during this raid, they destroyed 60 German planes (the British calculated that they had shot down 185), and it was clear that the Luftwaffe had not established air superiority, the prerequisite for Operation Sea Lion.

On September 17, Hitler postponed Sea Lion "until further notice," and on October 12 it was cancelled for the winter. Germany did keep up invasion preparations until March, 1941, but after September 15 passed, there was small likelihood of a German attack. England had won the battle for control of her skies and was safe from invasion for the duration of the conflict.

The Battle's third phase has often been referred to as the Blitz, although German attacks did not regularly maintain the pressure suggested by that term. In this phase, German raids consisted primarily of night bombing—mainly against British cities—the object being to break civilian morale. These raids did do a great deal of damage. Three and a half million homes were damaged or destroyed, the House of Commons and Buckingham Palace were hit, and much of London and several provincial cities devastated. Some 30,000 people were killed. Still, morale was basically unshaken and the British people united as never before in their history. When an American worried about civilian morale in London, he was told that there were no civilians in London. The worst night of the attacks proved to be the last. On May 10, 1941, a German attack on London killed nearly 1500 people and injured over 1700, but this raid was really a cover for the coming Nazi invasion of the Soviet Union and was used to camouflage the movement of German aircraft to the Eastern Front. After May, 1941, German air attacks on England declined greatly both in number and in effect.

Reasons for the British success in the Battle of Britain are numerous and interrelated. In the first place, the Luftwaffe was not designed for strategic air operations. Its previous successes were illusory in that they came in the role of support for ground troops, not in combat with an enemy airforce. Secondly, the Luftwaffe's shifting of targets from airfields to the cities came at a time when British fighter strength was near depletion. And although British cities were to suffer severely under the Nazi onslaught, Fighter Command was able to rebuild its bases, train new pilots, and replenish its lost aircraft. Thirdly, German overestimation of British aircraft destroyed probably led them to believe that they could shift targets since their figures indicated that RAF fighter strength was virtually nonexistent. The Germans believed that they had shot down 3058 British planes when in fact they had destroyed about 650.

On the British side, a number of factors contributed to success. Radar enabled British pilots to be waiting for German planes and relieved them of the necessity of doing standing patrols. The strategy of Dowding in not allowing Fighter Command's strength to be eroded, either in France or over the English Channel, was another major contribution to British success. Dowding was often criticized for his overly cautious strategy and after the battle was replaced as head of Fighter Command. His handling of men and machines, however, minimized losses at a time when England had to count the costs every day, so close was she to extinction. Just by remaining intact, Fighter Command won the Battle of Britain and for this Dowding deserves major credit. Finally, the spirit of Fighter Command's pilots, the quality of its aircraft, and the surge in fighter output under the able direction of Lord Beaverbrook were important contributors to British success.

The RAF and particularly Fighter Command greatly enhanced Britain's world prestige by winning the battle that Hitler probably never wanted. It may also have been a factor in luring Hitler into a major blunder, his attack on the Soviet Union. Since there were no enemy troops on the European mainland, Hitler argued, an attack on the Soviet Union would not involve Germany in the feared two-front war. Indeed, he suggested that by defeating the Soviet Union and depriving the British of their only possible continental ally, he would force Great Britain to surrender. The way to defeat England was to defeat the Soviet Union. Such was the delusion under which Hitler labored as he turned his attention towards the Soviet Union in the Spring and Summer of 1941.

Chapter VI

The German Invasion of the Soviet Union

❖ ❖ ❖

Hitler began his political career as an anti-Communist, and early expressed his desire to annihilate Soviet communism. In *Mein Kampf* Hitler also wrote about the need for living space (*lebensraum*), "...to guarantee to the German nation the soil and the territory to which it is entitled on this earth," and when thinking about these lands, he stated, "...we are bound to think first of Russia and her border states." Not only would the conquest of Russia provide *lebensraum* for the vigorous, expanding German people, but would also give Germany control of the Euro-heartland, and in Hitler's geopolitical views, whoever controlled the vast raw materials and food resources of this heartland, would control the world. Hitler, in fact, often expressed his interest in expanding to the east. Shortly after becoming Chancellor, he told German commanders that one of his primary goals would be to gain new territories in the East and to "Germanize" them.

Hitler's long-held beliefs about communism and the Soviet Union, did not prevent him from signing the Non-Aggression Pact with the Soviet Union in 1939. This allowed him to attack first Poland, and then Western Europe without worrying about fighting the Soviet Union and waging a two-front war. In addition, the agreement provided for Soviet food and raw materials to be shipped to Germany. But Hitler never intended the pact to last. Even as the document was being signed, he was telling leading Nazis that the pact was just to buy time and that ultimately he intended to crush the Soviet Union.

It is also doubtful that Stalin believed that the pact would endure for very long, which may explain why he quickly took advantage of it to add to the Soviet Union. Once the so-called "Phony War" ended in May, 1940, and the Germans became heavily involved in the West, the Soviets extended their holdings by incorporating the Baltic States, Latvia, Lithuania, and Estonia into the Soviet Union; they also added Northern Bukovina at the expense of Rumania. Thus by the time the Non-Aggression was one year old, Stalin had added an area of some 175,000 square miles, containing nearly 20 million people, to the territory of the Soviet Union.

This expansion worried Hitler, who was not yet ready to attack the Soviet Union. To help protect his northern flank, he signed a treaty with Finland and sent German troops there; in the South, he reached an agreement with Rumania, which permitted German soldiers to be stationed in that country.* It was obvious that Hitler would tolerate no more Russian expansion to the West, and he told Viacheslav Molotov, the Soviet Foreign Minister, that any further Russian expansion should be to the East, toward the Persian Gulf and India.

In July, 1940, Hitler ordered his generals to prepare for an invasion of the Soviet Union, noting that the sooner Russia was crushed, the better. Encouraged by Russia's poor military showing in the 1939–40 war against Finland, he told doubting generals that Russia was so weak that she could be conquered in 8–10 weeks. Against objections that an attack on the Soviet Union would mean a two-front war for Germany, Hitler argued that as soon as Russia was conquered, a demoralized Britain would sue for peace. "England is beaten," he said, although "a little still remains to be done."

---

*Germany's main source of oil was Rumania, whose Ploesti refineries provided the German war machine with the bulk of its fuel.

By December, the invasion plans were ready. The operation was to be called Barbarossa (Red Beard) after the nickname for Frederick I, who had campaigned against the Slavs in the 12th century. The date for the invasion was set for May 15, 1941, and throughout the early months of 1941, preparations moved forward. Tanks, artillery, and troops were moved into East Prussia and Poland. The build-up was stalled for a while when German troops were forced to put down an insurrection in Yugoslavia and to assist the Italians in Greece (See Chapter VII), and the attack date was moved from mid-May until June 22, a delay that some historians think may have doomed Barbarossa to failure. This meant one month less of good fighting weather, and because the Wehrmacht was not prepared for winter fighting, heavy pressure was now placed on the German military for a quick victory.* The main cause for the delay in the attack seems to have been shortages of equipment, particularly motor vehicles. According to British historian, A.J.P. Taylor, even at the time of the attack, forty percent of the German divisions were either wholly or partially supplied with captured French equipment.

Perhaps the greatest mystery surrounding Operation Barbarossa is the failure of the Soviets to take much heed of it, even though they received numerous warnings about an imminent German attack. Marshall Vasilevsky, who went with Molotov to Berlin in November, 1940, returned convinced that Germany was going to attack the Soviet Union. Daily bulletins from the Soviet General Staff, as well as from the Naval Staff, carried items about German preparations for war against the Soviet Union. German reconnaissance over-flights of Soviet territory were frequent occurrences. The United States and Great Britain also sent warnings about the likelihood of a German attack.

Perhaps the most convincing warning of all came from a brilliant Soviet agent by the name of Richard Sorge. Sorge had fought in the German army in World War I, but afterwards became a dedicated Communist and began to work for the Soviet Union. In 1933 he went to Japan, allegedly as a German journalist, and became a confidant of the German Ambassador in Tokyo. In May, 1941, Hitler revealed his blueprint for conquering the Soviet Union to the Japanese (undoubtedly hoping that they also would attack through Siberia). Sorge soon heard about the plan and wired the details to Moscow.**

Despite all of these warnings, the Soviet Union took few if any steps to prepare for a German attack, although the Chief of Intelligence for the General Staff at the time, F.I. Golikov, insists that all reports bearing on German plans were forwarded to Stalin; but Stalin did nothing. War games predicated on the possibility of a German attack were discussed, but the generals were reprimanded for "Germanophobia." Lavrentia Beria, head of the Soviet Secret Police, issued orders forbidding border generals or any military units to fire on German planes. It was simply not healthy for military men to speak their minds openly about Germany or to make any preparations to guard against a German attack.

Why, when confronted with such overwhelming evidence about a coming German attack, did Stalin ignore or refuse to believe it? There is no obvious answer to this question. One suggestion is that Stalin trusted Hitler and believed that the German generals were the ones who wanted war with the Soviet Union. Over-flights and border violations were viewed by Stalin as attempts to provoke the Soviet Union into retaliating, so that the generals could complain to Hitler and demand that Russia be punished.

A second possible explanation for Stalin's reticence when faced with the likelihood of a German attack, is that he was stalling, trying to buy time, at least until the Spring, 1943, in which to build up the Soviet military. It is also possible that Stalin believed that the German buildup opposite the Soviet Union was a feint to cover the real Nazi plan, the invasion of Great Britain. According to this view, Stalin did not believe Hitler would attack the U.S.S.R. until England was defeated, and in Spring, 1941, that event seemed a long way off.

---

*A.J.P. Taylor argues that the delay may actually have helped the Germans because in mid-May, the Russian soil was still very heavy after the Spring thaw. By mid-June, it had dried out.

**Five months after relaying his information to Stalin, Sorge was arrested by the Japanese and in 1944 he was hanged.

Finally, some historians have suggested that Stalin's inaction was a reflection of his paranoia concerning the West. "If the Western countries tell you one thing, then you must believe the opposite," was the way Stalin often approached the West. If they warn you about a German attack, it must mean that they wish to embroil you in a war with Germany while they profitably stay out of the affair. Western warnings were thus not to be believed, or at best taken with great skepticism.

Whatever Stalin's reasons for ignoring warnings about the German attack, there is no doubt that the attack, when it did come, was a complete surprise to him. Nikita Khrushchev has depicted Stalin as literally collapsing when informed of the German attack and ceasing to do anything whatever. He didn't direct military operations (and Stalin was the Supreme Commander of the Soviet Military), and he didn't issue instructions to Soviet Ambassadors around the world. He reportedly returned to activity only when the Politburo (the Political Bureau of the Communist Party) persuaded him that he must do so because of the national crisis. The Soviet Ambassador to Great Britain at the time, Ivan Maisky, paints a similar picture. "Stalin," he said, "locked himself in his office and refused to see anyone for the first four or five days."

Operation Barbarossa was based on a hierarchy of threes: Three German armies were to accomplish three main objectives in three phases. The main objectives of the plan were: 1. Destruction of Soviet Armed Forces; 2. Capture of the political and industrial centers of the Soviet Union (namely Moscow and Leningrad); and 3. the occupation of coal, iron, and grain centers of the Ukraine and the Caucasus.

The Germans hoped to achieve these objectives in three phases: In phase one, the German air and ground forces were to thrust deep into Soviet territory, create chaos, disrupt supply lines, encircle and destroy Soviet forces west of the Dvina-Dnieper River line, and prevent the organization of new defenses. Phase two called for the capture of Leningrad, Moscow, and the Ukraine in order to deprive the Soviet forces of political direction and economic support. In the final phase German troops would advance and hold a line running along the Volga River, from the Caspian Sea in the South to Archangel in the North.*

To execute this plan, the Germans divided their forces into three groups: 1. Army Group North in East Prussia, under Field Marshall Von Leeb, was to "liberate" the Baltic States and attack Leningrad; 2. Army Group Center in Northern Poland, under Field Marshall von Bock, was directed against Moscow; and 3. Army Group South, in southern Poland and Rumania, under Field Marshall von Rundstedt, was to concentrate on the Ukraine. This Army Group contained three Italian divisions, two Rumanian armies, and Hungarian and Slovak units.

Facing these German Armies were three Soviet Forces: 1. the Northwestern Front, under Marshall Voroshilov, was responsible for the defense of the newly acquired Baltic states and the city of Leningrad; 2. Forces of the Western Front, under Marshall Semen K. Timoshenko, guarding the approaches to Smolensk and Moscow; 3. the Ukrainian Front, defended by the forces under the command of Marshall Budenny.

Whatever the Soviet plans for meeting a German attack (if indeed there were any), the surprise dawn attack on June 22, quickly destroyed them. Bombing and strafing Soviet airfields, the Luftwaffe gained air superiority in one day. Most Soviet fighters were caught on the ground because they were not given permission to take off until the Germans had been bombing Soviet territory for nearly four hours. Over 1500 Soviet aircraft were destroyed on the ground that first day, and by the end of August, Russian aircraft losses probably reached 5000 planes.

On the ground the Russian front was broken in several places within hours of the beginning of Barbarossa. German panzer groups struck swiftly, disrupting the Soviet forces. They were followed by the German infantry, which encircled and trapped Russian forces in isolated pockets. Russian defenders were overwhelmed as German troops advanced as much as 50 miles per day.

---

*The Germans had no plans to occupy the whole of the Soviet Union.

It appeared that the Soviet Union was going to crumble under the weight of the German military. By mid-August, 700,000 Russian soldiers had been killed or wounded and another one million taken prisoner. The Germans had "liberated" the Baltic states and were only one hundred miles from Leningrad, while Finnish forces had recaptured most of Karelia and were pressuring Leningrad from the North. In the center, German forces had captured Minsk and Smolensk, and were within 200 miles of Moscow.* And in the South, half of the Ukraine was in the hands of the Germans, who were ready to cross the Dnieper and seize the Ukraine's main industrial areas. The first phase of Operation Barbarossa had been completed successfully.

Phase Two proved more difficult to carry out. Soviet land resistance stiffened and supposedly "sub-human" Slavs suddenly seemed "super human" to many German soldiers. Gaps opened up among the advancing German forces, allowing many Russian soldiers to escape and fight again. The Soviet Air Force, operating from more secure bases, were now at least able to harass the German advance. More important in slowing the Germans, however, was their inability (more correctly Hitler's) to fix the priority of the next strategic objective of the campaign. The generals insisted that Moscow should be the primary objective because it was the capital of the Soviet Union, a vital communication center, and an important industrial base. At first, Hitler wanted Leningrad to be the main objective in order to link up with the Finns, establish a new line of communications by sea and clear the Baltic of the Soviet fleet. By mid-August, however, he changed his mind and relegated both Moscow and Leningrad to secondary importance and gave priority to the Ukraine in order to place the resources of the region at the disposal of Germany. But no sooner had this plan gotten underway than Hitler developed a new plan of attack. It called for the reduction of Leningrad through siege and starvation; the encirclement and capture of Moscow; the conquest of the Crimea and above all, the Don River basin and the Caucasus Mountain area in order to gain the coal and oil resources of these regions for Germany.

The Germans began to threaten Leningrad as early as August 20, and by the 30th had cut off the city from the rest of the country. By September 8, Leningrad was totally encircled, except for one opening on Lake Ladoga. This set the stage for one of the most heroic and tragic events of the Second World War. Leningrad was to be virtually isolated and besieged by the Germans for the next 900 days, its only supplies coming from across Lake Ladoga (during the winter months a road was built across the ice). No one knows, or probably ever can know, the exact number of Russians who died in this siege, but estimates run between one and one and a quarter million, *i.e.* about the same as the entire losses the U.S. has suffered in the whole of its history, including the Civil War. Hundred of thousands of civilians died from starvation, after trying to stay alive by eating sawdust, glue, and rats. Cannibalism was also reported in the city, and many starvation-crazed people murdered to get food. In the winter months, the cold intensified the suffering. Oil and coal supplies were soon dissipated, and central heating disappeared. Pipes froze and the water supply was cut off. Yet the people of Leningrad never gave up. Perhaps in the short run they were saved by Hitler's decision not to attack but to besiege the city. In the long run, however, it was undoubtedly the heroism of the Leningraders, their capacity to suffer and their determination not to give in to the German aggressors, which saved the city.

It was only when the Soviet Army launched its massive counter attack in 1943–44 that the siege was lifted. German shells actually fell on the city as late as January 23, 1944, but by that time the Soviet counter-offensive was underway, and on January 27, 1944, a salute of red, white, and blue rockets marked the liberation of the city and the end of nearly 900 days of encirclement. The Leningrad writer, Vera Inber, found it impossible to write about the end of the siege, noting in her diary on January 27, "The greatest event in the life of Leningrad: full liberation from blockade. And I, a professional writer, have no words for it. I simply say: Leningrad is free. And that is all." But Olga Bergolts' words etched on the wall beside the eternal flame at Piskarevsky Cemetry do sum up the meaning of Leningrad:

---

*Finnish forces attacked the Soviet Union on June 25, 1941. Their aim was to reclaim what they had lost to the Soviets in the 1939–1940 Winter War. After winning back the part of Karelia, which had earlier been taken by the Russians, Marshall Mannerheim, the Finnish Commander, refused to take part in the capture of Leningrad.

Here lie the people of Leningrad,
Here are the citizens—men, women, and children—
And beside them the soldiers of the Red Army
Who gave their lives
Defending you, Leningrad,
Cradle of Revolution.
We cannot number the noble
Ones who lie beneath the eternal granite,
But of those honored by this stone
Let no one forget, let nothing be forgotten.

The German attack on Moscow was no more successful than their siege of Leningrad. German forces did score some initial successes on the Moscow front and captured important communication centers in Moscow's vicinity: Orel, Viazma, Briansk. By October 16, Muscovites began to panic as German forces appeared in the city. Many fled and government offices were moved some 500 miles away to Kuibyshev, although Stalin stayed in Moscow. His presence and the institution of martial law helped to restore order to the city, whose inhabitants now began to prepare for the German attack.

One German battalion managed to reach the suburb of Gorky, while another blew up the railroad station at the suburban village of Lobnia. Field Marshall von Bock even got close enough to see the spires of the Kremlin through his field glasses, but ten miles was as close as the Germans got to Moscow.

A number of factors contributed to Moscow's ability to withstand the German attack. First among them was the weather. Early October rains became downpours, which turned Russia's dirt roads into quagmires and the fields into seas of mud, often three or more feet deep. Trucks and wagons sank into the ooze. The tanks, which were able to move soon became stalled because the fuel they needed (and the supplies for the troops) could not reach them. German forces were now lucky to move 10 miles a day. German commanders openly wondered when they would be allowed to stop. Hitler's response was not "until they reached Moscow."

By the middle of November, temperatures had dropped enough to congeal the mud and allow the tanks and trucks to roll forward once again. Still, most German field commanders favored digging in for the winter, but once again Hitler ordered his armies forward toward Moscow.

This advance soon ran into a new obstacle, "General Winter" as the Germans came to call it. The first snows fell in October and by November the temperatures plunged, freezing trucks and tanks to the ground. Strong winds often caused the temperature to drop to the equivalent of –40 degrees F. Oil froze in German trucks, grease froze in guns, and railway engine boilers froze up. Airplane motors had to be kept running continuously because once stopped, they could not be restarted. Frostbite became common, and many wounded soldiers froze to death, sometimes in railway trains stalled in snowdrifts.

The German army was not prepared for this kind of fighting because Hitler had believed Russia would be defeated before winter came. Thus, German vehicles and weapons lacked the proper lubricants for the cold weather. Winter clothing and boots were also in extremely short supply. Many German soldiers went through the winter wearing summer uniforms and without any gloves. They were even reduced on one occasion to sawing off the legs of dead Russian soldiers and thawing them until their felt-lined boots could be removed. "Colonel Mud" had slowed the German advance; "General Winter" now stopped it.

As the advance ground to a halt, many German commanders began digging in for the winter, ignoring Hitler's directives to forge ahead. Instead of blaming the real culprits, *i.e.* the weather, the terrain, or Russian resistance, Hitler blamed his generals. Before December was over, he relieved more than 30 of them, including Guderian, von Rundstedt, and von Bock, of their commands.

Not only did the weather conspire to halt the German advance but so too did fresh Russian troops, whose presence in Moscow had gone undetected by German intelligence. These were the troops of the Soviet Far Eastern Army, some three-quarters of a million in number. They had been stationed, with strong tank and air support (and equipped for winter fighting), in the area around Lake Baikal in Siberia in order to guard against a possible Japanese attack from Manchuria.

In early October, however, Sorge sent a report to Stalin indicating that Japanese interests lay not in Siberia but in southeast Asia and in the Pacific. This time, Stalin believed his agent and ordered over half of his Far Eastern Command—18 divisions in all—to Moscow to aid in its defense. Russian troops were also given a new commander, Marshall Gregory Zhukov, who had recently been organizing the defenses of Leningrad.

These fresh, well-equipped troops not only helped to stop the German advance but launched their own winter offensive. Intending only to relieve the pressure on Moscow, they found German forces so weakened that they pushed them back as far as 135 miles. As the Russian winter offensive stalled in March 1942, the front reached a stalemate.

The one area where the Germans achieved some success in the second phase of their attack was in the south in the Ukraine. In late September, the capital of the Ukraine, Kiev, fell and with it some 600,000 Russian soldiers. The Germans soon added Odessa, Kharkov, Rostov, and the whole of the Crimea. The Russian winter offensive managed to recapture Rostov, but Germany still controlled most of the Ukraine and its food and mineral wealth.

In the Spring, 1942, the Germans unleashed a new offensive. Realizing by this time that his resources could not maintain a continuous attack all along the front, Hitler decided to concentrate German efforts on the flanks. There would be a secondary offensive in the north to capture Leningrad, but the main effort was to be in the south, where Hitler hoped to take the rest of the Ukraine, the oil fields of the Caucasus and the city of Stalingrad on the Volga River.

The Leningrad offensive managed to destroy the Soviet's Second Shock Army and capture its commander, General A.A. Vlasov.* The ring around Leningrad was further tightened, but the city continued to hold out. In the Fall, the Russians even launched a counter-offensive, which although it did not lift the siege, at least it removed the threat of immediate German capture of the city.

The German offensive in the south was launched at the end of June, 1942, and by the end of July, German armies had crossed the Don River on a broad front. On August 23, German troops reached the Volga River, and on September 9 approached the Volga port of Stalingrad. Hitler considered Stalingrad's capture to be important in order to provide flank cover for the German offensive in the Caucasus. It was also an industrial city of some 500,000 that controlled navigation on the Volga, and it was the communications center between central Russia and the oil fields of the Caucasus.

While the attack was being mounted on Stalingrad, German troops of Army Group B, under General von Kleist, fanned out into the Caucasus. The Maikop oil fields, although wrecked by the Russians, were captured in early August and on September 10, the Soviet's Black Sea Naval base at Novoroossisk fell. At this point the campaign stalled with the Germans not able to penetrate the Caucasus mountain barrier. Their attention now turned toward capturing Stalingrad.

The assault on the city began on September 15, and for the next month attack after attack was directed against it. Because of staunch resistance by Soviet forces under General Chuikov, none of the German attacks gained more than a temporary advantage. The more the Germans struggled to take Stalingrad, the more its psychological importance increased. The very name, "Stalingrad (Stalin's city) both inspired the Russian defenders and attracted the German aggressors. Hitler became so hypnotized with it that he lost all sight of strategy. As long as the supply lines to Stalingrad were open and reinforcements and reserves available to the city, the repeated German attacks were foolish. The Germans would have done better to have captured the left bank of the Volga (crossing down stream from Stalingrad) and attempted to starve out the Stalingrad garrison by cutting its supply lines. As it were,

---

*Vlasov was willing to be used against his former associates, but until 1944 he was employed only for the purpose of making propaganda. In September of that year, Hitler allowed the formation of a "Russian Liberation Army" under General Vlasov. Made up of Soviet prisoners willing to fight against Stalin's regime, the Army was to fight for the "creation of a new People's political system without Bolsheviks and exploiters." Vlasov was returned to the Soviet Union after the war and was executed.

all they did with their repeated bombing and shelling of the city was to create more rubble to be used for defensive purposes by the Russians. German shelling and bombing actually converted Stalingrad into a fortress.

In November, General Friedrich von Paulus took over command of the German Sixth Army, which was besieging Stalingrad. On November 19, he was greeted with a series of surprise Russian attacks against the flanks of the German salient, which was dangerously exposed in front of the city. Proper German action would have been to withdraw to better defensive positions in order to protect their communications and to keep from being surrounded, but Hitler vetoed such a move. With Rommel's recent defeat at El Alamein and with the British and American landings in North Africa (See Chapter VII), Hitler could not afford another failure.* Instead, he ordered von Paulus to take Stalingrad and promised him a relief force. Although German reserves were nearly depleted, an army of some 150,000 men was put together under General Manstein, but it ran into stiff Russian resistance and never reached the Sixth Army.

Meanwhile, the plight of von Paulus' forces worsened. His army was short of food and munitions, weakened by disease, had no winter clothes, and by November 23, was encircled by Russian troops. Paulus wanted to attempt a quick breakthrough of the Russian lines, costly though it might be, in order to reestablish his supply and communication lines, but Hitler refused. Instead, he promoted von Paulus to Field Marshall, making it clear that no German Field Marshall had ever surrendered. On the 31st of January, 1943, tradition notwithstanding, von Paulus and eight of his generals surrendered, and two days later the rest of the Sixth Army capitulated. Altogether, 100,000 Germans died and over 90,000 were captured, including 24 generals in the battle for Stalingrad. At the time, it was the worst defeat ever suffered by a German Army. These sacrifices did allow von Kleist's army to withdraw from its exposed salient in the Caucasus. In this case, Hitler did not oppose withdrawal, agreeing with Manstein's belief in the necessity of "trading space for time."

Stalingrad was the farthest penetration of German armies into the Soviet Union, and although they launched a new offensive in the Spring, 1943, the myth of German invincibility was now shattered. Stalingrad did not mark final Russian victory by any means, but the Soviet Union gained enormous worldwide prestige for what she had achieved, basically on her own.** Stalingrad was not just a victory for the Red Army but for the Soviet economy and for the Communist regime as well. The Russian people now drew more closely together and the early collaboration with the Germans (see below) basically disappeared after Stalingrad.

At the time of the Stalingrad battle, German troops had been in the Soviet Union for a year and a half, considerably longer than Hitler had anticipated, and they had failed to gain most of their major objectives. The reasons for this failure were many. In the first place, the enormous distances in Russia made it difficult for the German blitzkrieg strategy to work effectively. After the initial surprise attacks, the Germans found it difficult to cut off and annihilate the Russian troops. There was virtually endless space in which the Russians could fall back and form new defensive positions. The distances in Russia were five times as great as in Western Europe. Also, every advance by German armies in France brought them closer together. In Russia, the advance of the three army groups pulled them further apart and the more the Germans advanced, the wider became the gaps along their front.

Primitive Russian road conditions also hampered the German attack. German-tracked vehicles could operate over open fields but their supply vehicles could not. Thus, the mobility of German armies depended on good roads, which in Russia did not exist. Moreover, Russian airfields were generally not paved and when captured by the Germans proved difficult, if not impossible to use (particularly by Bf 109, with its unstable landing gear). In addition to the terrain, the weather conditions also

---

*Some historians suggest that Hitler feared that another German military failure might be siezed upon by disgruntled generals to discredit him and to carry out a coup d'etat.

**Material assistance from the U.S. and Great Britain had not yet reached the Soviet Union in very large quantities.

hampered the Germans. They were simply not prepared for a winter war or for the rainy, muddy conditions that preceded the cold and snow. The early onset of winter in 1941 gave the better-prepared Russian troops a major advantage by neutralizing the German superiority in equipment.

The Germans also failed to exploit divisions existing within Russian society, particularly strong anti-Soviet and anti-Great Russian feelings. In Western Russia (Belo or White Russia) and the Ukraine, many people looked to the Germans as liberators from the Communist yoke imposed upon them by the Great Russian majority of the country. Many Russians believed that the Germans would put an end to collectivized agriculture and possibly reopen churches closed earlier by the Communist regime. In the Ukraine, the German armies were often greeted with bread and salt, the traditional Ukrainian signs of welcome, and many Ukrainians willingly cooperated with the Germans as did numerous White Russians. There were partisan bands operating behind Russian lines as well as German ones. Hitler, however, considered all Slavs to be *untermenschen* (lesser beings) who should be eliminated. Because of Hitler's peculiar racial views, an opportunity to hamper the Soviet war effort by courting and supporting internal opposition against the regime was lost. In fact, so arrogant and brutal were the Germans in their treatment of the local population—murdering them, shipping them back to Germany as slave laborers—that they soon alienated most of the Soviet population, who more and more looked upon the Stalin regime as the lesser of two evils when compared to the Germans. Inability to fix objectives also hurt the German armies in the Soviet Union. Many historians believe that Hitler should have concentrated on one target—particularly Moscow—instead of trying to achieve a host of objectives, stretching from the Baltic Sea in the North to the Black Sea in the South. Hitler also made numerous strategic blunders, often going against the sound military advice of his own generals. Stalingrad was perhaps the most glaring of such instances.

Russia's recent economic and material progress also helped to stop the Germans. The series of five year plans begun by Stalin in 1928 had placed strong emphasis upon building up Russian heavy industry, in particular war-oriented industries. Additionally, new industrial centers were begun beyond the Urals where they would be safe from an enemy attack. Out of reach of German air attacks, these plants furnished most of Russia's military production in the early war years.

Finally, the heroism and the almost superhuman obstinacy of the Russian soldiers played a major part in the German defeat. They would fight to the death (perhaps aware that Stalin considered any Soviet soldier who was taken prisoner to be a traitor). They fought even when their supplies were cut off and often attempted desperate and hopeless counter-attacks.

Russian partisans also harassed German troops behind their own lines, mainly in the forest of White Russia and the Ukraine. Partisan numbers increased as instances of German brutality increased. They would blow up bridges, derail trains, cut telegraph and telephone lines, and attack small German detachments. So hated were the partisans by the Germans, that if captured they suffered horrible deaths. Germans would break their fingers, burn the soles off their feet, and even amputate womens' breasts, before finishing off the maimed or the dying. Anyone assisting or even suspected of aiding the partisans stood to die as well. In one pro-partisan town the Germans set fire to every house and then trained guns on their windows and doors to prevent the inhabitants from fleeing alive.

By the winter of 1942–43, all of these factors had combined to halt the German advance into the Soviet Union. The Russian offensive was to get underway that summer, but unlike the Germans, Soviet troops were not stopped until they reached Berlin.

Although Hitler often talked about Operation Barbarossa as if it were a sure thing, it was, from the beginning, a desperate gamble. The gamble was that German armies could defeat the Soviet Union in six months time, without the necessity of a long winter campaign. When that gamble failed, Germany was doomed because Hitler had made no preparations for a lengthy conflict. Germany had prepared for a short war, it could not win a long one.

German failure to defeat the Russians was the turning point of World War II in Europe. England now had a new ally and renewed hope. The Germans had a new implacable enemy. Although one cannot ignore later Allied bombing raids on Germany and Allied landings in France in June, 1944, as factors in defeating Germany, in final analysis, it was the Red Army that played the major role in destroying Hitler's Third Reich. Eighty-five percent of all casualties suffered by the German military were inflicted by the military forces of the Soviet Union.

Many historians believe that it was a blunder for Hitler to attack the U.S.S.R., and that he should have concentrated on winning North Africa, the Suez Canal, and the oil resources of the Middle East instead. But Hitler was so obsessed with Communism and the Soviet Union, that he put his major effort and the bulk of his supplies into the Russian campaign, and relegated North Africa and the Middle East to a vast holding operation against the British armies. He passed up a war that he might have won in order to fight one he could not.

Although the *Wehrmacht* never did recover from the disaster at Stalingrad, it still had many battles left in it. In fact, on February 19, 1943, German armies on the south-central front launched a counterattack aimed at the city of Kharkov, which Soviet forces had seized only three days before. By March 15, the Germans retook the city, and the Soviet winter offensive was stopped and the front stabilized. Thus, by the spring, 1943, a lull had fallen upon the front that now stretched for some 1750 miles, from Leningrad in the North to Novorossiisk on the Black Sea in the South.

As summer approached, Hitler turned his attention toward a possible limited offensive against the Soviets which would demonstrate that his troops still had the power to inflict punishment and inspire fear among the Russians. The area which stood out as the target for such an attack was a Russian bulge or salient about 90 miles into the German lines near the city of Kursk between Belogorod in the South and Orel in the North.

Code-named *Zitadelle* (Citadel), the Nazi plan called for short operations in the north and the south to snip off the Bulge at its base, which stretched nearly 70 miles from north to south. The battle, however, assumed proportions far greater than ever imagined by the Germans. For one thing, the forces aligned against each other were enormous. Around the salient's front, the Germans assembled nearly 570,000 men, 2500 tanks and self-propelled guns and about 10,000 field guns and mortars, all supported by nearly 2000 aircraft. Opposing this force were 977,000 Russian troops with more than 3300 tanks and assault guns, 20,000 guns and mortars, and nearly 3000 aircraft. In addition, the Soviets were protected by six concentric defensive belts, totaling more than 6000 miles of trench works and sown with an average of 2400 anti-tank and 2700 anti-personal mines for each mile of front.

German plans stressed the need for absolute secrecy and surprise. However, from the very inception of the operation, German plans for Citadel found their way into the hands of *Stavka*, the Soviet military intelligence agency, thanks apparently to an extraordinary Soviet spy known as Lucy.*

On July 5, 1943, the Wehrmacht began its all-out offensive, hoping that the sheer weight of their attack force would bring victory. Instead, Soviet forewarnings had prepared them for the German attack. Soviet minefields channeled the advancing Germans into the Red Army's fields of artillery fire. Soviet air supremacy and anti-tank guns halted the German panzers.**

The German attack in the north was held from the very beginning and by July 10, the Germans were forced onto the defensive. General von Manstein, the German commander in the south, was initially more successful, but as Soviet reserves were brought forward, the Germans were stopped in the biggest tank battle of the war, near the city of Kursk. By July 12 it was all over. The next day Hitler

---

*Lucy was the code name for Rudolf Rossler, a German World War I veteran. Rossler was an anti-Nazi who managed to establish himself in the espionage community in Switzerland.

**The 72-ton Ferdinands were slow and possessed no machine guns. Soviet infantrymen could thus attack them from almost any direction. The sleek new Panther tanks had extremely vulnerable oil and fuel systems and were easily set afire.

ordered a halt to Operation Citadel, in order to transfer units to Italy to meet the expected Allied invasion there. Manstein fought on alone for six more days but mostly as a delaying action.

In the battle for Kursk, German casualties included nearly 30,000 dead and more than 60,000 wounded. Russian losses have never been revealed. The German panzer force never recovered. Soviet General Ivan Konev described the Battle of Kursk as "...the swan song of the German armor." It was the last significant offensive in a campaign which had begun two years earlier. But perhaps even more significantly, Kursk set into unstoppable motion the Red Army steamroller. The Russian counterattack took Orel and Kharkov and in the Fall of 1943, extended the fighting along the whole front from the Baltic to the Black Sea. Their gains also included Kiev, which they recaptured in November, 1943.

Chapter VII

The Mediterranean Conflict

❖   ❖   ❖

World War II in the Mediterranean area primarily involved fighting in three main regions: the Balkan Peninsula, the Mediterranean Sea itself, and North Africa. Although the fighting in these areas often overlapped and interrelated with each other, for purposes of clarity they will be considered independently. When appropriate, the relationship of one area (*e.g.*, the Balkan Peninsula) to another (*e.g.*, North Africa) will be pointed out.

German involvement in the Balkans predated the outbreak of World War II. The waning of French influence in the area in the 1930's forced these states to turn more and more to Germany and in November, 1940, three of them, Rumania, Hungary, and Slovakia, adhered to the Tri-Partite Pact, joining Germany, Italy, and Japan. Hitler was thus able peacefully to exert German economic and political control in the area and to acquire much needed raw materials (*e.g.*, oil from Rumania) for his war machine. Two developments, however, forced the Germans to intervene militarily in the Balkans.

The first of these was a coup in Yugoslavia against the pro-German government of the regent Prince Paul. Paul's signing of the Tri-Partite Pact on March 25, 1941, triggered the uprising led by General Dushan Simovic. Although Simovic and King Peter, who now proclaimed himself of age, promised to steer a neutral course in European politics, this was not good enough for Hitler, who decided to send troops into Yugoslavia. On April 6, 1941, seven Panzer divisions and over 1000 aircraft attacked the country. An extremely savage bombing of Belgrade forced its capitulation on April 13, and on April 17, Yugoslavia surrendered. The price of the rebellion for the country was dismemberment. Hungary, Bulgaria and Italy took parts of Yugoslavia that they considered theirs, while a separate Croatian state was set up by the pro-Fascist Croatian leader, Ante Pavelic, who had been in Italy and was a favorite of Mussolini. The Serbian part of the Yugoslav state became a German controlled-puppet; King Peter and his government, however, managed to escape the country and make their way to England.

At the same time he sent troops into Yugoslavia, Hitler also launched a German attack on Greece. His concern over Greece dated back at least to October, 1940, when Mussolini, without Hitler's knowledge or approval, sent Italian troops from Albania, which he had seized in April, 1939, into Greece. His motive seems to have been no more than jealously of Hitler's victories and a desire to gain glory for himself.*

Eleven Italian divisions were used in the first attack, although this force was later increased to 16 and then to 25 divisions. The Greeks had only four frontline divisions, and by the end of October the Italians had won some early successes. However, autumn rains, the rugged mountains, and resistance from the local population soon halted the Italian attack. In mid-November, the Greeks counter-attacked and within 10 days had pushed the Italian forces back to their starting point in Albania.**

---

*Mussolini has been described as a solitary individual with few friends or intimates. Jealously and suspiciousness were apparently strong features in his character.

**French historian, Henri Michel, notes that the whole of occupied Europe was splitting its sides with laughter at the Italians' military ineptitude. Placards were put up along the French Riviera, facing towards Italy: "Greeks stop here: this is France."

Mussolini's set back in Greece, along with the others in North Africa and at sea (see below), finally motivated Hitler to assist the Italians; his plans for Italy to dominate the Mediterranean were dashed, but he couldn't allow his ally to go ignominiously down to defeat. Accordingly, he ordered the OKW to prepare a plan for aiding the Italians.*

At the same time, the Greeks appealed to the British—who had been pressuring them to receive British troops—for assistance. The British War Minister, Anthony Eden, and the commander in North Africa, General Archibald Wavell, did not want men and material diverted from North Africa to Greece, but the impulsive Prime Minister, Mr. Churchill, favored such a move in order to get at the Germans. Beginning on March 4, 1941, British troops, taken from the front lines in Libya and from reserves in Egypt, were transported to Greece. An Italian attempt to stop the convoys met with disaster off Cape Matapan in southern Greece, when a British naval force from Alexandria sank three Italian cruisers and two destroyers and damaged the 35,000 ton battleship, Vittorio Veneto.

The British presence in Greece as well as the continued military humiliation of his ally, Mussolini, hastened Hitler's decision to send in German troops. On April 6, the same day as the offensive in Yugoslavia, the Germans invaded Greece from Bulgaria. So swift was the German attack that by April 20, the Greek General, Alexander Papagos, asked the Germans for an armistice. On April 27, the Germans occupied Athens and King George and his government left for Cairo. A large part of the Greek navy and merchant fleet took refuge in Alexandria. The British, meanwhile, evacuated almost without a fight, leaving most of their equipment behind. The British still held the island of Crete, off the southern coast of Greece, which they considered important for control of the Western Mediterranean. When British troops were sent into Greece, it was used as a supply base; but with the fall of Greece, Crete suddenly became a refuge for 50,000 troops; British, Australians, New Zealanders and Greeks. Feeling that the Royal Navy insured it against any invasion, the British never seriously prepared to defend the island. What the British did not count on was a German air invasion. Existing airstrips were not mined and proposals to build hidden airstrips in the hills had not been carried out. There was only one squadron of modern aircraft on the island; there were hardly any tanks; and there was a sorry lack of radio and telegraph equipment.

The German attack came on May 20 with glider and paratrooper landings; a whole division was landed, comprising three mountain-infantry regiments, one armored battalion, and a motorcycle battalion. Casualties were high for these German troops with whole units being wiped out on landing or soon thereafter. Still, they managed to seize Maleme airfield and fly in troop carriers and gliders with additional troops and supplies. The British navy managed to turn back two German convoys, stopping seaborne supply attempts, but German control of Maleme was the decisive factor in the battle for Crete.

By May 26, the British Commander of Crete, Sir Bernard Freyberg, was convinced the battle was over and decided to evacuate the island.** Altogether, 18,000 British troops were taken off, but 13,000 remained behind and became prisoners-of-war. The Royal Navy suffered rather severe losses trying to defend the island: Three cruisers and six destroyers were sunk and two battleships, one aircraft carrier (the only one), two cruisers, and two destroyers were badly damaged. German losses were so high, a third of the airborne invaders being either killed or wounded, that Hitler now abandoned plans for similar airborne attacks on Malta and the Suez Canal. He turned his parachute units into infantry regiments.

The loss of Crete cost the British control of the Aegean Sea and gave the Germans a secure route from Greece to Constantinople and the Black Sea for the next three years. Crete's loss also had a considerable impact on British morale, coming as it did, on the heels of losses to Rommel in North Africa (see below) and the recent loss of Greece; these combined with a spring renewal of the air blitz on England, made many Englishmen wonder how much more their country could take. The British did

---

*The OKW—Oberkommando der Wehrmacht—was the inter-service planning headquarters of which Hitler himself was head.

**Freyberg was a New Zealander who had won the Victoria Cross, Britain's highest and rarest honor during World War I. Freyberg was popular with his men, although even those who admired him, thought him to be impulsive in his decisions and a sloppy administrator.

enjoy successes in two peripheral areas in 1941: the Middle East and East Africa. In the Middle East they recovered control of Iraq in June, 1941, following a pro-German military coup the previous April. Also, the British managed to seize Syria from the Vichy French who held it, and they set up a Free French government there. Thus, by the end of June, 1941, the British had established control over the vast oil resources of the Arab world.

The other area of British success was in East Africa. In January, two British armies, one under General William Platt from the Sudan, and the other under General Sir Alan A. Cunningham, from Kenya, converged on the Italian troops in Ethiopia. Within four months time, Ethiopia and all of East Africa were back in British hands. Italian military conduct in the region was really quite mysterious. They simply retired, putting up neither an active nor a passive defense. Even more surprising was their failure to utilize their superior air power in the region.

Britain's naval fortunes in the Mediterranean were mixed in 1940–41. Her major successes came against the Italian navy, which the British fleet harried all over the Eastern Mediterranean. In July, 1940, clashes near Calabria and Crete cost the Italians one cruiser sunk and a battleship and cruiser damaged. Italian bombers tried several times to assist their fleet, but usually arrived too late; in one instance they dropped bombs on their own ships. In November, 1940, the British launched 24 aircraft from the carrier *Illustrious* in a surprise attack on the Italian battleships at Taranto.* Three of the six were seriously damaged and two cruisers disabled. At the same time, British ships also attacked Italian ships in the Straits of Otranto (between southeastern Italy and Western Albania). The Italians then moved their fleet to Naples, which allowed them to operate in the Western, but not the Eastern, Mediterranean. British ships also successfully bombarded the Italian seaport of Genoa in February, 1941, escaping detection from nearly 200 Italian aircraft. And in March, 1941, the British won their victory over the Italians off Cape Matapan.

The main British setbacks in the Mediterranean came at the hands of German airpower during the battle for Crete. As noted above, British losses here had been significant, and ended in what Admiral Cunningham called, "...a disastrous episode in the history of the Royal Navy." The loss of Crete meant that the British navy could no longer operate in the Eastern Mediterranean. Mastery of the seas was of little use without control of the skies. The Italians had been made aware of the same thing in the Fall, 1940, as British planes operating from Malta were able to bomb Italian shipping operations between Italy and North Africa. These attacks became so serious that the Germans sent a squadron of 400 aircraft to Sicily to be used in bombing the air and harbor installations on Malta. These intensive attacks did cut down on Italian naval losses in the Western Mediterranean, but did not solve the problem of Malta and its use as a sort of Mediterranean aircraft carrier by the British. Malta was to prove quite important to the British in the fighting in North Africa.

That a war among European powers should be fought out, in part at least, in North Africa seems at first glance a bit incongruous. The conflict there, however, was really a legacy of nineteenth century imperialism. Libya had been in Italian hands since 1911 and contained 250,000 Italian soldiers at the time Italy entered the war in June, 1940. Neighboring Egypt, although technically an independent country, was in fact controlled by the British, whose concern about the Suez Canal led to the presence of some 36,000 men there by June, 1940.

Outnumbering the British by nearly seven to one, Mussolini was determined to take advantage of England's precarious position in the summer of 1940 (see Chapter Five). It seemed the ideal time to seize British holdings in North Africa, and on June 28, 1940, Mussolini ordered the invasion of Egypt. Preparations for the attack dragged on for two and a half months until September 13, when the Italians launched their attack with five infantry divisions and seven tank battalions. The attack force resembled a massive

---

*The Japanese profited a great deal from the British feat in planning their attack on the American fleet at Pearl Harbor.

military parade—first came the motorcyclists, then the light tanks, followed by the trucks and other vehicles, all drawn up in neat rows. The trucks carried marble markers to chart the progress of the Italian army—the same procedure used centuries earlier by the Roman armies. Behind all of the motorized vehicles came the Italian infantry, mostly on foot. This formidable looking fighting force was in reality a paper tiger (to use a more contemporary phrase). Italian tanks were armed only with machine guns, and were so flimsy that they split apart under fire; the solid rubber tires on Italian trucks could not withstand the desert boulders and broke apart when they hit them. Most of the Italian army was made up of infantrymen who were to prove of little use against the more mobile British forces. They were also poorly trained, armed with outdated weapons (some cannons and rifles dated from the 19th century). Italian planes, anti-tank and anti-aircraft guns, and even mines were mostly obsolete.*

Still, when it came at dawn on September 13, 1940, the Italian attack went remarkably well, and within four days, they were 60 miles inside of Egypt. What the Italians did not realize was that the British were falling back according to plan, trying to force them to overextend their supply lines. General Wavell, British Commander in Chief of the Middle East, also was waiting for troop reinforcements and a shipment of tanks before launching a counter attack.** In the meantime, General Graziani, the Italian Commander, halted at Sidi Barrani and built fortified outposts along the front with the British, "dwadling" away three months in the process.

In December, Wavell was ready to counterattack. Under the command of General Richard O'Connor, a 30,000 man, motorized army attacked the Italians. The broad desert enabled O'Connor to use naval-type tactics to outflank the Italian outposts and attack them from the rear. Wavell, perhaps unaware of the Italians' intrinsic weaknesses, had not contemplated a major offensive; he had planned only a five-day attack that would carry the British some 25 miles beyond Sidi Barrani. Instead, the operation lasted for 62 days and carried the British Desert Army right across Cirenaica—a distance of 500 miles—and ended with the destruction of Graziani's army. With a strength never exceeding more than two divisions, O'Connor destroyed ten Italian divisions, captured 130,000 prisoners, and seized the major fortresses of Bardia and Tobruk; only 438 of his force were killed, 353 of them Australians. O'Connor was prepared to end the conquest of Italian North Africa by taking its capital, Tripoli. But he was ordered to halt and to return the bulk of his forces to Egypt from which they were to be sent to Greece to help counter the anticipated German intervention there.

In retrospect, it was probably an unfortunate decision to halt the advance on Tripoli. After the war, O'Connor was to chide himself for not continuing. It would have been possible to first take Tripoli, and then aid Greece, he said, and he blamed himself for not doing so. British failure to take Tripoli provided a base for the remaining Italian forces in North Africa and a site for German intervention in the desert war. On February 9, 1941, the German military attache in Rome informed Mussolini that one panzer division and a light mechanized division—the so-called Afrika Corps—were to be sent to North Africa. Commanded by Erwin Rommel, who had commanded the 7th Panzer Division in its dash to the Atlantic Coast during the Battle for France, the Afrika Corps was told simply to hold Tripoli and the remaining Italian holdings in North Africa. It was not instructed to launch an offensive or to roll back the British gains.

Rommel, who arrived in Tripoli on February 12, was not the type to fight a defensive war. His maxim was *Sturm, Swung, Wrecht*—attack, impetus, weight. He was an aggressive and audacious soldier and he proceeded to ignore Field Marshal Walther von Brauchitsch's order to fight a defensive war.*** One of the divisions allotted to him, the 5th Light Division, began its move to North Africa in

---

*Italian night patrols often dug up and stole British mines so that they could sow their own minefields.

**The tanks were dubbed Matildas. Each weighed 30 tons and had armor plating, impenetrable to Italian guns.

***Brauchitsch was the Commander-in-Chief of the German Army. Rommel thought him to be "an overly sensitive, withdrawn patrician." Rommel also had little use for Franz Halder, the Army Chief of Staff.

mid-February, expecting to complete the transfer by mid-April. The other division, the 15th Panzer, was not due to arrive until the end of May. Fearing that the British would continue their offensive during this period of German weakness, Rommel resorted to a ruse. He had dummy tanks constructed of wood and canvas mounted on Volkswagen chassis, hoping to make the Germans appear "as strong as possible and to induce the maximum caution in the British."

But the British were already committed to aid the Greeks and in the process, stripped their defenses in eastern Libya to the bare bones. They did not think that a German attack would be possible in the near future, and in fact, the German High Command had ordered Rommel to do nothing before the end of May. Rommel promptly disobeyed his orders.

Rommel believed that the growing British weaknesses should be exploited, and at the end of March, 1941, he attacked. The effect of this audacious decision was, as Liddel-Hart has noted, "magical." Utilizing the flanks as the British previously had done against the Italians, Rommel encircled British units, often deceiving them by raising huge clouds of dust with trucks to conceal his weakness in tanks. On April 3, the British had to abandon Benghazi and on April 6th, a German patrol captured General O'Connor and Lieutenant General Sir Philip Neame.* By April 11, the British, with the exception of a force at the Libyan port city of Tobruk, were back in Egypt.** Rommel had driven the British out of Cyrenaica even faster than the British had expelled the Italians from the same area. His success raised the tantalizing prospect of a German advance to Suez and the Middle East, but Hitler ordered that the attack on the Soviet Union be given priority. So, without adequate supplies and reinforcements, Rommel was forced to pause on the Egyptian frontier.

In November, even though outnumbered, Rommel again attacked, driving 15 miles inside of Egypt, but by the first week of December, afraid of being encircled and running low on fuel, he pulled back, under heavy and nearly continuous British attack. The British attack, Operation Crusader, forced the Germans back out of Egypt, all the way to El Agheila, where they had started in March, 1941. Rommel had suffered his first serious defeat. Between November 18 and mid-January, the British took 33,000 Axis prisoners and destroyed 300 enemy tanks. British tank losses were actually greater than the German and Italian losses, but they lost only about one-half the men.

Once again, however, events outside of North Africa had a major influence on the desert war. In December, 1941, Japan bombed the American fleet at Pearl Harbor, and almost simultaneously began its expansion into Southeast and Southwest Asia. Among their targets were several British possessions. England quickly declared war on Japan and began to divert men and material marked for North Africa to the Far East, particularly to Singapore. In addition, increased German bombing of Malta, the arrival of German submarines in the Mediterranean, and raids by Italian midget submarines, combined to cause the British serious supply problems.*** These same factors helped to ease the German supply difficulties, enabling Rommel to receive new tanks and large supplies of fuel.

At the end of January, 1942, Rommel struck again. The weakened British fell back, abandoning Benghazi once again on January 19, 1942. By February 6, Rommel was at Gazala, half-way back across Cyrenaica, where stalemate was reached with the British and the Axis forces on their respective sides of the Gazala Line, a 60 mile-long chain of defenses built by the British. The line was densely sown with mines that linked a number of strong points, or boxes, each a mile or two square. There were six of these boxes in all; each had enough stores to last a week, and each was protected by mines, barbed

---

*O'Connor had been given a rest at the end of February and was replaced by Neame, an engineer unversed in desert warfare. When the German attack came at the end of March, O'Connor was sent to advise Neame. Their unescorted car happened to drive into an area of the desert where a German patrol had been sent.

**Tobruk was isolated and besieged by the Germans until the first week of December, 1941.

***The Italian midget subs were little more than manned torpedoes. On December 19, three of them attached their warheads to the only British battleship in the Mediterranean, as well as to a tanker, in the harbor of Alexandria. The tanker was sunk and the battleship put out of action for some time. British ability to cut Rommel's supplies, and to carry their own, were seriously weakened.

wire, slit trenches, and pill boxes. British tanks were to move freely behind the boxes, aiding any that came under attack.

Along the line, the British had a 3–1 superiority in tanks and a 3–2 advantage in guns, but they lacked a commander to compare with Rommel. The Desert Fox, as he had come to be known, feigned an attack in the north at Gazala, in order to occupy the British forces stationed there. His main thrust, however, came in the south. Early on May 27, attacking in the dark, the German and Italian forces went around the British flank at Bar Hacheim and fanned out to the north and east. Some Italian units were left to deal with the Bar Hacheim box, whose Free French defenders managed to hold out for two weeks. The decisive factor in the battle turned out to be the German concentration of armor as opposed to the dispersed British armor. According to Rommel, "...the British threw their armor into the battle piecemeal and thus gave us the chance of engaging them on each separate occasion with just enough of our own tanks." Indecision among British commanders also assisted Rommel. When Rommel's supply line was cut and his forces temporarily immobilized, the British delayed the attack that might have turned the tide in their favor. Rommel quickly recovered, massed his forces, cut through a new supply line, and continued his offensive. By mid-June the Germans had gained the upper hand in the battle, and the British began to fall back.

The British withdrawal dangerously exposed their strategic port of Tobruk, which so valiantly had withstood the German siege the previous year. Tobruk's defenses, however, had been neglected because no British Commander had thought it would have to withstand a second siege. In addition, it was dangerously short of anti-tank weapons. The British probably would have been well-advised to have abandoned Tobruk, since its importance as a supply base had declined when the British fleet began to have difficulty operating in the Mediterranean. Churchill, however, telegraphed the British Eighth Army Commander, Major General Neil M. Ritchie, that he presumed "...there is no question...of giving up Tobruk."* Ritchie, therefore, left a considerable force at Tobruk, but pulled the rest of his troops back to the Egyptian border. Tobruk's isolation proved fatal, and Rommel captured it in one day, June 20. He took 35,000 prisoners (more that his own entire force), and much needed supplies: fuel, vehicles, and other provisions. An admiring Hitler promoted Rommel to Field Marshal, the youngest in the history of the German Army. Churchill, who received news of Tobruk's fall while in Washington at the White House, called it a "disgrace."

General Claude Auchinleck, Commander of all British Middle Eastern forces, dismissed Ritchie and took over personal command of the Eighth Army. Rather than make a stand on the frontier, which offered Rommel the possibility of outflanking the British to the south, he decided to fall back to El Alamein, 240 miles inside of Egypt, and only 60 miles from Alexandria. Unlike most other desert areas, El Alamein was defensible, because it was bordered on the north by the Mediterranean and on the south by the Qattara Depression. The biggest such depression in North Africa, Qattara was 400 feet below sea level and had a salt marsh bottom, impassable to wheeled or tracked vehicles; surrounding it were hills, up to 700 feet high. Thus, there was no way to outflank El Alamein, as had been so often done in previous desert battles.

For the rest of July, Rommel hammered away at the El Alamein line. Living and fighting almost solely on captured British supplies, he was down to 26 tanks, was short of fuel, and his overextended supply lines were now being harassed by British bombers.** Still, Auchinleck was not sure he could stop Rommel, and panic seized the British in Egypt. The fleet left Alexandria and passed through the Suez Canal to the Red Sea. The British Embassy began to burn its files and the British Ambassador

---

*The British Army's youngest general, Ritchie had succeeded General Alan Gordon Cunningham on November 26, 1941. Cunningham had earlier taken the place of the unfortunate General O'Connor, who had been captured in April, 1941.

**The Russian campaign had drained away much of the Luftwaffe's Mediterranean Air Force. This allowed Malta to breathe more freely, opened up Rommel's supply convoys to increasing British attacks, and gave the British Desert Air Force a marked superiority over the Germans.

prepared to flee to Palestine. Yet the worst was over. In a letter home on July 4, Rommel told his wife that German strength was exhausted; they had run out of resources. He couldn't break through the British lines and the so-called first battle of El Alamein went to the British.

Despite his success in stopping Rommel, Auchinleck was replaced in August by two British officers. General Sir Harold Leofric Rupert Alexander, the last British commander to leave the beach at Dunkurk, was made commander-in-chief of the Middle East. Lieutenant General Bernard Law Montgomery, the son of a Tasmanian clergyman, was put in command of the Eighth Army. Alexander gave him only one order, "Go down to the desert and defeat Rommel."

At the end of August, Rommel made one last bid to break through at El Alamein, telling his troops, "In three days we shall be at Alexandria." In fact, the battle lasted until September and British air superiority, coupled with Rommel's shortage of supplies (particularly fuel), clinched the matter for the British. The Germans did push a small gap into the Allied lines, but it was quickly closed. At this point, Rommel went back to Germany for rest and recuperation.*

Montgomery quickly came under pressure to launch an immediate counter-attack against the weakened German forces, but he resisted. He was well aware of the ups and down that the Eighth Army had been experiencing since 1940, and he was determined that the next British offensive would bring them final victory in North Africa. Thus, he slowly proceeded to buildup his forces, train new troops, and retrain old ones. He also worked on tactics and developed elaborate plans of concealment and deception. He combined command of the army and air force and created an armored force similar to the Afrika Corps. At last on October 23, Montgomery was ready to launch Operation Lightfoot—the code name for the British attack.

This second, and perhaps more famous Battle of El Alamein, began with British tanks attacking the German-Italian line at its strongest point. But the British tanks were halted and Montgomery had to pull back and try again. Once again, Rommel stopped him. The British, however, were wearing down his forces and exhausting his material. By November 2, Rommel was down to 30 tanks, and he prepared to withdraw, but Hitler ordered him to hold the line at any costs; on November 4, the British tanks broke through. An opportunity to cut off and encircle the Germans was lost when the British moved too slowly, but they still bagged 10,000 German and 20,000 Italian prisoners.

The official British history of World War II in the Mediterranean and the Middle East states that "The Battle of El Alamein may be said to have ended at dawn on 4 November, with the enemy breaking away and the British setting out to catch him." Yet El Alamein was hardly the end of the war in North Africa; it was rather the beginning of a series of events that would lead to that victory. It took seven more months to drive the Germans from the continent, and Rommel still had some surprises in store for the Allies, but never again, with the exception of a few local offensives in Tunisia, would the Axis forces regain the military initiative.**

Tipping the balance against the Axis was what Hitler at the time called, "...the largest landing operation that has ever taken place in the history of the world." On November 8, 1942, British and American forces began landing troops in French North Africa, in Morocco and Algeria. Commanded by the then relatively unknown General Dwight D. Eisenhower, Operation Torch, as the plan was called, sought to create a pincer movement against the Germans and drive them from North Africa. The first major hurdle for the operation was the French. Both Morocco and Algeria were French colonies under the control of Vichy France, which had pledged to Hitler that the French themselves would

---

*Rommel had driven himself hard for 18 months despite suffering from chronic stomach and intestinal inflammation, in addition to circulatory troubles and nasal diphtheria.

**Following the defeat at El Alamein, Rommel proceeded to carry out perhaps the most difficult of all military tasks—an orderly, combative retreat following a major defeat. Although he was continuously pushed back across the desert, Rommel would periodically stop and fight, making the British Eighth Army pay for every bit of desert.

defend these territories in the event of an Allied invasion. The actual French reaction to the invasion when it came was mixed. Some Frenchmen fought to the death against the Allied invaders, while others hailed the Allies as liberators and deliverers from Vichy oppression. Admiral Jean Francois Darlan, Commander-in-Chief of all French forces—naval, land, and air—ordered a cease fire for all French troops in North Africa on November 10.* On the evening of that same day, German troops—10 German and six Italian divisions—moved into Vichy France, assuming full control of all of France.

The Allies hoped to advance the 450 miles into Tunisia in about two weeks. The arrival of fresh German and Italian troops in Tunisia and the inexperience of the Allied troops and their commander, however, brought the Allied offensive to a halt by Christmas, 1942, far short of their goal. In the middle of February, 1943, Rommel inflicted one of the worst defeats of the war on the Americans at the Kassarine Pass. However, continued pressure from the British Eighth Army to the East made it impossible for Rommel to exploit his victory. In order to protect Tunisia from the Eighth Army, he fell back to the Mareth Line, a belt of fortifications earlier built by the French to protect Tunisia. On March 9, 1943, Rommel flew to Germany to try to persuade Hitler to pull out of North Africa and save his soldiers from complete annihilation. Hitler refused to listen and ordered Rommel to go on sick leave and not to return to North Africa. According to Rommel's journal, "I emphasized as strongly as I could that the African troops must be re-equipped in Italy to enable them to defend our southern European flank. I even went so far as to give him (Hitler) a guarantee—something which I am very reluctant to do—that with these troops, I would beat off any Allied invasion in southern Europe. But it was all hopeless." General Jurgen von Arnim then assumed command of all Axis forces in North Africa.

The Germans fought on against the Allies until May. But by the beginning of that month, the Allied naval blockade, coupled with overwhelming Allied superiority in the Mediterranean, served to completely exhaust the Axis forces, who ran out of oil and, for all practical purposes, out of food. On May 8, a Free French force entered Tunis, and on May 13, the remaining Axis troops in North Africa surrendered; a few hundred of them managed to escape, but about 150,000 Germans and Italians surrendered, the last of the Axis combatants in North Africa.

The Allied victory in North Africa was only the half of the close of the Mediterranean campaign. Unquestionable Allied control of that Sea would not be secured until the island of Sicily and its airfields were in Allied hands. In addition, Italy's military strength had been depleted early in North Africa and its once vaunted fleet almost ceased to exist as a fighting force. Thus, it seemed to Allied planners that the invasion of Sicily was the logical sequel to their victory in North Africa.

---

*An earlier admirer of the German military, Darlan agreed to switch sides in exchange for being named High Commissioner of French North Africa, in charge of civil administration. On Christmas Eve, 1942, Darlan was assassinated by a young French royalist. His successor was General Henri Giraud, who was himself ousted some five months later by the French leader, Charles De Gaulle.

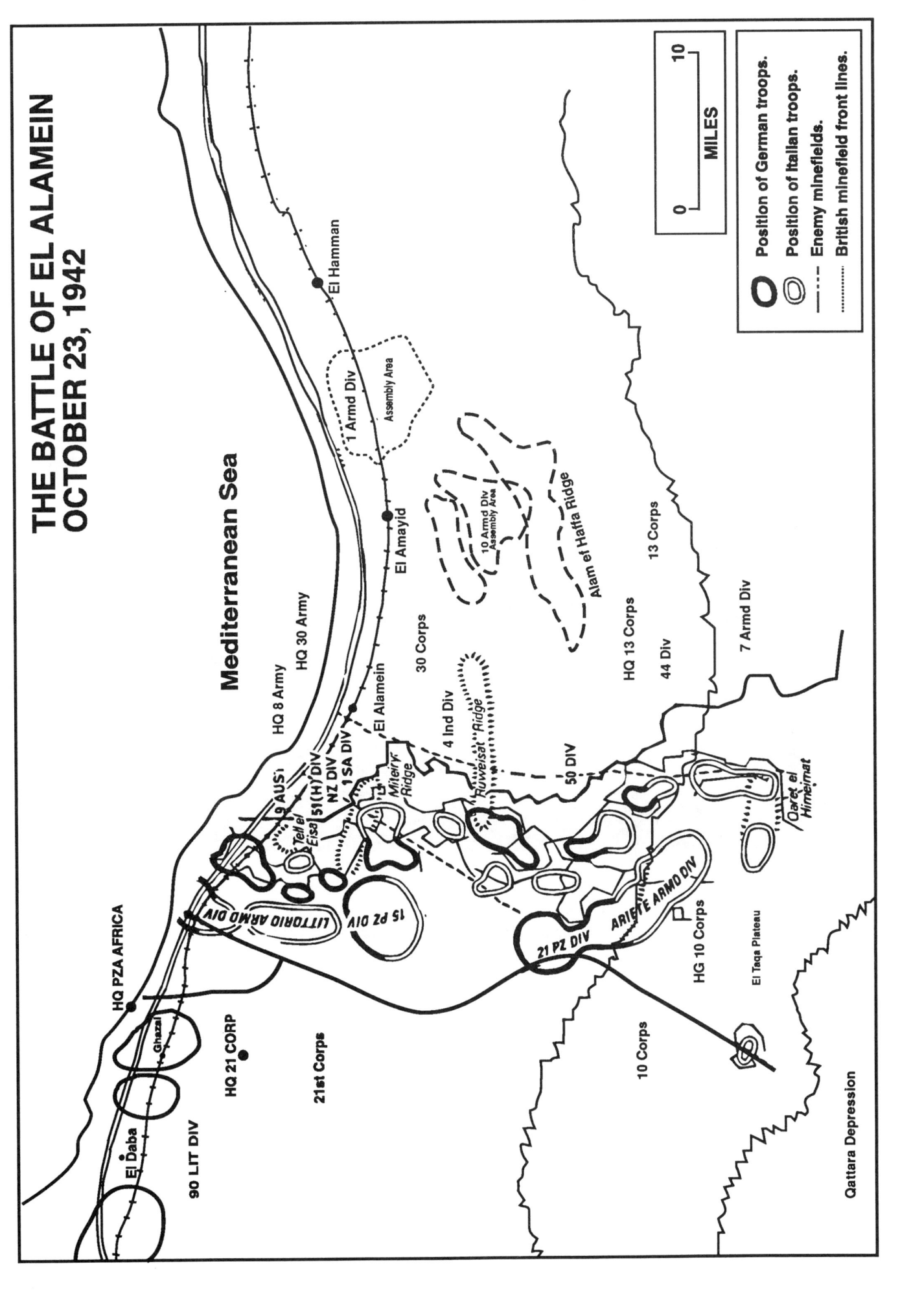

U.S. ARMY

Chapter VIII

The Italian Campaign

❖ ❖ ❖

In January, 1943, four months before the fighting in North Africa ended, American President Franklin Roosevelt and the British Prime Minister Winston Churchill held an important conference in the Moroccan city of Casablanca. Roosevelt's hope that the Soviet leader, Joseph Stalin, would also attend, were dashed because Stalin did not wish to leave Moscow while the fighting at Stalingrad and the area beyond the Don River was in full swing. Three important decisions were taken at the Casablanca Conference: 1. A decision to fight the war to unconditional surrender; 2. a decision to carry out massive bombing raids on Germany in 1943 and 1944; 3. a decision to invade the island of Sicily following the North African campaign.*

The decision to fight the war to unconditional surrender came as a result of a rather off-hand suggestion by Roosevelt, hesitantly agreed to by Churchill, that the only acceptable conclusion of the war would be the unconditional surrender of Germany, Italy and Japan. Roosevelt was apparently influenced by General Grant's use of the term in 1862 as an ultimatum to General Buckner. Germany's claim that she never really had been defeated in World War I probably caused Roosevelt to make sure that she could not make such a claim after World War II.

Churchill seems to have seen the declaration as a way to placate Stalin, who was disappointed and angry that no second front had been opened on the continent and was not likely to be until 1944. Unconditional surrender at least would assure him that the British and Americans would negotiate no separate peace with the Germans. Churchill also thought more importantly that it might prevent Stalin from negotiating a separate treaty with the Germans, since there had been some hints that Italy and Japan were working to arrange one between Germany and the Soviet Union (a policy which was favored by von Ribbentrop, the Nazi Foreign Minister).

Both the short and long term effects of unconditional surrender were not particularly advantageous to the Western Allies. In the short run, unconditional surrender probably stiffened the German peoples' will to resist and weakened any anti-Nazi movements in Germany. Propaganda Minister Goebbels made wide use of the term to strengthen the morale of the German army and people by pointing out the barbaric and uncompromising nature of the enemy. Anti-Nazi forces in Germany were weakened because it appeared that even if they did get rid of Hitler and the Nazis, they could not negotiate a separate peace with the Allies. Why get rid of Hitler and his henchmen when total annihilation would still be the result? In the long term, unconditional surrender was to change the balance of power in Europe. The destruction of Germany was to leave the Soviet Union as the greatest military power in Europe and in a position to dominate the continent.

The second decision taken at Casablanca was to bomb Germany in an attempt to destroy and dislocate "...the German military, industrial and economic system," and to undermine "...the morale of the German people to the point where their capacity for armed resistance is fatally weakened." The full

---

*Charles De Gaulle, leader of the Free French forces in England, was persuaded to come to Casablanca in an attempt to unify his forces and those of General Giraud. Neither man was enthusiastic about the effort, although they did pose, albeit ungraciously, for Allied photographers. Within a few months De Gaulle had maneuvered Giraud out of office.

implication of this decision will be explored later in this text. But it is worth noting here that the air offensive that followed this decision proved to be one of indiscriminate bombing, which killed thousands of German civilians but affected German war production and her ability to wage war very little.

The third decision, *i.e.* to invade Sicily, is of particular concern to this chapter. Although agreeing at Casablanca to the joint invasion of the island, the Americans and the British had rather different perceptions about the meaning of such an attack. The Americans considered the Mediterranean as really a side show to their central objective, a cross-Channel invasion of Nazi-dominated Europe. Since they did not believe that was possible in 1943, they accepted the Sicilian invasion only as a way to make the Mediterranean more secure for Allied shipping and as a way to draw German forces away from the Russian front. The British saw Sicily as the first step in finishing off Italy and perhaps as a way of getting at Germany through the "soft underbelly" in Italy and the Balkans, not through a cross-Channel invasion. These differences, which would surface again a bit later, were deferred for the moment. Sicily was to be the next objective, but whether it was a prelude to the invasion of mainland Italy was for the time left unresolved.

Operation Husky was the code name given to the invasion of Sicily, which was to be under the overall command of General Eisenhower. In order to deceive the islands' defenders, an elaborate deception campaign was devised by Allied planners. The corpse of a young man who had died of pneumonia and exposure was dressed in a naval officer's uniform and provided with fake plans indicating that an Allied attack on Greece and Sardinia, to be accompanied by a feint towards Sicily, was imminent. The body was then put in the coastal waters near Spain in hopes that Spanish authorities would discover it and turn the plans over to the Germans.* In fact, the Spanish did just that.** The Germans swallowed the bait, sent reinforcement to Greece and Sardinia, sent Rommel to Greece to command Axis forces there, and transferred naval forces from Sicilian waters to the Aegean.

On July 10, 1943, two Allied armies, the American Seventh Army under General Patton, and the British Eighth Army under General Montgomery landed on Sicily. The British landings came along a forty mile stretch of coast at the Southeast corner, while the Americans hit a forty mile stretch of the southern coast. In all, 160,000 thousand men were put ashore in the first wave, with 600 tanks and 14,000 vehicles; they were supported by a fleet of 1400 vessels of all types. An airborne assault that preceded the amphibious landing ran into problems from the very beginning. The pilots of the 366 planes were inexperienced in airborne and overwater operations and none had ever approached an enemy-held position at night. High winds caused navigational problems, and some planes became lost and turned back, while others simply disappeared. Some gliders were released prematurely and fifty of them landed in the sea. The paratroopers, commanded by Major James Gavin, were scattered across a sixty mile stretch of southeastern Sicily; for a long time, Gavin and others were not even sure they were in Sicily. The chaotic scattering of the airborne troops was confusing to the Germans and Italians, who got so many reports of landings at so many points that some assumed the Americans and British had dropped between 22,000 and 30,000 men on them (the actual total was 4600).

The seaborne landings began early on the morning of July 10. Defending against the Allies were five Italian Infantry divisions, five Italian coastal divisions and two German divisions, including the crack Hermann Goering SS Division. Most of the Italians, however, were war weary, disliked the Germans, and offered little resistance. "The Italian coastal divisions, whose value had never been rated very high, disintegrated almost without firing a shot and the field divisions, when they were met, were also driven like chaff before the wind. Mass surrenders were frequent." In the British sector, one observer noted that the Italian coastal troops "...stampeded to the safety of our prisoner of war cages on

---

*Although given the identify of Acting Major William Martin of the Royal Marines, the true identity of the corpse has never been revealed. The body was released from a submarine but made to appear as if he had crashed on a flight from London and had floated in the water for several days.

**Although theoretically neutral, the Spanish in practice were pro-German.

the beach in such terrific disorder that our troops faced greater danger from being trampled upon than from bullets." On the morning of the second day, however, German tanks counterattacked and managed to get within one mile of the beaches. Shells from the Allies' newest portable anti-tank weapon, the bazooka, were far too small, and simply bounced off the tanks, and it took the American navy to save the day. The cruisers *Boise*, (and) *Savannah*, and a host of destroyers stopped the tanks with well-directed eight- and five-inch shells.

On the night of July 11, an attempt was made to reinforce the beachhead with paratroopers.* Since German planes had been periodically bombarding the fleet during most of the day, when the American planes appeared about 10:30 P.M., the navy gun crews assumed they were Luftwaffe planes and opened fire. Many of the planes crashed in flames, as panicked and wounded paratroopers frantically bailed out. Some were shot as they floated to earth. In all, 23 planes were lost and 37 badly damaged. The airborne force suffered 318 casualties—88 dead, 162 wounded, and 68 missing—at the hands of Allied gunners.

The initial plan after the beachhead was secured was for the British to push up the east coast of the island towards Messina with the Americans protecting their left flank. However, the flamboyant Patton was unwilling to play a subordinate role to anyone, least of all Montgomery. So when Montgomery got stuck on the slopes of Mt. Etna in the south, Patton pushed out along the west and then the north coast of the island. He took Palermo on July 22 and reached Messina, the goal of the Sicilian campaign, on August 16. When British troops arrived the following day, they were greeted with shouts of "Where've you tourists been?" by the Americans. Patton had made the taking of Messina a horse race in which the prestige of the U.S. Army was at stake (in his mind at least). "We must take Messina before the British," said Patton. General Omar Bradley, who commanded II Corps under Patton, noted that toward the end of the operation, "...Patton became nearly irrational in his determination to beat Monty to Messina. He stopped me on the road and exhorted: 'I want you to get to Messina just as fast as you can. I don't want you to waste time on...maneuvers, even if you've got to spend men to do it. I want to beat Monty into Messina.' I was shocked. The orders sickened me...."

Although Sicily was won, the Germans were able to evacuate the bulk of the 15th Panzer Grenadier Hermann Goering Division and most of their heavy equipment, across the Straits of Messina to the Italian mainland. Also, the Italians were able to evacuate nearly 7500 troops and 75 to 100 guns to the mainland. According to an American officer, "They retreated very much at their own speed and with insignificant losses." This was a remarkable achievement in view of the Allies almost complete air superiority, and has led General J.F.C. Fuller to suggest that, "It appears...that someone in the Allied Air Force...blundered." In fact, an Allied landing on the toe of Italy, in Calabria, prior to the attack on Messina might have prevented the successful German withdrawal. And the American naval historian Samuel Eliot Morison wrote: "I cannot avoid the conclusion that the entire Husky plan was wrong; that we should have attacked the Messina bottleneck first..." Even General Eisenhower later told his private diarist Captain Harry C. Butcher that the Sicily plan had been a mistake—that the Allies should have landed simultaneously in Sicily and Calabria.

Allied casualties on Sicily were high: 5,542 killed, 14,410 wounded and 2,869 missing. At the time, Allied forces thought that they had inflicted heavy losses on the Germans, but postwar records showed them wrong; at most, a few thousand Germans were killed. Still, the Allies did achieve certain gains from the Sicilian invasion. They gained practice in amphibious and airborne landings. And most importantly, Allied successes in Sicily brought down Mussolini and went a long way in knocking Italy out of the war.

On July 25, 1943, fifteen days after the Allies invaded Sicily, King Victor Emmanuel III dismissed Mussolini as head of the Italian government, and "El Duce" was then hustled off under arrest. The

---

*The air drop was originally planned for the night of July 10 in the First Division area, but it had to be postponed for one day, partly owing to the confusion at the beachhead.

reasons for his demise were numerous. Italy had obviously grown weary of Mussolini's rule. Her economy was in shambles—her industry crippled and her daily rations down to 900 calories a day. Strict rationing allowed each Roman only 3 ½ ounces of bread per day and that same amount of meat per month. The Germans often commandeered food supplies to feed their soldiers and fuel supplies to heat their billets. Two events, however, probably precipitated Mussolini's downfall: First and foremost was the success of the Allied campaign in Sicily; Second was an Allied bombing raid on the rail yards in Rome, which killed and wounded over 4,000 civilians. Even the Grand Council of the Fascist Party realized that Mussolini had to be deposed and its alliance with Germany ended, or Italy would be dragged down to utter ruin. The Council's no confidence vote in Mussolini was all the king needed to officially end his twenty-one year rule. Mussolini's successor was Field Marshal Pietro Badoglio. Seventy two years of age, he had served as Chief of the Armed Forces General Staff under Mussolini.*

Badoglio's first pronouncement upon assuming office was that Italy would stay in the Axis camp, but he secretly began to work to take Italy out of the conflict. He was very cautious, because he did not want Italy to become another German occupied country with the arrests and shootings which that would entail. What he offered to the Allies was Italian surrender, predicated on two conditions: Allied troops would be landed in the north near Genoa where they could cut off northern Italy from German invasion; and an Allied airborne invasion of Rome to prevent that city from being occupied by the Germans.

Churchill had long supported an invasion of Italy and had at one time proposed an operation through the soft underbelly of Europe as the main Allied thrust against Nazi Germany. The Americans supported, on the other hand, a cross-channel invasion of Europe as the most feasible way of knocking Germany out of the war and looked at an Italian operation as a peripheral one, draining men and supplies from any cross-channel landing. In May, 1943, at a meeting in Washington (known as Trident), Churchill agreed to the cross-channel attack on Germany. At a meeting in Quebec, in mid-August, however, the Americans agreed to invade southern Italy in order to assure Italy's surrender and to secure air bases for bombing Germany from the south. Attracted by Italy's war weariness and desire for surrender by Mussolini's downfall, and lulled by the ease with which they captured Sicily, the Allies thought that an invasion of Italy would be a relatively easy matter. But as the Allies dragged out their discussions about Italy, the Germans were alerted to the likelihood of Italian defection and began Operation Axis, a scheme whereby German soldiers, at any clear sign of Italian defection, were to disarm the military and take over defensive positions themselves to repel any Allied landing. On July 30, Rommel, now in command of German forces in northern Italy, ordered German troops to take control of all Alpine passes leading from Italy to Germany in order to safeguard German supply routes.

Despite the Allied rejection of a landing in northern Italy and a last minute cancellation of the airborne assault on Rome, Badoglio agreed to surrender on September 3.** The public announcement of the surrender was not to be made until September 8, however. The time was so calculated because the Allies planned to land in the Gulf of Salerno, 30 miles south of Naples, early on September 9. The cancellation of the Allied air drop on Rome meant that the city was quickly occupied by the Germans. This forced the Badoglio government to flee for their safety to southern Italy. The formal Italian surrender was completed at Malta on September 9, and on October 13, 1943, Badoglio's government formally declared war on Germany.

The first Allied landing on the Italian mainland came on September 3, when General Montgomery's forces crossed the Straits of Messina into Calabria (the toe of Italy). Following a heavy and prolonged bombardment which one author has noted, "...seemed intended not merely to soften up the opposition but to blow off Italy's toe," the 5th British and 1st Canadian divisions made their crossing. They

---

*After serving 11 months, Badoglio was replaced by Ivanhoe Bonomi, the man Mussolini had ousted when he came to power in 1922.

**General Maxwell A. Taylor secretly slipped into Rome on September 8 in order to determine the feasibility of such a plan. He recommended against it because he did not believe that the Italian troops would be able to secure the airfields against the Germans.

encountered no Germans, only some bedraggled Italian soldiers, who seemed more interested in helping the Allies to unload their landing craft than in fighting. The movement of the 8th Army to the north was to be a difficult operation, however, as German engineers blew up bridges, tunnels, and mountain passes; actions that held up the Allied advance.

There were several factors that influenced the Allied decision to land at Salerno. In the first place, it was about at the range limit for fighter planes flying out of Sicily. Troops landing any farther north would have to operate without ground-based air support. Secondly, Salerno was considered the gateway to Naples, the major Italian westcoast seaport and certainly important for Allied supply purposes. Salerno itself was a small port, capable of handling modest tonnage for the Allies, and it lay astride a railway and a coastal highway leading to Naples and to Rome. Finally, there was a good airfield at Montecorvino, within the Salerno beachhead area. There were also certain drawbacks to Salerno. Particularly serious were the mountains that enclosed the beachhead. Enemy artillery here could be trained directly on the beaches. Also, once a beachhead was secured, an Allied advance north to Naples would have to pass through the Sorrento hills, in which there were only two easily defended passes. Still, Allied planners did not dwell on Salerno's disadvantages, because it was generally thought that the landing would be largely unopposed. As the invasion fleet neared Salerno on the evening of September 8, General Eisenhower made the radio announcement that Italy had surrendered. Shipboard celebrations quickly broke out as the men contemplated waltzing ashore against little or no resistance. Field Marshal Albert Kesselring, commander of German forces in southern Italy (south of a line running from Pisa to Rimini) and perhaps one of the most intelligent and effective generals in any of the armies engaged in World War II, reacted quickly to news of Italy's surrender. He ordered his field commander, Colonel General Heinrich von Vietinghoff genannt Scheel, to disarm those Italians who refused to fight and replace them with German troops.* Vietinghoff knew that Montgomery's Eighth Army was advancing up the coast from Messina and he was determined to throw the forces at Salerno back into the sea before the Eighth Army would arrive. He very nearly succeeded.**

The Allied force that landed at Salerno was commanded by Lieutenant General Mark Clark, at 47 years of age, one of the youngest men of his rank in the army. His force, the U.S. Fifth Army was divided into two corps: The U.S. VI Corps, under Major General Ernest J. Dawley, and the British X Corps, under Lieutenant General Sir Richard L. McCreery.*** The Salerno landings began at 3:30 A.M. on September 9. After the initial success of getting ashore, the Allies were quickly thrown on the defensive. Troops were pinned down on the beaches by artillery and mortar fire and by machine gunners and snipers. German tanks also moved back and forth along the line, pouring heavy fire into the invaders. The Luftwaffe added to Allied difficulties, launching almost 600 attacks in three days on the beachhead and on Allied shipping in the Gulf of Salerno. They utilized a new weapon, first unveiled at Salerno: a controlled glide bomb. Released from high-flying planes and guided by radio to their targets, these weapons combined with conventional bombs to sink four transports, one heavy cruiser and seven landing craft.† Numerous other ships were damaged, including the British cruiser *Uganda*, the British battleship, H.M.S. *Warspite* and the U.S. cruiser, *Savannah*.

---

*Vietinghoff commanded the German Tenth Army, composed of 6 divisions. An old and expert Prussian infantryman, he was another tough and extremely capable German commander.

**On the same day as the Salerno landing, British troops landed at Taranto, on the heel of the Italian boot. Two days after landing, these troops occupied the seaport of Brindisi (to which King Victor Emmanuel and Marshal Badoglio had fled). Bari, another 60 miles farther north, was also seized.

***Dawley, who had fought with distinction in World War I, did not prove out in combat in Italy. He was relieved of command, reduced in rank to colonel and returned to the States.

†Hoping to upset the guidance controls of the glide bombs with interference from electrical motors, whenever a glide-bomb attack was though to be imminent, an order was given to turn on all the electric razors in the fleet. How effective this tactic was has never been discerned.

So heavy was the German resistance, that General Clark proposed re-embarking. But the Allied units held their ground and were reinforced by parachute units that actually landed on the beach. This force and the arrival of the British Eighth Army in the Salerno area on September 16 forced the Germans to fall back.*

While the Salerno battle was still undecided, Mussolini was rescued from his confinement in a ski lodge on Gran Sasso d'Italia in the Apenine Mountains about 75 miles northwest of Rome. German intelligence had learned of his whereabouts and under the direction of Captain Otto Skorzeny, 90 German commandos landed in gliders near the ski lodge and made good the rescue without firing a shot. A small Storch observation plane took Mussolini and Skorzeny first to the safety of Rome; then Mussolini was flown to the Wolf's Lair, Hitler's headquarters in East Prussia. He returned to northern Italy on September 27 and established a new Fascist republic whose foreign policy was controlled by the Germans as was its economic resources.

Bad weather, German demolition of ridges and roadways, and German counter-attacks hampered the Allied advance and caused heavy Allied casualties. The sequel to the invasion of Italy had been very disappointing. Allied planners had thought that Italy could be occupied in six month's time, but in four months they had advanced only 70 miles beyond Salerno and were still 80 miles short of Rome. There was obviously to be no quick victory in Italy.

Narrow, mountainous, and bisected by fast flowing, flood-prone rivers, Italy was an ideal country for fighting a defensive war. As the Germans fell back from Salerno, they made good use of Italy's geography to hinder their pursuers. Their basic plan was to create two defensive lines, the Gustav and the Gothic, which would take advantage of Italy's difficult terrain.

The first major defensive line was the Gustav Line, which ran the width of Italy between Rome to the north and Naples to the south. Utilizing the mountainous terrain and fast flowing rivers, the Gustav Line was fortified to the point where it was so strong that Kesselring did not believe that the Allies could break through. The central point of the Gustav Line was the town of Cassino, site of the famous monastery, Monte Cassino.**

North of Rome the Germans had constructed a second defensive line, the so-called Gothic Line. Twenty miles north of Florence, the Gothic Line ran diagonally across Italy, winding through the northern Appenines. It was composed of a wide belt of fortifications consisting of anti-tank minefields, barbed wire entanglements and artillery and machine gun emplacements carved into rock. If the Allies managed to break through the Gustav Line and take Rome, they would then have to assault these mighty fortifications.

The Allied assault on the Gustav Line didn't begin in earnest until January, 1944. Repeated attacks by the multinational Allied forces were stopped cold by the tough German defenders.*** Wrongly believing that the Germans had fortified the monastery and were using it as an observation post, the Allies bombed it into destruction. The rubble provided excellent cover for the Germans, who now did occupy the monastery ruins. Failure to penetrate the Gustav Line led to a new Allied plan to outflank it by landing troops behind it at Anzio, only 35 miles south of Rome. It was hoped that his landing would cause the Germans, afraid of having their supply and escape routes to the north cut, to retreat to their prepared positions north of Rome.

---

*While the Allies were bogged down at Salerno, the people of Naples rose up against the Germans and fought them for 3 days. By the time the Allies arrived (October 1) the people of Naples had suffered terrible reprisals from the Germans.

**Monte Cassino was the site of St. Benedict's most famous monastery and his famous library. St. Benedict's bones had been removed to France 13 centuries earlier.

***Despite the widespread impression in the U.S., the Italian campaign was never primarily an American effort. Allied forces included: Canadians, British, Indians, New Zealanders, Poles, South Africans, Italians, Free French (mostly Moroccans and Algerians) and Brazilians. This mix of nationalities caused a number of problems: there were communication difficulties, dietary differences, differences in types of weapons and differences in combat preferences and characteristics.

The Anzio landing on January 22 caught the Germans by surprise and encountered little opposition. Kesselring had known that an expedition was in preparation in Naples, but he thought it was destined for Civitia Vecchia or points north of Rome, which would have been more dangerous to him strategically. The American commander, Major General John Lucas, who had taken over the command of the VI Corps during the last part of the Salerno battle, was a cautious individual who was quite pessimistic about his chances of success at Anzio. A daring commander, in the style of George Patton, would have made a lightning dash to Rome that first day. But Lucas was not Patton. As one author has noted, "...on discovering that there were no Germans in his path, he behaved as though there were." General Clark, the overall Allied commander, was also cautious. "Don't stick your neck out, Johnny," he told Lucas, "I did at Salerno and got into trouble." He thought that Lucas should simply seize and hold a beachhead without making a risky dash inland. Thus Lucas concentrated on building up the beachhead for the first week and made no attempt to move inland until January 30. By then it was too late.

Field Marshal Kesselring, a skilled strategist, quickly and resolutely reacted to the Allied landing. He ordered his forces in the Gustav Line to stand fast and shifted the Hermann Goering Division and available units in Rome into the Alban hills overlooking Anzio. In all, elements of eight German divisions were brought to the Anzio sector while Lucas was still consolidating his beachhead. When he finally tried to move inland, Lucas found that the Germans were too strong for him. They could now harass the whole beachhead with artillery fire and air attacks. On the small beachhead, where there was little cover from the constant barrage of German bombs and shells, 2,000 Allied troops were killed and 8500 wounded in the first month of the operation.* However, German attempts to drive the Allies into the sea as Hitler wanted, failed. The result was that stalemate prevailed until May, 1944.

Allied forces battled at the Gustav Line for five months, beginning in January, 1944. Although the casualties were high, the attackers finally began to wear down Kesselring's defenders. The German position was never more than a defensive one in a country of secondary importance to Berlin. Kesselring could thus expect little in the way of reinforcements or supplies. When British, Polish, and French forces opened a new attack in May, he was finally forced to abandon his positions south of Rome. French forces made the Germans evacuate Monte Cassino on May 17 and the next day, Polish troops entered the ruined monastery and the British entered the town of Cassino. On that same day, the Germans began to retreat all along the line. This weakened the German position around Anzio and allowed Allied troops there to break out on May 22, exactly four months after they had landed. Allied success in breaking through the Gustav Line relieved the pressure on Anzio. Ironically, the Anzio landing, which was intended to enable the Allies to breakthrough the Gustav Line, was itself saved by the event it had originally hoped to bring about.

Allied planners intended that the breakout from Anzio would be followed by a rapid thrust to Valmontone, to cut Route Six—the main inland road—and thus cut off most of the German Tenth Army, which had been holding the Gustav Line. But General Clark, now in overall command, wanted the glory of liberating Rome. Disregarding orders, he left the German line of retreat open and went straight for the Italian capital, which he entered on June 4. German troops meanwhile got away and moved into new defensive positions in the Gothic Line to the north. The fighting in Italy, which could have been shortened by a more audacious commander at Anzio in January, or a more obedient one there in May, was now destined to go on for nearly one more year.

Two days after Clark entered Rome, Allied troops landed in northwest France, along the Normandy coast. Italy was now a backwater operation for the Allies. The United States refused to reinforce its troops in Italy and even withdrew forces to invade Southern France (Operation Anvil) in August, 1944. "Victory in Italy in 1943 was beyond the Allies" grasp and victory in 1944 was pointless because there was never any thought of making the winning thrust anywhere but in France. By 1944 no other front could hope for...men and material...."

---

*Allied medical facilities also came under heavy German fire. Six American nurses were killed and four became the first women ever to win the Silver Star.

The campaign for Italy continued until the end of April, 1945—a grinding, bloody, slog through mud and mountains, that seemed to go on forever.* The end finally came when General Karl Wolff, head of the S.S. in Italy, after a series of clandestine meetings with Alan Dulles, head of the American O.S.S. (Office of Strategic Services—forerunner of the C.I.A.), agreed to negotiate a surrender. On April 23, he and General Vietinghoff, Kesselring's successor in Italy, decided to disregard Hitler's orders for continued resistance and a final stand in the Italian Alps. On April 29, German forces in Italy surrendered unconditionally, effective May 2, only 6 days before the overall German surrender in the West.

Partisan activity in northern Italy made a large contribution to Allied victory. As Allied troops advanced in the area, bands of urban partisans in the major industrial cities rose up and staged insurrections in Genoa, Milan, and Turin. They seized power stations, factories, offices buildings, German command posts and radio stations. Rural partisans blocked roads to prevent a German retreat and then the Allies found thousands of already captured Germans. All in all, partisans killed, wounded, or captured 50,000 Germans. Their losses were also high, as 35,000 partisans lost their lives and another 20,000 were wounded.

Partisans also captured Mussolini and his mistress of 13 years, Clara Petacci, as they fled towards Austria on April 27. The next day a Communist partisan machine-gunned them to death. Their bodies were strung upside down for everyone to see.

Many people have questioned the value of the Italian campaign to overall Allied victory in World War II. The frustration of the expected quick victory, the high casualty rate, and the secondary importance of Italy following the Allied landing in France have helped to diminish Italy's importance in the war. Yet, the Italian campaign was not just a peripheral operation. It occupied up to 26 German divisions that could have fought in Russia or France, and it provided Allied air bases from which the Balkans and southern and central Europe could be bombed. The campaign also eliminated Italian armed forces from the war, not just in Italy, but in the Balkans and on the Russian front as well. As the Germans had taken over the defense of Italy themselves, they were forced to pour resources southward, resources that were later badly needed on the Eastern front against the Russians and on the western front in Normandy. J.F.C. Fuller has pointed out that, "Relative to its own strength, the Allied force in Italy absorbed a higher proportion of the German's resources than those on other fronts."

---

*Churchill called it "...dragging the hot rake of war up the Italian peninsula."

U.S. COAST GUARD

Chapter IX

The Second Front

❖ ❖ ❖

In October, 1941, Winston Churchill appointed Admiral Lord Louis Mountbatten to head Combined Operation Headquarters (COHQ), whose task was to carry out commando raids along the whole of the enemy coastline. A cousin of the King and commander of a destroyer at the start of the war, Mountbatten was told that his major objective was to prepare for re-invasion of France and the establishment of a second front in Europe.

Accordingly, the commando raids on the continent carried out under Mountbatten's leadership, were important not so much for the damage they inflicted but rather for the experience and information they provided for planning a full-scale continental invasion. Mountbatten was also told to develop devices to make the invasion possible, to select and build-up bases from which to launch the invasion, to create training centers, and to select the place for the attack. Although Churchill later was to have doubts about a cross-channel invasion of France, his appointment of Mountbatten set into motion a planning group which would lay the groundwork for the Allied landings in Normandy in June, 1944.

Commando raids carried out by COHQ had mixed results. A British commando raid on St. Nazaire on March 28, 1942 was considered a "smashing success." Despite heavy British casualties, the raid destroyed the largest German drydock on the Atlantic coast and killed more than two hundred Germans. A second commando raid by British and Canadian soldiers at the German-held Channel port of Dieppe, however, was a "bloody failure." Of the 5,100 Allied troops who landed there, 3,648 failed to return. The two strategic goals of the attack, to force the Luftwaffe into a decisive battle over the beaches and to relieve German pressure on Russia by drawing troops and war planes away from the Eastern Front, were not realized. But the Dieppe failure did serve a major purpose. It taught those planning a second front in Europe that no invasion could succeed if it was directed against a fortified port rather than open beaches; that attacks on heavily fortified areas should be launched from the flanks, not head on. Dieppe also showed that massive and prolonged bombardment from sea and air were necessary (more so than surprise) for a successful landing. The need for many technical innovations in equipment and their use—from special armored vehicles to better landing craft—were also indicated by the Dieppe operation. As Mountbatten was later to note, "For every soldier who died at Dieppe, ten were saved on D-Day."

In March, 1943, the work of COHQ was superseded by the establishment of COSSAC (Chief of Staff to the Supreme Allied Commander) which was given the task to start planning a return to the Continent. The head of COSSAC was British Lieutenant General Sir Frederick E. Morgan, a former tank-force commander in the invasion of North Africa and a chief architect of the plan for invading Sicily. Described as a "self-starter with extraordinary executive ability," Morgan's orders directed him to plan a large-scale invasion of the continent, to be launched as early as possible in 1944. The master plan which emerged from COSSAC was later code-named, *Overlord.*

Planning for *Overlord* was hampered by the lack of a Supreme Commander of the invasion forces. Since it would be primarily an American operation, it was generally accepted that the commander should be an American. At first, the American Chief of Staff, General George C. Marshall, seemed to be the leading candidate for the position. But Roosevelt decided that he was too valuable in Washington and would not part with him. Finally, in December, 1943, Roosevelt selected General Dwight Eisenhower (Ike), who had commanded three previous invasions in the European theater: North Africa, Sicily, and Italy. COSSAC now gave way to a new organization, SHAEF (Supreme Headquarters of the Allied Expeditionary Force).

When Eisenhower arrived in London in January, 1944, to take up his duties, he found that an excellent groundwork for the invasion had been laid by COSSAC. Experiments with, and development of, landing craft, artificial harbors, and new tanks, were already underway. Also, much intelligence information, necessary for final planning of the operation, had been accumulated.

Eisenhower's initial task was to appoint a staff to assist him. His selections were: Deputy Supreme Commander—Air Chief Marshal Sir Arthur Tedder, who had been head of the Royal Air Force in the Middle East and Allied Air Forces in the Mediterranean; Naval Commander—Admiral Sir Bertram Ramsey, who had organized the rescue of British and French troops at Dunkirk in 1940; Head of the Allied Air Forces—Air Chief Marshal Sir Trafford Leigh-Mallory, a Battle of Britain Commander. Lieutenant General Walter Bedell Smith, Eisenhower's Chief of Staff in the Mediterranean Campaign, was retained as Chief of Staff for Overlord; while General Morgan was named Deputy Chief of Staff. General Montgomery, the hero of El Alamein, was named ground commander of all the Allied Armies.*

One of the crucial decisions which SHAEF inherited from COSSAC, was that of a landing site. In fact, there were only two areas suitable for the invasion: The Pas-de-Calais coast; and the Normandy Coast, to the west of the Pas-de-Calais in the Bay of the Seine River. The Calais area had two major advantages. The first was its proximity to England. Only 21 miles from Dover, Calais could be seen, and shelled, from there. The short distance had other advantages: The area could be blanketed by Allied air power; and there would be a short turnaround time for ships and landing craft. The second advantage to a landing at Calais was that it provided a shorter, more direct route to Germany than any of the beaches further west. COSSAC planners, however, felt that the disadvantages of a Calais landing outweighed its advantages. For one thing, British ports across the Channel were too small to accommodate the invasion forces. Additionally, the capacity of the French ports of Calais and nearby Boulounge, was too small to meet Allied supply needs. Since the beaches in the Calais area were narrow and had restricted exits, it would have been very difficult to maintain a build-up on the beaches. Therefore, immediate possession of a major port in the area (of which there were none) would have been a necessity. In addition, the Dieppe experience had shown the difficulty of taking a port with a quick, head-on attack. Finally, since most Germans expected an attack at Calais, it was the most heavily defended area of France. Any advance following a successful landing, would have been dangerously exposed to a German counterattack on the flanks.

A Normandy landing would have none of these drawbacks. The area was weakly held and defended, at least in comparison to Calais. Its beaches were expansive enough to support a large invasion force and they were protected against the prevailing westerly winds by the Cotentin Peninsula. The beaches could also be strategically isolated by bombing the bridges over the Seine and Loire Rivers. Two large ports—Cherbourg and Le Havre—lay on the flanks of the Normandy area, and particularly Cherbourg could handle large amounts of material, and it could be attacked from land. Finally, the whole area was within easy fighter range of England. Thus, the Normandy coast was selected for the attack; and although much work remained on the Overlord plan, it would have been difficult in 1944 to have changed the landing area, even if Eisenhower had so desired.

German forces in Normandy were under the overall command of Field Marshal von Rundstedt, Commander-in-Chief of the Western Front. Field command of German troops in France, however, fell to Rommel, who in February, 1944, was put in charge of Army Group B, which consisted of the Seventh Army in Normandy and Brittany, and the Fifteenth Army in the Pas-de-Calais and Flanders.

---

*Montgomery's forces consisted of the United States First Army, including the 82nd and 101st Airborne Divisions, under General Omar Bradley; the 21st Army Group, comprising the First Canadian Army, under Lieutenant General H.D.G. Crearar; the British Second Army, under Lieutenant General Sir M.C. Dempsey; the 6th Airborne under Lieutenant General F.A.M. Browning; and various Allied contingents.

Unfortunately for the Germans, Rommel and von Rundstedt did not agree on the way to counter an Allied invasion. Rommel favored stopping an Allied landing on the beaches. The Allies must be prevented from establishing a beachhead, he argued, or Germany would lose the war. He advocated mining the shore and beaches, strengthening beach defenses and beach garrisons, and moving reserves close to the front line troops. Rommel had had the painful experience of Allied air supremacy in the western desert and knew well the fate of armored columns attempting to move by daylight. If the armor was not close at hand, he doubted its ability to get there, and certainly not in time to be effective.

Rundstedt saw little likelihood of preventing an Allied landing, so his strategy was to accept it and then throw the enemy back into the sea by a counter-attack. This meant keeping the bulk of German troops well in the rear of the coastal defenses, bringing them to bear on the Allied flanks once they began to move inland off the beaches.

Although Hitler favored Rommel's view, he still held large forces back from the beaches, particularly German armor. Of the seven armored divisions in Western Europe, three were assigned to Rommel as tactical reserves, but only one was even near the invasion area on D-Day. The remaining four were held in strategic reserve near Calais and could be moved only with Hitler's approval. The result was what General Fuller has called "...the very worst thing in war: the infantry was kept forward and the armour was kept back." Under the circumstances, Rommel had to rely on the Atlantic Wall and its static defenses to repel any invasion, and he set out to strengthen the wall by speeding up the construction of bunkers and gun emplacements.* Anti-tank obstacles were placed along the beaches and logs and steel beams were driven into the sand and tipped with mines and metal cutters designed to destroy landing craft. Czech-hedgehogs—twisted steel girders welded together—were strewn in the tidal flats to hinder the invaders. Behind the beaches, tall, thick poles, known as Rommel's asparagus, were implanted so that "enemy aircraft and gliders will break-up while landing." All through the spring of 1944 the Germans worked feverishly on the Wall. Allied bombing raids hampered their work—e.g. only 10 percent of the projected 50 million stakes were in place by D-Day. Still, by the end of May, 1944, Rommel had transformed the Atlantic Wall into a formidable obstacle.

Allied officers were well aware of Rommel's plans and became particularly concerned with his progress in the invasion area of Normandy. As a result certain changes were made in the assault plan. In order to get through the obstacles it would be necessary to see them, and a daylight landing was necessitated, not a night landing as originally proposed. Also, a landing at high tide, as originally suggested was now impossible because many of the obstacles would be invisible, just below the water line. The landing would have to come at low tide so that demolition engineers could clear a path. Special weapons were also designed by Major General Sir Percy C.S. Hobart to overcome many of the obstacles. He and his staff eventually produced an amazing variety of specialized armored vehicles, including flame throwing tanks, tanks that could "swim" ashore under their own power, tanks designed to clear minefields, tanks that could roll out a carpet over soft, slippery soil and many more. It was decided that these specially designed tanks would go in first, followed by the infantry, contrary to the standard amphibious invasion techniques.**

Along with these tactical innovations, Allied planners made great efforts to catch the enemy by surprise. Only if Hitler was kept guessing as to the place and time of the invasion, could the assault hope to be successful. Consequently, a plan, code-named *Fortitude*, was developed to deceive the Germans about the attack and to tie down their land and naval forces in areas far removed from the Normandy

---

*Hitler had conceived of the Atlantic Wall as an awesome defense line of concrete and steel bunkers, heavily fortified with men and guns, stretching the 2400 miles from Norway to the Spanish border. Begun early in 1942, the heaviest concentration of the defenses was between Holland in the north and Le Harve in the south.

**In fact, American commanders rejected as unproven the specialized armor developed by Hobart. A few floating tanks were used at Omaha Beach, but the mine-clearing tanks, flame-throwing tanks and pill box busting tanks were utilized only by the British. Following the bloody encounters at Omaha, the Americans came to regret their decision not to employ the whole array of these so-called "Funnies."

invasion site. To bottle up the German units in Norway, the plan called for the creation of a fictitious British Army in Scotland. Fake messages and requests for various items were sent out by this army and were intercepted by German intelligence (as intended), which believed them. To guard against a possible invasion by this bogus army, twenty seven German divisions in Norway stayed put and did not move south.

Fortitude was specifically designed, however, to make the Germans believe that the main invasion would come at the Pas-de-Calais. To this end, a fake army of some 50 divisions was created and established in southeastern England across from Calais.* Under the command of General Patton, whom the Germans thought would be in the vanguard of any continental invasion, this army was provided with rubber-inflated tanks, gliders made of canvas, fake ammunition dumps, etc. German reconnaissance planes were allowed to fly over the area and report their findings back to German intelligence. Again, the Germans swallowed the bait and disposed their forces accordingly in the Calais area. So effective was the Allied scheme that for as long as six weeks after the Allied landing in Normandy, Hitler continued to believe that it was a feint and that the real attack was going to come in the Calais region. Both Hitler and von Rundstedt believed an invasion likely in Calais because the V-1 launching sites (see Chapter 11) which the Allies had difficulty bombing, were located there. Allied air power contributed to the deception campaign by concentrating most of its pre-invasion activity in the Pas-de-Calais. For every Allied reconnaissance and bombing mission and for every ton of bombs dropped in Normandy, there were at least two in the vicinity of Calais. This bombing pattern reinforced the Germans' suspicion that Calais was to be the target. Air power was also effective in eliminating German radar stations along the coast of France. By D-Day, not more than 18 percent, according to one estimate, of the enemy apparatus in northern France was operational. This deprived the Germans of their most important tactical warning system.

The deception campaign also utilized German spies in England, who were bribed or forced into sending erroneous information to their German superiors. In fact, the Germans learned very little about the actual invasion plan. German reconnaissance aircraft could not safely operate over southwestern England where Montgomery's invasion force was assembling.**

The *Overlord* assault plan, code named *Neptune*, called for 20,000 airborne troops, the British 6th, the U.S. 82nd, and the U.S. 101st, to land on the continent at 2 A.M. Their tasks were to protect the flanks of the assault and to open exits from the beaches for the seaborne troops (particularly behind Utah Beach). The amphibious landings were due to begin at 6:30 A.M. along the Normandy coast, at five designated beaches: Utah and Omaha for the Americans; and Sword, Juno, and Gold for the British and the Canadians. In all, one hundred and seventy thousand seaborne troops were to be landed the first day, the vanguard of some two million troops from a dozen nations who would land in France in the next months.

Of the 60 divisions making up von Rundstedt's forces in the west, forty three were assigned to Rommel's Army Group B; only three of these division—the 709th, the 352nd, and the 716th were in the Normandy area. Of the three armored divisions under Rommel's control, only one, the 21st was actually in the Normandy area at the time of the Allied invasion. Thus, the outcome of the first day of fighting was to lay with the coastal batteries and with the three divisions entrenched along the Normandy coast. Although there were some crack, hard-core, battle-hardened units among the defenders, e.g. the 352nd, many of the defenders were over-aged and/or suffering from some physical ailment—stomach trouble, poor eyesight. Also, many of the gun crews were composed of impressed "volunteers" from occupied countries—Poles, Hungarians, Czechs, Yugoslavs, and even two Russian divisions, composed of men who preferred fighting for the Nazis to remaining in prison camps.

---

*Although most of these divisions were imaginary, two forces, the American Third Army and the Canadian First Army, did exist and eventually landed in France for post-D-Day operations.

**After early Spring, 1944, the Luftwaffe was unable to make any photo-reconnaissance flights over Great Britain.

Overlord's launching date—"D-Day"—was originally set for May, but because of a shortage of landing craft, was put back to June 5. By June 3, all the assault troops were aboard and by June 5, the 5,000 ships of the invasion armada had assembled 13 miles southeast of the Isle of Wight for the journey across the Channel. Minesweepers led the armada, clearing 10 lanes through the Germans' mid-Channel mine field. They were followed by warships, freighters, landing vessels, swarms of tugs and, among the troop transports, converted yachts and luxury liners.

At the last minute, however, the invasion force was halted. Stormy weather and high winds in the English Channel made the operation too risky. Initial forecasts indicated a continuation of the bad weather. Another day's postponement would mean the whole operation would be set back for two more weeks when the tides would again be right for an invasion. But Allied meterologists, using reports coming from across the Atlantic, saw the likelihood of a lull between two storm fronts, and General Eisenhower decided to "go" with the attack on June 6.

Across the Channel, German meteorologists, who did not have the benefit of weather stations in the Northwest Atlantic, predicted a continuation of the bad weather—"rough seas, poor visibility, force 5 to 6 wind, rain likely to get heavier." The Germans even cancelled their torpedo-boat patrols for the night and General Friedrich Dollman, commander of the 7th Army, believed that because of the bad weather, the invasion wouldn't come for two more weeks when the tides and the moon were once again favorable. He thus ordered his divisional and regimental commanders to leave their units and attend a staff war game at Rennes on June 6. The game's subject was "Enemy landings in Normandy, preceded by parachute drops." Rommel took advantage of the bad weather to leave his headquarters at La Roche-Guyon to celebrate his wife's birthday on June 6 and then to proceed to Berchtesgaden to plead with Hitler to transfer two armored divisions to Normandy.

General Walter Warlimont, Deputy Chief of Operations at Supreme Headquarters, was later to write that "OKW" had not the slightest idea that the decisive event of the war was upon them. Yet, German headquarters for all troops in Western Europe, located in Paris, did receive advanced notice of the pending attack. German intelligence had penetrated the French resistance movement, which was supposed to carry out certain sabotage activities—blowing-up bridges, railroads, cutting communication lines—just prior to D-Day. They would be readied for action by the first line of a poem by Paul Valery, broadcast over the French language service of the B.B.C. (British Broadcasting Corporation). When they heard the line, "The long sobbing of the violins of autumn," the resistance knew that the invasion was imminent. When the second line of the poem, "Wound my heart with monotonous languor," was broadcast, it meant that invasion would occur within 48 hours. From their spy, the Germans learned of the code and monitored all B.B.C. transmissions. At 9:15 P.M. on June 5, the second line of the poem was aired. Within two hours this important information had been sent to Supreme Headquarters at Berchtesgaden. Incredibly, nothing was done; von Rundstedt, the Commander-in-Chief in the West, did not believe that the invasion could take place in such bad weather conditions; he also apparently did not believe that the Allies would broadcast their plans in the open over the B.B.C.

The first Allied troops to land in France were the pathfinders, whose job was to mark the way for the main airborne forces. They landed shortly after midnight on June 6 and were soon followed by two American airborne divisions, the 82nd and the 101st; and by the British 6th Airborne Division. For the most part, the British were dropped on or near their objectives along the estuary of the Orne River and proceeded to liberate the first village in France from German rule, Ranville.

American operations, however, were confused from the outset. Many of the pathfinders marked the wrong landing zones. In addition, haze and clouds caused many of the planes to stray off course. And to make matters worse, heavy German antiaircraft fire forced the planes even further off course. The result was that three-fourths of the 6500 men in each division were widely scattered—thousands were simply lost. Yet, the remarkable fact is that so great a confusion was created in the enemy by this scattering of men in their midst, that there was no possibility of reserves supporting the beach defenders or launching a counterattack. It seemed to the Germans that they were surrounded on all sides by hostile troops, and they could not assess their numbers or the directions from which to expect an attack. This bewilderment which the widespread air drop created in the enemy was perhaps of greater effect than would have been possible if all had gone according to plan.

Both the British and American airborne units successfully completed their principal assignments in good time. The British were firmly astride the Caen and Orne bridges, which carried the main road leading inland from the beachhead on the eastern flank of the nearly 70 miles invasion front. They also destroyed five bridges over the Dives River, needed by the Germans to carry equipment and reinforcements to the beachhead area. And the 9th Parachute Battalion, under Lieutenant Colonel Terence Otway had knocked out the seemingly impregnable four-gun German battery at Merville, which commanded the left flank of the British landing beaches. The Americans, despite their initial problems did equally as well. The key communications center of St. Mere Eglise was captured; the main Cherbourg highway running down the Cotentin Peninsula was cut; the rear of the Utah beachhead was held; and although none of the causeways leading off of Utah Beach had been reached by the time of the seaborne landing, groups of soldiers were advancing on them by dawn on June 6. Casualties among all the airborne units were high, about 10 percent, but still considerably lower that Eisenhower's fear of between 70 and 80 percent.

At about the same time that the airborne landings began in Normandy, the Allies began a series of deception operations. RAF bombers dropped hundreds of life-size dummies by parachute, all over Normandy. The purpose was to make the actual airdrop look like a feint or a diversion.* The Allies also began to jam German radar stations in Normandy in order to mask the approach of the invasion fleet. Bombing attacks were concentrated near Calais to reinforce German beliefs that it was the Allies' invasion target. The British also used an electronic ruse to make the German radar in the Calais area pick up what appeared to be an enormous Allied sea and air armada bound for Calais. Meanwhile, the real invasion fleet was steadily sailing toward Normandy. It wasn't until after 4 A.M. on June 6, when Allied landing craft were already beginning their runs to the beaches, that von Rundstedt realized that Normandy was the target of the massive invasion effort. He tried to bring the strategic reserves—the 12th S.S. Hitler Youth and the Panzer Lehr—to Normandy. But his orders were countermanded by General Alfred Jodl, Hitler's Chief of Operations, who thought the Normandy attack was a diversion and that the main target was Calais. According to von Rundstedt's operation officer, General Zimmerman, this meant that "the first critical day was lost!" The success of the invasion was already decided.

Shortly after dawn on June 6, following a massive preliminary aerial and naval bombardment of the German shore defenses, the seaborne assault divisions began landing on the five beaches.** These forces were to secure their respective beachheads on the first day; on the second day, D plus 1, the beachheads were to be joined; and on D plus 2 to D plus 9, the Allies were to expand northwest, west, and south to form a staging area for a breakout toward Paris and the Rhine. The key to the plan was for the British and Canadians to take Caen, engaging in the process the bulk of the German forces, including their armor. Meanwhile, the Americans would swing to the west, cut the Contentin peninsula, secure Cherbourg and build up their resources for the breakout from Normandy.

Things did not go as planned, despite what Field Marshal Montgomery was to say at a later date. Perhaps Liddel Hart best summed it up when he said that, "It was an operation that eventually went according to plan but not according to timetable....The ultimate triumph has obscured the fact that the Allies were in great danger at the outset, and had a very narrow shave. To illustrate this point, it is helpful to look at fighting on the five beaches.

---

*Most of the deception operations worked according to plan. The dummy parachutes, for example, persuaded German commanders to disregard reports of real paratrooper landings.

**Nearly 200,000 men were engaged that day in naval operations and 11,000 air sorties were flown. In 1940, the Germans invading France had 19 aircraft for each assault division; in 1941, invading Russia, they had 26. On June 6, 1944, the Allies had 260 aircraft per division.

American fortunes on Utah and Omaha were almost diametrically opposed. On Utah beach, where the first amphibious assault troops landed in France on D-Day, there was only sparse opposition from the Germans.* Many of the defenders had been killed and their weapons destroyed in the pre-invasion naval and air bombardment. In addition, the smoke and dust from the preliminary shelling and a strong cross current threw most of the landing craft off course, causing the Americans to land in the wrong place. As it turned out, it was a fortuitous error as the assault troops landed in an area of weak German defenses. A landing 2,000 yards further north at the intended site, would have been in the teeth of German defenses.

Exiting from the Utah beachhead proved a slow process. The Germans had flooded a large area behind the beachhead, confining American movement to three causeways. As the assault forces moved out over these passages, German guns zeroed in on them. Still, American casualties on Utah were relatively light: 197 killed or wounded and 60 missing (presumed drowned) on the first day.

The American landings at Omaha were nearly a disaster, earning it the title, Bloody Omaha. Even the American land commander, General Bradley, called it "a nightmare." The beach fortifications and terrain at Omaha were formidable. There were underwater steel and concrete obstacles, most of them mined. At low tide, when the Americans landed, the beach was over two hundred yards wide with no cover. Then came a low sea wall and behind it, sand dunes and bluffs: between the two, thousands of mines had been laid. There were five possible exit ways through the dunes and bluffs, all covered by German gun emplacements.** American historian Samuel Eliot Morison, was to later write about Omaha: "Altogether, the Germans had provided the best imitation of hell for an invading force that American troops had encountered anywhere. Even the Japanese defenses of Iwo Jima, Tarawa and Peleliu are not to be compared to these."

Although troops were landed at the wrong spots as at Utah, in this case it did not work to their benefit. Almost the entire length of the beach was swept by German fire, and there was no cover for the Americas, who instantly came under a hurricane of enemy machine gun, mortar and artillery fire. Six hours after landing, the Americas held only ten yards of beach. Not until the principal commanders got ashore did the men, pinned down on the beaches, begin to move forward to the cover of the seawall and the bluffs. Brigadier General Norman Cota, assistant division commander of the 29th Division, rallied his men by shouting: "Two kinds of people are staying on this beach, the dead and those who are going to die. Now, let's get the hell out of here."*** Slowly, the troops began to advance. Covering fire from American ships, including destroyers which came so close to shore they nearly ran aground, allowed the deadlock on the beach to begin to breakup. At one thirty in the afternoon, General Bradley, who had privately considered evacuating the beachhead, received the following message, "Troops formerly pinned down on beaches...advancing up heights." By the end of the day, American troops had moved one mile inland. American casualties—dead, wounded, and missing—were about 2500 that first day, although no exact accounting has ever been made."

---

*Among American troops who landed on Utah was the oldest man to land in any of the initial waves on D-Day, fifty seven year old, Brigadier General Theodore Roosevelt, eldest son of the former president, Teddy Roosevelt. He had persuaded General Bradley to allow him to take part in the landings. On July 12, just after General Eisenhower appointed him commanding general of the 90th Division, General Roosevelt suffered a fatal heart attack. He was posthumously awarded the Congressional Medal of Honor for his heroism and courage under fire at Utah beach.

**The German 716th Infantry Division, low in morale and composed of fifty percent transcripts, most Polish or Russian, had primary responsibility for defending the Omaha area. Preceding D-Day, however, American intelligence confirmed that the German 352nd Infantry Division, a mobile unit battle hardened on the Eastern Front, had been moved into the Omaha Beach area. American troops, already on their way to the area were not informed and they went into battle believing that Omaha was weakly manned.

***General Bradley credits Cota with making this statement. Others, including Cornelius Ryan in his book, *The Longest Day*, have attributed it to Colonel George A. Taylor, Commander of the 16th Infantry.

Three miles off of Omaha Beach, early on D-Day morning, two hundred and twenty five Americans of the 2nd Ranger Battalion landed below the cliff at Pointe du Hoc. Their task was to scale the 358 foot high cliff and destroy a German coastal battery which Allied intelligence said contained guns powerful enough to cause heavy damage on the American landings at Omaha. When they finally got to the top, the Rangers found that there were no guns in the battery, but they paid heavily for this faulty intelligence; only 90 of them were still able to bear arms, after reaching the top.

British landings of Gold, Juno, and Sword, were less difficult and bloody than Omaha. The German 716th Division also was responsible for defending this area, and here is where they concentrated most of their foreign conscripts. British troops at Gold quickly overran the defenses, and pushed four miles inland, still short, however, of their D-Day objective. The Canadian 3rd Division, which landed at Juno, also penetrated four miles inland, with some of their patrols reaching the vital Bayeux-Caen road. At Sword, the British 3rd Division lost 28 of its 40 seagoing tanks in the rough water.* The remaining twelve helped overrun German beach defenses and allowed British troops to link up with the British 6th Parachute Division along the Orne River. However, the British failed to take their D-Day objective of Caen. Altogether, 75,000 British and Canadian troops went ashore on June 6, along with 8,000 paratroopers; of this force they suffered 3,000 casualties, one-third of whom were Canadians.

British failure to take Caen, which was not to be secured for more than a month, was caused by a number of things: a traffic jam on the beaches; overly cautious commanders, who failed to move when there was hardly anything to stop them (similar to General Lucas at Anzio).** Also hindering Montgomery's hope of capturing Caen that first day, was the arrival on the scene of the one German panzer division in Normandy. Part of the division even broke through the British front to the beach, but the effort was too small to have any lasting effect. By D-Day plus 4, there were three panzer divisions in the area, blocking the British advance on Caen. To illustrate just how tenuous Allied D-Day operations were, the British military historian, Liddel-Hart, has pointed out that if the three panzer divisions had been at hand to intervene on D-Day (as Rommel had wished) "...the Allied footholds could have been dislodged before they were joined up and consolidated."

General Eisenhower was certainly aware of the possibility of failure at Normandy and had drawn up a message to be broadcast in case this happened. In the note, which was naturally never aired, Eisenhower assumed full responsibility for the decision to launch the invasion and for its failure.

All in all, Allied commanders were elated with the events of D-Day. Their beachheads were small and thinly-held, a seven-mile gap still separated the British and American beachheads, and Caen remained in the hands of the Germans. Yet, Hitler's Atlantic Wall had been smashed and Rommel's strategy of repulsing the invasion on the beaches had failed. Allied mastery of the air was complete; the few Luftwaffe attempts to interfere with the operation had been driven off. So effective had been the *Fortitude* deception plan, that the German High Command (including Hitler) was still looking toward Calais for the main attack.***

SHAEF officials had predicted 10,000 Allied dead in the initial assault. Although exact losses have never been calculated, probably no more than 2500 men lost their lives and total casualties—wounded, missing and prisoners—were fewer than 12,000. There are no figures on German losses, but they were

---

*Called DD's for duplex drive, these "swimming tanks" were dubbed "Donald Ducks" by the Americans.

**General Bradley was later critical of the British. "...the British and Canadian assault forces sat down. They had Caen within their grasp and let it slip away."

***Hitler was asleep at the time of the invasion and his aides refused to awaken him. It was late morning before Hitler heard about the landings. He was reluctant to release reserves because he considered Normandy a preliminary to the main attack which would come at Calais. General Bradley wrote that if Hitler had thrown all his reserves against the Allies in the first few days, or within the first week, "...he might well have overwhelmed us."

probably about 4,000. One British writer has pointed out in comparison, "33,000 men perished at Towton Field on March 29th, 1461 and nearly 20,000 British troops were killed on the first day of the Battle of the Somme in 1916.

From this day on, the Third Reich had less than one year to live. Soon the whole of Hitler's Europe would be liberated. Above Omaha Beach, at the American Cemetery where many of those who fell on D-Day are buried, there is a chapel with this inscription on it wall:

> *Think not only upon their passing.*
> *Remember the glory of their spirit.*
> *It was the spirit of free men fighting for the cause of freedom.*

This is the true legacy of June 6, 1944, what the late Cornelius Ryan called the Longest Day.

THE ALLIED INVASION OF EUROPE JUNE 6, 1944
ALLIED POSITIONS AND MOVEMENTS
First U.S. Army
United States assault units
Follow up units
British 2nd Army
Follow up units
Beaches
A. Utah
B. Omaha
C. Gold
D. Juno
E. Sword
German Installations
German Headquarters
3rd U.S. Army
ENGLISH CHANNEL
CONCENTRATION AREA
Guernsey
Jersey
A B C D E
Paris
0 50
MILES

The Allied Landings
US 1 Army
Bradley
21 Army
Montgomery
British 2 Army
Dempsey
US 7 Corps
Collins
US 5 CORPS
Gerow
British 30 Corps
Bucknail
British 1 Corps
Crocker
Montebourg
St. Mere Eglise
UTAH
BAY OF SEINE
OMAHA
Port-en-Bessin
GOLD
JUNO
SWORD
Vierville
Colleville
Carentan
Isign
Douvres
Cabourg
Bures
Ballroy
VII Army
0 5

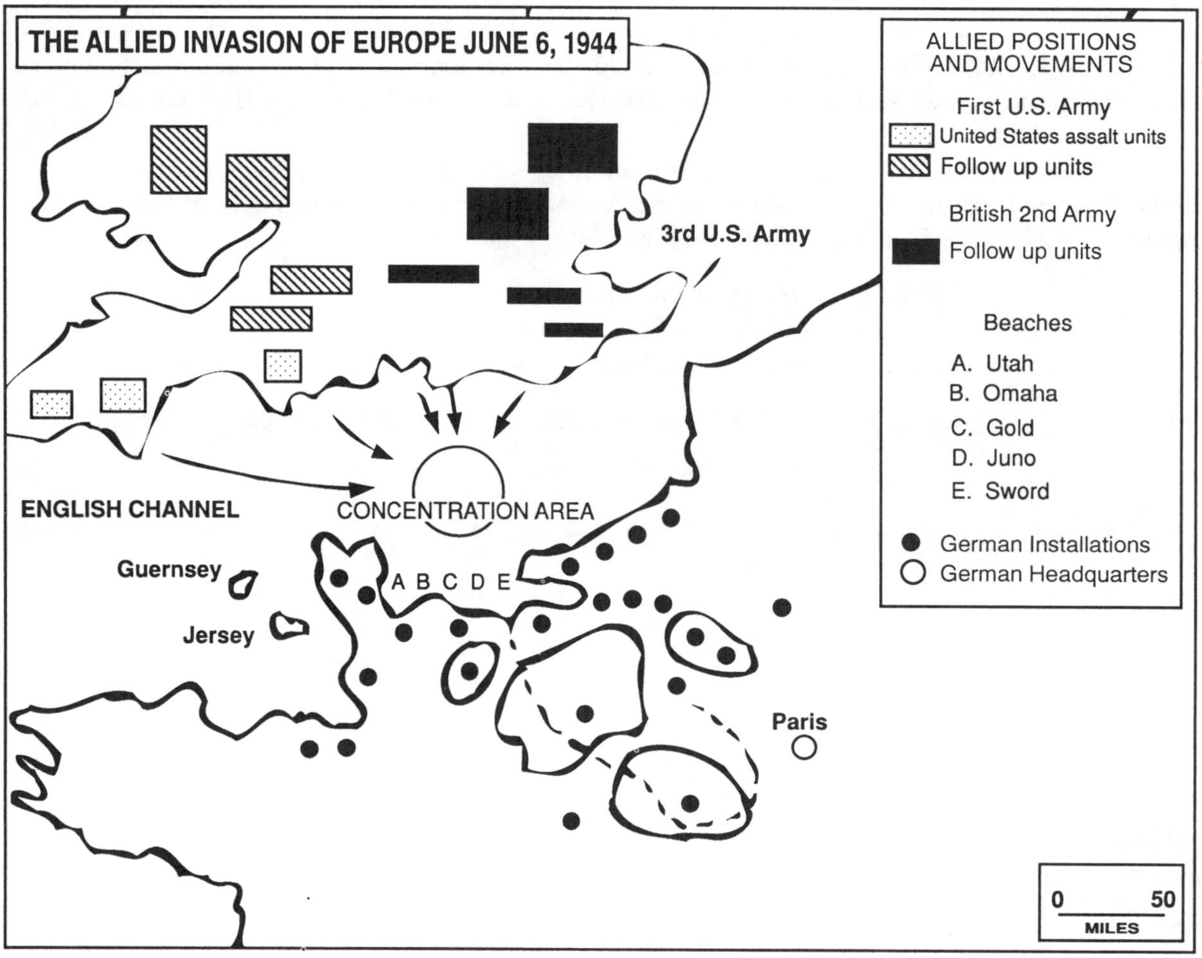

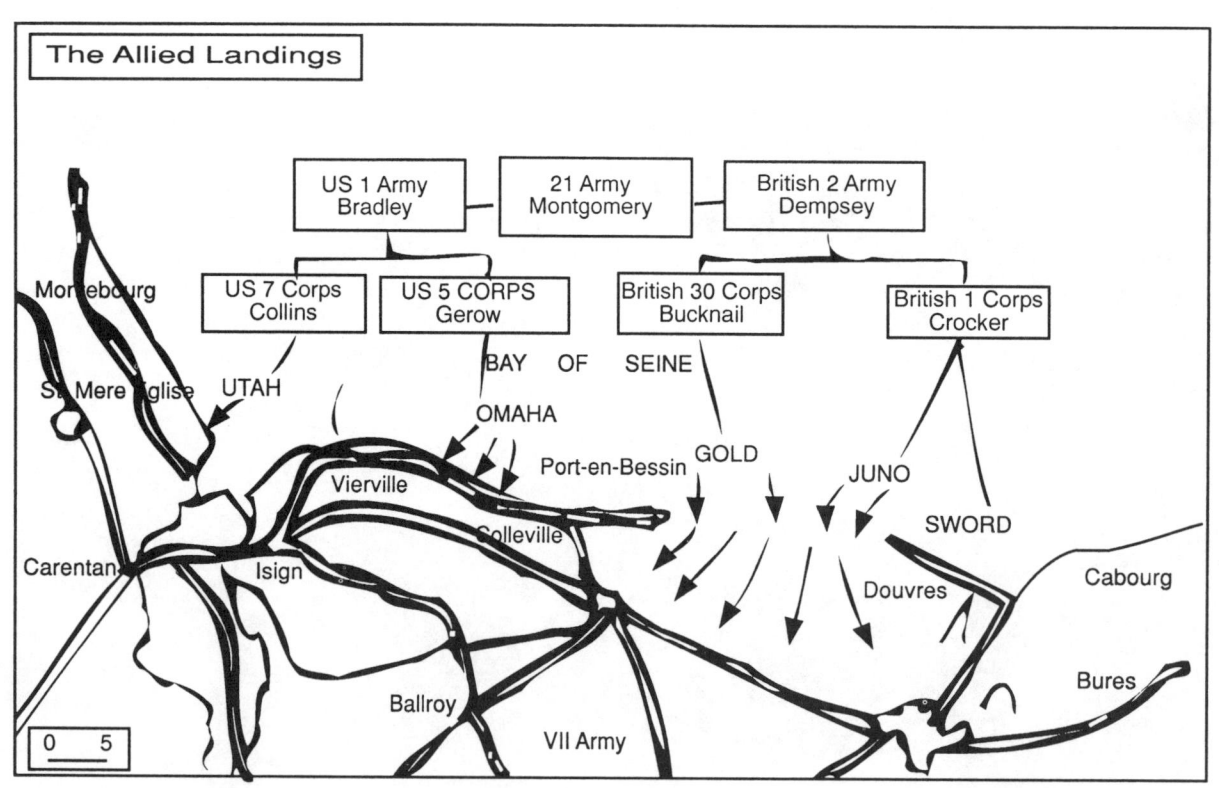

Chapter X

Victory in Europe

❖   ❖   ❖

While Western armies were consolidating their beachheads in Normandy, Soviet troops were clearing Russian land of German troops. The 1943–44 Russian winter offensive had bogged down in mud caused by the spring thaw, leaving Belorussia still under German control. Soviet advances to the north and south had liberated most Soviet territory but the central front was relatively unchanged since 1941, when German troops were pushed back from the gates of Moscow. Although the flanks of Army Group Center, under Field Marshal Ernst Busch, were dangerously exposed, the Germans were not worried because their intelligence expected the Soviet 1944 summer offensive to liberate the Balkans. Hitler also believed this to be the Soviet plan and accordingly took 15 percent of Busch's divisions, 33 percent of his heavy artillery, 50 percent of his tank destroyers and 88 percent of his tanks to reinforce the southern sector of the Russian front.

German intelligence and Hitler, however, had made a monumental mistake. Since April, 1944, the Soviet High Command had been preparing a major blow against the German line in Belorussia, not the Balkans. Operation *Bagration*, as it was called, began with an attack on the German northern flank on June 22, followed by attacks in the central sector on June 23 and the southern flank on June 24. Aided by partisans, operating behind German lines, who crippled the vital railroad network needed to move reinforcements behind the German lines, four Soviet army groups slammed into the Germans at six separate points along a 450-mile front. Spurred on by evidence of German atrocities—razed villages and mass graves, Soviet troops advanced relentlessly.* By early July, they virtually annihilated Army Group Center. Twenty-eight German Divisions were destroyed and between 300,000 and 350,000 men were killed or captured. As Wehrmacht power on the Eastern Front waned, Soviet forces prepared to carry the campaign both into the Balkans and into Poland.

In August, Soviet armies of the Second and Third Ukrainian Fronts burst into Rumania along a 250-mile line and soon fanned out into Bulgaria, Yugoslavia, and Hungary. Rumania accepted Russian terms on August 23 and immediately declared war on its former ally, Germany. The Bulgarians, who had participated in the invasion of Russia, did not resist the Soviet attack, and also declared war on Germany on September 9. Soviet forces didn't attack Hungary until late December, but quickly established a pro-Soviet government in Budapest, which also turned against Germany on December 29, 1944.

The Soviet attack on Poland began in mid-July, 1944. By July 26, units of the First Belorussian Front under the command of Marshal Konstantin K. Rokosovosky were within 60 miles of Warsaw. Four days later, they were only five miles away. As their troops neared the Polish capital, Soviet radio stations broadcast appeals to the people of Warsaw, urging them to rise up against their Nazi occupiers. One broadcast closed with the words, "Poles, the time of liberation is at hand! Poles to arms! There is not a moment to lose!" On August 1, the Polish Home Army, loyal to the Polish Government in exile in London, responded.** For the first few days, it seemed that the Home Army might triumph over

---

*It is estimated that the Germans killed over one million Belorussians during their 3-year occupation. According to a Soviet officer, "The infantry has its own mechanization now: its heart. They see what the Germans have done and they're in a hurry."

**The Soviets did not recognize the London government as the legal government of Poland. Instead, they recognized the so-called Liublin Committee, a pro-Soviet institution, as the *de jure* government of Poland.

their German occupiers, but by August 5, the Germans moved to the offensive. The Poles and the Allies appealed to the Soviets to press their attacks on Warsaw to relieve the German pressure. But the Soviets settled down along the east bank of the Vistula River, refitting and resupplying their divisions. It wasn't until September 11 that Stalin granted longstanding Allied requests to fly supply missions over Warsaw and then land at Soviet bases for refueling. By then it was too late; the insurgents had reached the end of their endurance, and on the evening of October 2, they surrendered. In accordance with the wishes of Hitler and Himmler, the Germans proceeded to virtually raze Warsaw to the ground, while the Soviets did nothing from their positions across the Vistula to stop them.*

It seems clear that Soviet calls for the Poles to rise up against the Germans were part of a concerted effort to weaken both sides, but more particularly the Polish supporters of the London government. A potential opponent of the Soviet-sponsored Liublin Committee was now virtually in shambles. When Soviet troops finally did enter the Polish capital in mid-January, 1945, Warsaw was dead as were the post-war hopes of non-Communist Poles.

The Soviet juggernaut continued to sweep on and by February 1, 1945, Russian troops were preparing to cross the Oder River; Berlin seemed to be virtually in Stalin's pocket. But Stalin ordered a postponement of the planned attack on Berlin; and it wasn't until April 16 that he finally unleashed the Soviet offensive against the city, a delay that was to dearly cost the Soviet armies. Mounting stories of Soviet atrocities struck such fear in the Germans that every German soldier and many German civilians were now ready to defend Berlin, not for Hitler and the Nazis, but for their own lives.

Allied advances in the West were not as rapid as those in the East. The breakout from the Normandy beachhead was not proceeding as quickly as planned, because the Germans were putting up a stiff defense and making good use of the terrain. The majority of German troops were concentrated in the area of Caen and strenuously resisted British efforts to take the city. West of Caen German forces were more thinly spread but the terrain greatly hindered the Allied advance. This was the *bocage*, or hedgerow country. These were small fields enclosed by dense hedges, vines, and trees, which grew up to 15-feet high, out of earthen mounds, themselves several feet thick, and three or four feet high with a drainage ditch on either side. Hedgerows made perfect cover for German defenders, who dug in at their bases, virtually hidden from attackers. It was also difficult tank terrain. On the sunken, narrow roads, tanks were easy marks for German anti-tank guns and rockets. In the fields tanks proved incapable of surmounting the hedgerow mounds without exposing their underbellies to anti-tank guns in the next row of hedges.

American armies did manage to capture the port of Cherbourg at the tip of the Cotentin Peninsular on June 26. Although Hitler was enraged because he had expected General Karl von Schlieben to defend the city until he and everyone else was killed, Allied possession of the port yielded little to them. Schlieben had seen to it that the port was destroyed. Mines were everywhere, sunken ships blocked the harbor, the electrical system and dock machinery were destroyed, and cranes toppled and twisted. It wasn't until September that all the obstructions were removed and the port could begin to operate. In the meantime, most Allied supplies continued to come across the Normandy beaches.

After the fall of Cherbourg, the American forces turned to the south, directly through the worst of the hedgerow country. Their two objectives were Coutances, where three major and two secondary roads converged; and St. Lo, where four major and four secondary roads met. The attack began on July 3 but after twelve days of fighting the Americans had progressed little, too little, in fact, for General Bradley, Commander of the U.S. First Army, who developed a new plan for breaking out of Normandy, Operation *Cobra*. After a preliminary bombing of the area, *Cobra* called for two infantry divisions to assault German positions, and force open a gap large enough for a motorized infantry division to come through. These divisions were to continue all the way to Coutances, followed by the two armored

---

*As a result, Warsaw was the most heavily damaged capital city of Europe during World War II.

divisions. While one division protected the flank, the other would strike for Avranches, some 30 miles away.

Cobra began on July 25, with a massive bombing attack by over 1500 heavy bombers. Since coordination between ground and air was still not perfected, some bombs fell short, causing a number of American casualties: 111 were killed and 490 wounded. But overall, the bombing was effective, killing over 1000 men of the Panzer Lehr Division; so deafening was the attack that some of the survivors could not hear for 24 hours afterwards. Only a dozen German tanks remained.

The Cobra ground attack began on July 26 and on August 1, the Americans, led by the American 3rd Army under General George S. Patton Jr., broke through at Avranches.* Some of Patton's forces were diverted south to liberate Brittany and secure the port of Brest, a campaign that yielded the Allies little.**

The task of retrieving the situation fell to General Gunther von Kluge, who had succeeded both von Rundstedt and Rommel. Hitler had dismissed von Rundstedt on July 1 and on July 17, Rommel was seriously wounded when his staff car was strafed by British fighters. Following Hitler's directives, Kluge launched an attack on Mortain on August 7, the purpose of which was to cut across the Cotentin peninsula to Avranches and cut off Allied forces there. Allied intelligence learned about the attack but allowed the Germans to move in a narrow corridor toward Avranches before launching a major counterattack that drove them back to the town of Falaise. If the British and Canadians, advancing on Falaise from the north and Caen (which they had finally captured on July 19) had moved faster, it is likely that the majority of German troops on the Western front would have been trapped. As it turned out, many Germans managed to escape through the gap between Falaise and Argentan before it was closed on August 20. Still, nearly 60,000 Germans were either killed or captured in the so-called Falaise Pocket. The battle of Normandy was finally over and Allied armies were spreading out over France.***

On August 15, two days before Model assumed command, Allied troops under the command of General Lucian K. Truscott, Jr. landed in Southern France. The purpose of Operation Anvil (later renamed Dragoon) was to drive up the Rhone River Valley and relieve German pressure on Normandy. This pincer movement from the south, it was hoped, would link up with forces in Normandy and liberate France by Fall. Although the ports of Toulon and Marsailles continued to resist for two weeks, most of the landings along the French Riviera went well.† The combination of American, Free French, and Resistance fighters moved quickly northward and on September 11 linked up with Patton's Third Army near the German frontier.

Patton's forces had been driving relentlessly toward Germany since August 1. While his VIII Corps raced westward 200 miles to reach Brest in six days, his XV Corps helped block the escape of more than 60,000 Germans in the Falaise Pocket. His XX Corps and XII Corps swung farther south and then north toward the Seine River, and by August 25, had crossed the Seine River, bypassing Paris. By August 31 they were at Verdun and the Meuse River.

Patton's fuel consumption, however, was enormous, between 500,000 and 600,000 gallons of gasoline every 50 miles. With no major Channel seaport yet fully operational, most supplies were still coming

---

*The breakout was aided by Sgt. Curtis G. Culin, who found the answer to the hedgerow problem. Sgt. Culin utilized the steel girders originally dumped by the Germans on the Normandy beaches as anti-tank obstacles. He had sharpened steel prongs made out of them, two of which were mounted on the front of the tanks to cut through the hedgerows.

**Brest didn't fall until September 19. By the time it was safe and operating, it was too far from the front lines to make much of a logistical contribution.

***Kluge committed suicide and was replaced by Field Marshal Walther Model. Kluge likely knew about the plot to kill Hitler on July 20 and had done nothing to stop it or inform authorities about it. Rommel, still convalescing from his wounds, was forced to kill himself for the same reason.

†Met on the beach by a Frenchman with a bottle of Champagne and glasses, Allied soldiers dubbed the attack "the Champagne Campaign."

across the Normandy beaches. As Patton raced East, the supply lines from these beaches stretched to the breaking point, and by the end of August, the Third Army ground to a halt, out of fuel. Patton complained, but by the time his supplies started again the Germans had gathered their forces and solidified their defenses.*

As Allied troops fanned out into the French countryside, they neared the French capital of Paris. General Eisenhower's initial impulse was to bypass the city, since his main objective was the Rhine River, 250 miles away. If he could get there before the German troops regrouped, he thought, the war might come to a quick end. Eisenhower also knew that liberating Paris could involve prolonged and costly street fighting, which would slow up his advances. And finally, once taken, Paris would be an enormous drain on Allied supplies, "...a civil affairs commitment equal to maintaining eight divisions in operation." The people of Paris were suffering from a variety of shortages and inconveniences, and were in dire need of food, electricity, and even municipal transport.

As Allied troops approached the city, however, Parisians rose in revolt against their German occupiers. Street fighting broke out between the Germans and the Resistance, causing heavy casualties on both sides, on August 19. Charles DeGaulle, who in July, 1944, had been recognized by Allies as the leader of a defacto French government in liberated territories, urged that the 2nd French Division, under General Jacques Leclerc, be sent forward from Argentan to liberated Paris. After some hesitation his request was granted.**

On August 21st the captain of a small tank detachment, Captain Raymond Dronne, arrived at the Hotel de Ville (City Hall) in the heart of Paris. The next day, Leclerc's main force, closely followed by the U.S. Fourth Infantry, entered the city.

The real hero of Paris, paradoxically enough, was the German commander of the city, Major General Dietrich von Choltitz, who refused to leave the city in ruins.*** At 3:00 P.M. on August 25, Choltitz surrendered the German forces in Paris to General Leclerc and to Colonel Roll (alias Tanguy) one of the Resistance leaders and the commander of the Communist military forces in Paris.

Eisenhower's plans for the advance beyond the Seine called for keeping pressure against the Germans along a broad front. To carry out this policy, he assumed the field command of the Allied armies in Northern France, with Generals Bradley and Montgomery as the two Army Group Commanders. On September 3, the British took Brussels, the Belgian capital, and on September 4, they seized the valuable port city of Antwerp.† Optimism swept Allied ranks and there was talk of ending the European War by Christmas, 1944. The British War Office even estimated that at their rate of advance, Allied troops would be in Berlin by September 28.

General Montgomery met with General Eisenhower in Brussels on September 10 and appealed for a single massive thrust into Germany to bring the war to a speedy conclusion. With supplies still being a major problem (most Allied supplies were still coming across the Normandy beaches), Montgomery argued that it would make more sense to funnel them into one major thrust, to be conducted by the British Second Army and elements of the American First Army.†† Those armies would together attack through Holland, cross the Rhine and sweep behind the Siegfried Line into the Ruhr, Germany's

---

*An angry Patton complained that too much fuel was going to the First Army to the North.

**According to Eisenhower, "My hand was forced by the actions of the Free French forces inside the city....For the honor of first entry General Bradley selected General Leclerc's French 2nd Division."

***His actions are the subject of both a book and a movie entitled *Is Paris Burning?* Choltitz' decision was heavily influenced by the arguments of Raul Nordling, the Swedish consul general in Paris.

†Antwerp was no immediate help to the Allies because the 60-mile Schlede Estuary, an outlet to the sea, was guarded by powerful German forces. It was not until November 28 that the first Allied ship sailed into Antwerp.

††Patton's Third Army in the south was to be halted, as was the Canadian First Army.

industrial heartland.* Montgomery further proposed dropping paratroopers along the highway connecting the Dutch cities of Eindoven, Nijmegen, and Arnhem. They were to seize a series of bridges along the road so that Allied land forces moving north could cross the bridges before the Germans could destroy them. The farthest drop was to be at Arnhem, where the British First Airborne Division was to secure the bridge over the Lower Rhine.

This operation, code named *Market Garden*, was launched on September 17 and initially went well. The American Divisions, the 101st Airborne and the 82nd Airborne Divisions accomplished their tasks, seizing their assigned bridges with the exception of the one at Nijmegen. Other aspects of the attack, however, soon ran into difficulty. The British landing at Arnhem, under Major General Robert E. Urquhart, experienced a number of unforeseen problems. Unknown to the British, two S.S. Panzer Divisions, the 9th and 19th, were refitting in the Arnhem area and were quickly committed to the fray. To add to the British woes, a few hours after the landing, the Germans found a copy of the entire Market Garden plan in a wrecked glider; it included the schedule and location of reinforcements and supply drops to take place over the next two days. In addition, British radios didn't work properly, and General Urquhart lost contact with most of his units. The British Second Army, commanded by Lieutenant General Brian G. Horrocks, was to move up the land corridor, hopefully reaching the Arnhem troops by September 11. The narrow, elevated roadway, however, made the British forces exposed targets for German gunners, and Horrock's troops ran into trouble almost immediately. But the real delay came at Nijmegen, just 11 miles from the Arnhem objective; here the Tenth Panzer Division held the highway bridge over the Waal, and only a heroic amphibious operation across the River by the American 82nd Airborne Division, finally secured the bridge.**

But the advance took too long. The beleaguered British paratroopers at Arnhem couldn't hold out long enough for the ground forces to reach them. Allied efforts to reinforce and supply the Arnhem troops were hampered by bad weather and by German knowledge of the Allied drop zones. Bundles of ammunition and food fell into German hands. Finally, on September 25, with Horrock's forces nearly exhausted, Field Marshal Montgomery ordered him to withdraw.*** On the night of the 25th, the exhausted survivors of the Arnhem landing tried to make their way across the Rhine to the Allied lines. Of the 10,000 British troops who landed in the Arnhem area on the north bank of the Lower Rhine, 2200 made it back across the river. As one author has noted, "The British 1st Airborne Division had ceased to exist." All in all, some 17,000 Allied troops were either killed, wounded or captured in Operation Market Garden, and with its failure, Allied hopes of a quick end to the war evaporated. Allied troops would not be home by Christmas.

---

*The Siegfried Line was a series of anti-tank barriers (concrete dragons' teeth) and concealed pillboxes, which ran some 400 miles from the Swiss border to Holland. It was incomplete along the Dutch border.

**General Horrock later termed this operation, "...the most gallant attack ever carried out in the war."

***Allied planners had estimated that the troops at Arnhem could hold out only four days without relief from the ground forces.

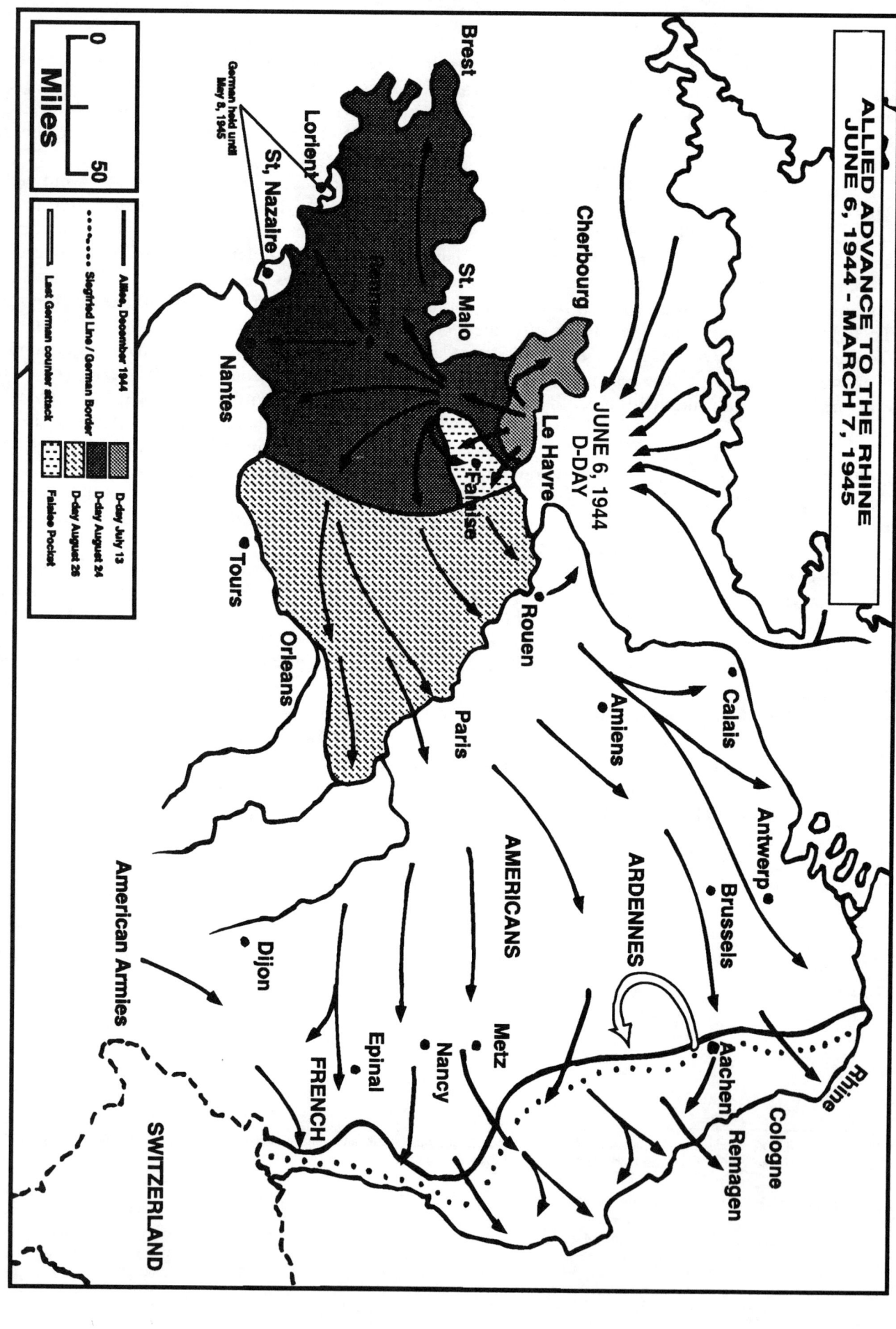

Chapter XI

Disintegration

❖   ❖   ❖

The failure of Operation Market Garden left Allied armies in Europe stretched out along a 450 mile front from the North Sea to the Swiss border, with supply lines that extended 350 miles back to the Normandy beaches. German suicide squads still held on to many of the Channel ports. Even those captured by the Allies had been so destroyed by German demolition squads that they were unusable. The superb Belgian port of Antwerp fell to the British on September 4, but German forces on both banks of the Scheldt estuary, which led to the port, blocked any Allied shipping from using the facility. The resultant Allied supply problems, together with the length of the Allied defensive line, which couldn't be strong everywhere, emboldened Hitler to contemplate a major strike at the Allied forces arraigned against Germany in the West.

Hitler's plan was to transfer German troops and equipment from the eastern front to the west, and to strike at a weak point in the Allied line. One such spot was in the Ardennes forest, where the Germans had struck France in 1940, and which was only 125 miles from Antwerp. Deployed along this 85 mile sector were only a lightly armed cavalry group, an armored division, and four infantry divisions, two of which were relatively untested in battle. A decisive blow here, reasoned Hitler, could break through the Allied lines, cross the Meuse River, and capture Antwerp. This bold thrust would deprive the Allies of the only major port they had captured intact, split the American and British armies, and isolate the British in the north, forcing them to contemplate an evacuation similar to that at Dunkirk in 1940. Deprived of their British ally, the Americans might very well consider a negotiated settlement in the west, which would allow the Germans to then concentrate all their forces and energy against the Russians on the eastern front.

The commander-in-chief on the western front—the recently recalled Kurt von Rundstedt—and other German commanders objected that the plan was too ambitious. But the only alteration to which Hitler would agree was to postpone the attack from late November until December 16, 1944.

Taking advantage of fog and mist, which curtailed Allied air reconnaissance, and operating under almost complete military secrecy, the Germans assembled 16 divisions north of the Ardennes, and 10 to the south. Another five were held in reserve. Even the Luftwaffe, which by this time had been pretty well written off by Allied intelligence, was ready to assist the Ardennes counter offensive. Hitler also personally organized an S.S. brigade under the command of Lieutenant Otto Skorzeny, who had rescued Mussolini from captivity in 1943. His men, who spoke English, were to be dressed in captured American uniforms and equipped with captured American tanks, jeeps, arms, and identification. Their task was to seize bridges, commit sabotage and generally to create chaos in the American rear areas. In addition, a 1000 man parachute force was to land behind American lines, open roads for German tanks, and block any enemy attempts to reinforce frontline areas.

At 5:30 A.M. on December 16, American units along the Ardennes front were awakened from their sleep by a thunderous German artillery bombardment. The Allied reaction was amazement and surprise. They had become so used to thinking the Wehrmacht was on the point of collapse that they did

---

*It wasn't until November 28 that the first Allied ship was able to dock at Antwerp.

not believe it capable of making an attack. When the shelling stopped, German tank and infantry units advanced toward the American positions. Thus began perhaps the worst day for American forces in the whole European war. It was also the day that General Eisenhower received word that he had been promoted to five star general (his 6th promotion in three and one/half years). As the Germans pounded into the Ardennes, Eisenhower was attending the wedding of his orderly. On that same day, General Montgomery requested leave in England for the upcoming Christmas holidays, and Allied headquarters reported that bandleader Glenn Miller's plane was missing.

Early reports about the German attack were confusing and General Bradley, who met with Eisenhower the evening of the 16th, underrated the gravity of the situation, thinking the offensive to be only a spoiling attack. Yet Eisenhower acted quickly, placing all Allied troops north of the German attack, including two American armies, under General Montgomery's command. He also ordered the Tenth Armored Division of Patton's Third Army north to the Ardennes, a move that Patton protested. The official Allied strategy mapped out on December 19 was to plug the holes in the line to the north and counterattack in the south. This meant building up and extending strong points along the flanks of the enemy salient (the bulge that this salient resembled gave the battle its name). The bulge would then be cut off by an American and British counterattack, which would initially be launched by General Patton's Third Army, whose headquarters lay in Nancy, 50 miles to the southeast. Patton's troops were to move northward and relieve the town of Bastogne, a vital and dangerously threatened road and rail juncture.

Even as Patton turned his forces to the north toward Bastogne, the battle appeared to be going badly for the Americans. Communications had broken down and confusion reigned. Skorzeny's forces, although failing in many of their objectives, did succeed in spreading much of the confusion and alarm. German saboteurs were reported in nearly every town east of the Meuse River. German tanks were said to be far behind Allied lines, and German paratroopers were reported in a number of places (they had landed in only one). As late as the evening of December 18, Allied commanders still did not know exactly where the front was located. The U.S. forces in front of Bastogne were all but destroyed, leaving the 101st Airborne to fight alone surrounded in Bastogne. On December 22, the Germans sent emissaries to the acting commander of the 101st Airborne Division, General Anthony McAuliffe, demanding surrender. McAuliffe's cryptic one-word response of "nuts" was to enter the folklore of American military history. Nevertheless, the situation continued bleak for the Americans as the fog and low snow clouds, which had neutralized their air superiority since the beginning of the battle, showed no signs of lifting.

By Christmas morning the Second Panzer Division was within three miles of the Meuse River, some 60 miles from its starting point. But this was the farthest westward German penetration of the battle, as their forces literally ran out of gas.* The clearing skies also permitted allied air power to come into use. Supplies were air-dropped at Bastogne and Allied fighter bombers were turned loose against German panzer units. The day after Christmas, Patton's 4th Armored Division broke through the German lines and relieved Bastogne; on that same day Hitler's advisors told him that Antwerp could not be reached under any circumstances.

From that point on, despite sporadic bombing raids by the Luftwaffe, the Germans were forced onto the defensive and began to suffer increasing casualties. The fighting continued through January, and the last vestige of the "bulge" did not disappear until January 28. In the end some 100,000 Germans were killed, wounded, or captured; the Allies suffered nearly 81,000 casualties, 77,000 of them Americans, the heaviest battle toll in U.S. history.** As testimony to the German brutality in the attack, about 300 American prisoners-of-war and 100 Belgian civilians were massacred by German S.S. units. The most infamous of these was in Malmedy, Belgium.

---

*German soldiers carried rubber hoses for the purpose of siphoning gasoline from disabled vehicles.

**American losses were about equal to those suffered on both sides at the Battle of Gettysburg during the Civil War.

In all probability the German Ardennes offensive shortened the war by at least a year. If German reserve units, which had been thrown into the offensive, had instead been put into defensive positions across the Rhine, later Allied advances would have been much more difficult. But now Germany had nothing to fall back upon to defend the homeland. Her best equipment had been lost and her last reserves squandered. In retrospect, it is surprising that Germany was able to hold out through February, March, and April.

The Russians were the ones who reaped the immediate benefit of Hitler's final gamble in the West. At the beginning of January, 1945, the Western Allies were directly engaging about 100 German divisions. In Poland and East Prussia, defending a 600 mile line, Germany had only 75 divisions, whose task it was to prevent the Red Army from advancing from Warsaw to Berlin. In addition, more than two-thirds of the Luftwaffe's aircraft were in the West. Taking advantage of the situation, the Soviets began their own winter offensive on January 12—the first stroke in the greatest Soviet offensive of the war, one which would carry them all the way to Berlin.

Some Germans hoped that an array of secret weapons might still salvage victory from defeat. But they all came too late. Hitler's strong emphasis on "Lightning War" (Blitzkrieg) caused him to forbid research on any weapon that could not be produced within 6 months. Although later abandoned, this edict seriously delayed the development of the Me 262 jet fighter (120 miles per hour faster than the best Allied planes), and the Me 163 rocket propelled fighter. He also tried to convert the Me 262 into a bomber to gain revenge on England for Allied bombing attacks on Germany. The famous V-weapons (the "V" standing for "Vergeltungswaffe"—an instrument of reprisal) also were delayed. These included the V-1, a jet-propelled pilotless aircraft, which despite much earlier testing, did not become operational until June, 1944; and the V-2, a rocket that could reach a speed of 3600 miles per hour and was used for the first time in September, 1944. The V-3, a long range gun designed to fire one shell on London every 12 seconds never became operational.

The V-1s and V-2s, aimed primarily at England (V-1s were also launched on Liege and Antwerp during the Battle of the Bulge), caused casualties as high as those inflicted by the Luftwaffe in September, 1940. The "V" weapons ultimately failed, but they were the forerunners of much that has been developed since the war. If their appearance had not been delayed, their impact on the war might have been far more dramatic, if not decisive. Indeed, at the end of the war, Germany was working on a multistage rocket that could have reached New York.

The one weapon that German scientists worked on but failed to produce during the war was the nuclear bomb. Allied scientists who moved into Strasbourg, the center of the German nuclear research effort, found somewhat to their surprise that Germany was not very far along in their research on this ultimate weapon.

Other expedients to which Hitler resorted were the *Volksturm*, a Home Guard under Heinrich's Himmler's command consisting of all available men between the ages of 16 and 60; and the *Werewolves*, armed bands that were to operate as marauding partisans after Germany's defeat. Although rather widely utilized, the *Volksturm* could not turn the tide of battle, while the *Werewolves* basically never functioned at all.

The first front to go for Germany was the one in Italy. Secret negotiations between the head of American Intelligence in Switzerland, Allen Dulles, and S.S. General Karl Wolff, led to the surrender of all German forces in Italy on May 1, 1945. On the main front, German forces were also collapsing. The Russians crossed the Vistula River in mid-January and reached the Oder and Niesse Rivers at the beginning of February. In the south, they captured Budapest on February 13, following a 50 day siege. Vienna fell on April 13, and the Russians made their plans for the final assault on Germany.

In the West the 9th U.S. Armored Division found the Ludendorff railway bridge, which crossed the Rhine at the town of Remagen, still intact, and became the first Allied force to cross that barrier to the heartland of Germany. A broken wire prevented the explosives on the bridge from being detonated from the other bank. The Germans then utilized artillery fire, air attacks, human torpedoes, and even V-2s in vain attempts to destroy the bridge. When it did finally collapse, it was too late for the Germans; by that time three American divisions were across the river and fanning out into Germany. But more and more, Eisenhower's attention was directed to the southern German Alps.

In the great map room near Eisenhower's office in Reims, there was an intelligence chart designated, "Reported National Redoubt." Depicted on it was an area of mountainous territory south of Munich straddling the Alpine regions of Bavaria, western Austria, and northern Italy. About 2000 square miles in area, its heart was Hitler's mountain headquarters at Berchtesgaden.

According to Allied intelligence, here in this craggy citadel the Nazis, with Hitler at their head, intended to make their last-ditch stand. The rugged stronghold was considered nearly impregnable, and the fear was that it might hold out for as long as two years. Through the early months of 1945, the specter of the Redoubt continued to grow. One assessment foresaw the possible creation in the redoubt area of "an elite force," predominantly S.S. and mountain troops, of between 200,000 and 300,000 men. General Bradley held the theory that the Germans would fall back into the Redoubt, where with 20 S.S. Divisions, supplied through a system of underground factories and supported by aircraft operating from underground hangers, they could hold out for at least a year.

To meet this expected final German stand, Eisenhower decided to divert American and British troops away from Berlin towards the south. If Hitler and the leading Nazis were going to make their stand in the Bavarian Alps, reasoned Eisenhower, then Berlin no longer had political and economic importance. And if it had no significance for the future of Germany, then there was no reason not to allow the Russians to take the city. On April 12, Eisenhower told General Patton that it was inadvisable for an American army to capture Berlin, that the city retained no tactical or strategic value and that taking it would require the Americans to care for thousands of Germans and displaced persons. Accordingly, he ordered Bradley's northern divisions to stop short of Berlin and Patton's forces to the south were likewise to halt. Patton protested as did many others. General Simpson wrote nearly 20 years later: "I really believe that the Ninth Army could have captured Berlin with little loss well before the Russians reached the city."* But instead, Eisenhower moved his armies to face the threat posed by the Redoubt, a threat which as it turned out was a myth. Yet, the American high command held to its belief in the existence of the Redoubt practically to the end, despite all the evidence to the contrary. General Bradley was to write after the war that: "Not until after the campaign ended were we to learn that this Redoubt existed largely in the imagination of a few fanatic Nazis. It grew into so exaggerated a scheme that I am astonished that we could have believed it as innocently as we did. But while it persisted, this legend of the Redoubt was too ominous a threat to ignore and in consequence it shaped our tactical thinking during the closing weeks of the war."

The Russian assault on Berlin was launched on April 16 with 2.5 million men, 6250 tanks, and 7500 aircraft. For their part, the Germans had been tardy in preparing to defend their capital city. It wasn't until March, 1945—with the Russians only 50 miles to the east—that the Germans began to develop a comprehensive defense plan for their capital. Hitler's designation of Berlin as a "fortress city"—*i.e.* a place to be defended until no one remained alive—did little to help. The hastily developed plan that did finally emerge, called "the Citadel" for a series of fallback positions, encompassed most of the main government buildings. Located here too was the Fuhrerbunker, Hitler's underground headquarters, where he spent the final months of the war. The entire structure was buried six feet underground, had a roof of concrete 16 feet thick and walls six and a half feet thick. It contained 19 rooms and besides Hitler, it housed a few guards, aides, personal servants and physicians. After mid-April, the residents of the bunker also included Eva Braun, Hitler's mistress, and Nazi propaganda chief Joseph Goebbels and his family.

---

*On March 28 Eisenhower sent an announcement for hand delivery to Stalin. In the message Eisenhower announced he was abandoning Berlin as an objective.

In specially designated areas of the city, people were to be deployed at fortified strong points. Overturned trucks, streetcars, and railway cars weighted with bomb debris were to link concrete walls, trenches, and natural barriers such as rivers lakes, and canals. These fortified positions were to slow down if not to halt the Russian attack. Unfortunately, Germany now lacked the manpower and the artillery to hold these defensive positions. There were about 75,000 German troops defending Berlin, but they were short of everything—tanks, guns, ammunition, fuel, and food.

Inspired by a desire to hold off the Red Army until they could surrender to the Americans, and threatened by roving S.S. squads, Berlin's defenders contested every foot of the city. Russian troops had to advance block-by-block, and clear buildings room-by-room. As a result the city was demolished. The human price, of course, was enormous. Berlin's civilians, mostly women and children, were caught in the crossfire and thousands of them died. The Russians suffered heavily as well. "Every step cost us lives," wrote Soviet General Vasilii Chuikov.

From time to time, Hitler seemed to have hoped that the Western Allies and the Soviets would split with each other and the West would rally to the defense of Berlin. Some of Hitler's staff compared President Roosevelt's death on April 12 to that of the Russian Empress Elizabeth in 1762. Her death had led to a pro-Prussian successor, Peter III, who recalled Russian troops from Prussia and saved Frederick the Great from defeat. Perhaps the death of the American president would produce a similar event, or at least a separate peace with the Western Allies. By April 28, even that hope had died for Hitler, and he prepared to end his own life.

First, however, he fulfilled the long-held desire of his mistress, Eva Braun, and had a wedding ceremony improvised on the night of April 28. Following a wedding reception attended by the other inhabitants of the Bunker, Hitler retired to dictate his last will and political testament. The will left most of his possessions to the German state, although his personal art work was to go to a gallery in Linz, Austria.

In his political testament, Hitler appointed Grand Admiral Karl Doenitz as President of a new German government. Hermann Goering, originally designated as Hitler's successor, was now under house arrest in his Bavarian castle. Martin Borman, head of the Nazi Party Chancery, had persuaded Hitler that Goering was trying to oust him from the post of fuhrer. Hence the choice of Doenitz as the new leader of the German state. The rest of the political testament contained nothing new, much to the surprise of Hitler's private secretary, Gertred Junge, to whom he dictated. It simply rehashed Hitler's old attacks on the Jews and the German generals, who Hitler collectively blamed for Germany losing the war.

On the afternoon of April 30, Hitler and Eva retired to the Fuhrer's rooms in the Bunker. Some minutes later when Hitler's valet pushed open the door, he was confronted by the sight of Eva curled up on the sofa, dead of cyanide, and Hitler slumped at the other end of the sofa. To make sure that he succeeded in the suicide attempt, Hitler had put a bullet into his brain just as he bit into a cyanide capsule. That night the surviving inhabitants of the Bunker escaped, with the exception of the Goebbels. The Nazi propaganda chief, in one last act of treachery, administered poison to his six children, then poisoned his wife and himself. On May 2, the Berlin garrison capitulated.

Doenitz, whose headquarters were in Plon in northern Germany, realized that there was no hope left for Germany. His major objective, as he saw it, was to enable as many Germans as possible (civilians and military alike) to escape from the Russian forces and to surrender either to the Americans or British. When Eisenhower threatened to drive the fleeing Germans eastward back into the arms of the Red Army, Doenitz gave in. At 2:41 A.M. on May 7, 1944, at Eisenhower's headquarters in Rheims, General Alfred Jodl signed the five-paragraph surrender document calling for the unconditional and simultaneous surrender of all German forces on all fronts at 11:01 P.M. on May 8.* Russian pressure

---

*Eisenhower was represented at the signing by his Chief of Staff, Lt. General Walter Bedel Smith. Eisenhower, who had recently visited a Nazi concentration camp, refused to meet with German representatives until they had signed a surrender document.

on the Allies caused the ceremony to be repeated and the unconditional surrender ratified on May 8 in Russian occupied Berlin. Field Marshal Whilhelm Keitel signed this final act of surrender by Germany and World War II in Europe was officially over.*

It took several days for isolated German garrisons to formally surrender, including those in such French ports as Dunkirk, Rocheport, La Rochelle, Lorient, St. Nazaire, and in the Channel Islands. The German garrison at Heligoland did not capitulate until May 11.

The Third Reich itself lived on until May 23 under the leadership of Admiral Doenitz and his aides, including General Jodl and Admiral Hans-Georg von Friedeburg, Doenitz' successor as Commander-in-Chief of German Armed Forces. Early on May 23, however, Doenitz, Jodl, and Friedeburg were summoned to SHAEF headquarters and were told they were now prisoners of war. Friedeburg went back to his quarters and committed suicide. Hitler's Third Reich, extended by Doenitz for three weeks beyond the Fuhrer's death, was now extinguished.

---

*Since the Soviets did not issue the surrender statement until the next day in Moscow, Russia celebrates May 9 as V.E. Day (Victory in Europe Day). The West celebrates the victory on May 8.

U.S. ARMY

Chapter XII
The War in Europe: Conclusion

❖   ❖   ❖

The Allied victory over Germany was a result of many factors. Perhaps the most fundamental of them was the Allied (particularly American) technical superiority, that offset the superior military qualities of the German soldier. Statistical evaluations of the performance of the German army during World War II show that German soldiers consistently out-fought the numerous Allied armies which ultimately defeated them. One historian has calculated that German combat effectiveness superiority over the Western Allies (British and American) was between 20 and 30 percent. On a man-to-man basis, the German ground soldiers consistently inflicted casualties at about a 50 percent higher rate than they incurred from the opposing British and American troops under all circumstances. On the Eastern front, in the early days of the conflict, German combat effectiveness superiority over the Russians was nearly 200 percent—*i.e.* one German division was at least a match for three Russian divisions, and as late as 1944 this superiority was still nearly 100 percent.

Offsetting this superior German combat effectiveness was Allied superiority in technology. An anecdote from retired U.S. Army Colonel David Hackworth speaks both to the German combat effectiveness and to Allied technical superiority.

I remember a German lieutenant captured at Salerno who I was guarding in 1946 in a prisoner-of-war camp. He was a real tough-looking Kraut and I was a young punk, a pimply-faced kid. He could speak perfect English, and I was riding him. I said, 'Well, if you're so tough, if you're all supermen, how come you're here captured and I'm guarding you.' And he looked at me and said, 'Well, it's like this. I was on this hill as a battery commander with six 88-millimeter anti-tank guns, and the Americans kept sending tanks down this road. We kept knocking them out. Every time they sent a tank we knocked it out. 'Finally, we ran out of ammunition and the Americans didn't run out of tanks.' And that's it in a nutshell.

The best answer to the question of why, with their combat superiority, the Germans did not drive the British and Americans back into the sea at Salerno, Anzio, or Normandy, is that the Allies simply had overwhelming military power that the Germans had no possibility of matching. A further illustration of this point is that at the Battle of El Alamein, General Montgomery had 230,000 men and 1100 tanks (many from the U.S.) facing Rommel's 80,000 men and 260 tanks. Yet when the battle was over, the British losses were triple those of the Germans.

From 1940 to 1945 the United States alone produced 296,429 warplanes, 102,351 tanks (including self-propelled guns), 372,431 artillery pieces, 2,455,964 trucks, 87,620 warships, 5,452 cargo ships, and 20,086,061 small arms. No wonder Stalin could propose a toast at the Teheran Conference in November, 1943, "To American production, without which the war would have been lost."

A second major factor contributing to Germany's defeat were the blunders of Hitler. Hitler is often said to have had the mind of a quartermaster—*i.e.*, he knew the names, types, etc. of weapons—but was particularly weak in global strategic thinking. His concept of world mastery was to conquer the land around him (the Eurasian heartland), but he lacked the vision to see the importance of seapower in accomplishing this goal.* It is ironic that the massive numbers of weapons that enabled the Allies to decisively defeat Nazi Germany came from across the Atlantic Ocean.

Hitler's constant interference with his generals, interference that often led to tactical blunders, further hampered German military efforts. His refusal to allow German troops to pull back and set up defensive positions for the winter outside of Moscow in 1941 or to fight their way out of the encirclement at Stalingrad in 1942 were serious errors. General von Manstein states in his memoirs that his troops could have captured Kursk in July, 1943, but that Hitler ordered a halt to his offensive so that reserves could be sent to the west. The substantial German losses in the Falaise-Argentan Pocket in 1944 (10,000 dead, 30,000 wounded, and 50,000 captured) would never have occurred if Hitler had not ordered his generals not only to stand and fight in untenable positions, but actually to move into the trap prepared by the Allies.

Some historians argue that Hitler's biggest blunder of all was his decision to invade the Soviet Union in 1941. They suggest that Hitler would have been better advised to have pushed the North African campaign to its logical conclusion, with Egypt, the Suez Canal, and the oil resources of the Middle East as the prime objectives. As it was, some 80 percent of the casualties incurred in land fighting by the Germans were inflicted by the Russians. It was the Red Army, according to Churchill, which "tore the Wehrmacht's guts." The most important front in World War II was the eastern one and here the Wehrmacht could not match the resilience and tenacity of the Soviet forces. Perhaps it is too much to say that the Soviet Union won World War II in Europe, but its contribution to victory was decisive.

Another significant factor in the Allied victory was superior intelligence operations. Most noteworthy here was the Allied prewar acquisition, thanks to Polish intelligence, of the German cipher (code) machine, a box about one cubic foot in size and appropriately named the Enigma. It had a typewriter keyboard from which a message was transmitted into a series of electrically wired rotors or wheels. Around the inside surface of each rotor were 26 electrical contacts, one for each letter of the alphabet. Each rotor multiplied by 26 the number of possible cipher alphabets the machine could produce. Three rotors—the original design—would yield 26 by 26 by 26 or 17,576 cipher alphabets. Other models used four rotors or 456,976 alphabets, and later even 5 rotors (308,915,976 alphabets) and 6 (8,031,815,374). Deciphering an Enigma message required an identical machine with identically wired rotors. The receiver had to know which rotors to insert, in what order to insert them, and at what position to set each one. This required a list of key settings shared by the sender and receiver, otherwise the receiving Enigma, operating in reverse, could not produce the letters of a plain-text message. Thus, a copy of the Enigma machine would do the Allies no good unless they could devise a means of determining the proper key settings. Long and diligent work by Allied cryptographers succeeded in unraveling the secrets of the Enigma system, and following the fall of Poland, Allied cryptographer working at Bletchley Park in rural Buckinghamshire, England, perfected a method for determining the proper rotor settings.

Believing that their cipher system was unbreakable, the Germans made wide use of it for the remainder of the war, and Allied intelligence was privy to the deepest of German military secrets.** Good intelligence, of course, does not guarantee military victories, *i.e.* knowing what the enemy is going to do does not necessarily mean you can stop them from doing it. But most Allied commanders who received information from the Enigma intercepts used it wisely, and it is clear today that the Allied ability to read most of the enemy radio messages was crucial to the outcome of the war.

Another factor, which has been long trumpeted as a contributing factor to Allied victory over Germany, is strategic bombing. Beginning in 1941 the British brought into action a strategic bombing force for use against continental targets. The effectiveness of this force was not great. For lack of long-range

---

*According to Albert Speer, the Minister of Armaments and Munitions, Hitler also lacked any deep grasp of aerial warfare—as perhaps illustrated in the Battle of Britain.

**The Enigma machine was not utilized during the Battle of the Bulge. Since German troops were backed up to their own borders, the military utilized land lines to send messages to the front.

escort fighters, the bombers operated at night and navigational problems resulted in over one-half of the crews not even being able to locate the cities, let alone the specific targets within the cities, which they were supposed to bomb. Even by the end of 1941, according to one estimate, only one-fifth of the bombers were dropping their bombs within a radius of three and a half miles of the spot at which they were aiming.

By 1943, the British had improved their performance through the use of electronic devices to deceive German radar and by marking targets with flares dropped by Pathfinder planes. But more ominous than the British technological improvements was a shift from aiming at specific military related targets to so-called area bombing. In other words, the British dropped the bombs over a wide area and hoped they hit something of military consequence. The effect, of course, was to cause great ruin and devastation and above all to terrorize the civilian population. Thousands of civilians were killed and millions made homeless by such a strategy.

Beginning in 1943, American bombers joined the British in the Air offensive against Germany. The Americans flew by day, endeavoring to pinpoint, and hit, specific targets, while the British continued to attack at night with their terror offensive of area bombing. One thousand bomber raids were not uncommon as Allied air attacks pushed deeper and deeper into Germany.

Allied losses were heavy. The British Bomber Command suffered, proportionally, the highest losses of any branch of service in England. In a two-month period in 1943, the American Eighth Air Force based in England lost 4700 aircraft; the average life of a bomber aircraft was estimated to be 160 days. The introduction in 1944 of long-range fighter planes that could escort the bombers and guard against German fighter attacks finally helped turn the tide and American bomber losses declined by nearly two/thirds between Fall, 1943, and Spring, 1944.

The peak (or depth) of the air war came with the bombing of Dresden in February, 1945. Over a period of fourteen hours, American and British planes repeatedly attacked the city—a cultural center in eastern Germany. The result was to create a literal firestorm, which burned for a week and gutted the city. Initial estimates placed the death toll at 135,000 (more than caused by the Atomic bomb at Hiroshima) but later studies reduced the figure to 35,000, fewer than an earlier fire-bombing raid on the city of Hamburg, which had killed 42,000. Yet the devastation of Dresden became one of the most controversial events of World War II. At best, Dresden, sometimes called the Florence of the North because of its role in the Northern Renaissance, was a marginal military target. The Allies apparently hoped that the raid would sow confusion among Germans fleeing the approaching Red Army and hamper the movement of German troops to the Eastern front. Subsequent judgment seems to be that Allied objectives and strategic goals did not warrant the massive destruction inflicted upon the historic city.

Between 1942 and 1945, the British dropped over one million tons of bombs on Germany and the U.S. Army Airforce another 600,000 tons. Nearly 160,000 Allied airmen—79,265 American and 79,281 British—were killed. The effectiveness of the bombing, as well as the morality of killing an estimated 305,000 German civilians, has been endlessly debated since the end of World War II. The impact of the bombing on the German economy was certainly not what the Allies had hoped for. In fact, the more bombs dropped on Germany, the more German industrial production increased. German armament production (heavy artillery, tanks, and aircraft) increased from 24,250 units in 1941 to 106,258 units in 1945. German fighter plane output increased from 3146 in 1940 to 28,925 in 1944. Bomb tonnage dropped on Greater Germany increased in the same period from 13,000 tons in 1940 to 915,000 tons in 1944. Obviously, strategic bombing did not cripple the German economy and did not win the war in Europe.

It did, however, contribute to the Allied victory. The German transportation infrastructure—particularly the railroads—was badly hit, as was the fuel industry. Tanks and aircraft might be produced but it was difficult to deliver them to the front by rail and impossible to use them without fuel.

Bombing also diverted workers from production to repair work, which perhaps kept industrial output from rising any faster than it did. Also, almost two million men were occupied in anti-aircraft positions, defending against air attacks, men who could have been used at the front. Bombing also had a demoralizing effect not just on those civilians who suffered it but on the troops at the front, who often worried more about their loved ones at home experiencing the Allied raids, than they did about themselves.

Strategic bombing may not have been enough to win the war as Arthur Harris ("Bomber Harris"), Head of the British Bomber Command, had hoped. But when combined with larger-scale ground operations, it made an important and singular contribution. Allied ground forces, which overran the Reich, were there in large part because of the destruction wrought by the Allied bomber offensive.

It is difficult today, nearly a half-century after the event, to imagine the horror generated by the Nazis in Europe, a horror which threatened the very fabric of civilized society.* Perhaps the best way to convey this horror is to recall the things that the Nazis did to individual human beings as they pursued Hitler's plan for a New Order in Europe.

The creation of this New Order or Greater Germanic Estate (*Grossraum*), involved territorial expansion, economic exploitation, and mass terror. The impact which this trinity had on the population is nearly indescribable. Large chunks of Europe and their populations were annexed to the Third Reich. German rule in the northern and western countries, although certainly not benign, was mainly directed toward an effective conduct of the war. In Eastern Europe, however, the Nazis were cruel in the extreme. The *Ostarbeiter* (Eastern Workers) program uprooted millions of workers to labor in German factories and on German farms. Conditions for these foreigners, mostly from the Soviet Union, were subhuman and literally millions of them died. But the worst fate of all befell those groups considered racially inferior by the Nazis, namely the Jews, who were exterminated, even if capable of working.

On January 20, 1942, at a conference in the Berlin suburb of Wannsee, the leaders of the Third Reich agreed to plans for the "Final Solution" of the Jewish question. Although Jews had suffered under the Nazis almost from the time Hitler came to power, and many had been confined to Concentration camps, the new policy called for the destruction of all European Jews. Under Heinrich Himmler's S.S., six extermination camps ultimately came into existence, all in Poland, for the expressed purpose of carrying out this most hideous of Nazi policies. At Auschwitz, near Krakow; at Chelmno, near Lodz; at Belzec, near Lublin; at Sobibor, at Majdanek; and at Treblinka, over 5 million Jews were murdered, often with the latest killing gas, such as Zyklon B, furnished by German industry.** So obsessed was Hitler with the so-called "Jewish question" that almost until the end of the war, trains of cattle cars from all over Europe carried Jews to the extermination camps. Trains which might have been more efficiently used to carry supplies and manpower to the front, were used instead to realize Himmler's desire that, "not only Jewish men but every Jewish woman and child must be destroyed." Among the millions killed were thousands of highly qualified specialists who might have contributed to Germany's war effort, though most of Germany's Jewish nuclear physicists, including Albert Einstein, managed to leave Germany for the West, before the "Final Solution." It seems likely, then, that for Hitler, destruction of the Jews took priority even over winning the war.

Many in the West have commented on the seeming passivity of the Jews who, according to some historians, went like "lambs to the slaughter." In fact, that is not completely true. Although many did meekly submit, many others resisted. There were uprisings at Auschwitz, at Treblinka, and a massive escape attempt from Sobibor. Jews who had been herded into the Warsaw Ghetto—a sealed-off district about 2.5 miles long by 1 mile wide— rose up in April, 1943, and fought the Nazis for forty-two days.

Although the primary target, Jews were not the only ones to fall victim to Hitler's genocidal policies. Gypsies and Slavs also perished, perhaps as many as nine million. Unlike other wartime atrocities, these killings were not spontaneous reactions carried out in the heat of battle. They were planned,

---

*This task is made even more difficult by modern day efforts to both popularize and trivialize Hitler and the Nazi era.

**Auschwitz managed to kill 12,000 Jews per day.

researched, and carried out as government policy. And such policy, argued the Allies, should not go unpunished.

Long before the war came to an end, in November, 1943, the United States, Great Britain, and the Soviet Union, declared that German war criminals should be brought to justice and in August, 1945, an International Military Tribunal was formally constituted in London on behalf of the above three powers as well as the Provisional Government of France. On November 20, 1945, the Tribunal opened its proceedings in the Bavarian city of Nuremburg. Although the site of impressive Nazi Party rallies, including the 1934 meeting enshrined in Leni Riefenstahl's film *Triumph of the Will*, the city was selected primarily because its Hall of Justice was one of the few in Germany to survive heavy Allied bombing raids.

The indictment received by the Tribunal named 24 Nazi war criminals, of whom 23 were then in custody. Martin Bormann, whose name was on the indictment, could not be found and he was tried in absentia. Two others, although named in the document, never stood trial. Robert Ley, an emotionally unstable labor leader committed suicide before the proceedings began, while Gustav Krupp von Bohlen was too ill to stand trial.

These former accomplices of Hitler were charged with three major crimes: (1) violations of the laws or customs of war—*i.e.*, acts that were illegal by custom or had been declared illegal by international convention. Included in this category were such things as the execution of prisoners of war and the use of certain proscribed weapons; (2) Crimes against humanity—i.e crimes clearly contrary to law in civilized states. This category included use of forced labor and killing of individuals because they belonged to certain categories; (3) Crimes against peace—this charge stated that starting and waging an aggressive war was contrary to international law and hence was illegal.

The Nazi defense centered on attacking the legality of the trial, pointing out that the victors were acting as both judges and jury, and that it was impossible for a defeated enemy to gain a fair trial, because it was the victors who determined what was and what was not a war crime. The other defense tactic was to lay the blame for the crimes on Hitler, who was dead, and Bormann, who could not be found. The Tribunal rejected these pleas and after sitting for nearly one year, returned its verdict on October 1, 1946.

Three of the defendants were acquitted; twelve (including Bormann) were sentenced to death; three were given life imprisonment; and four received prison terms ranging from ten to twenty years. Goering, who lost 70 pounds during the trial, escaped his execution by committing suicide. The other executions were carried out on October 16, 1946.

Although there may have been legal shortcomings to the Nuremburg trial—Senator Robert Taft was one critic of the proceedings—it did manage to show to the whole world the horrors and sufferings inflicted upon innocent men, women and children by the Nazi regime. It would indeed be difficult to convince one who survived a Nazi Concentration or Extermination camp, or a young soldier who liberated the concentration camps at Dachau or Buchenwald, that the verdicts reached by the Tribunal were not fair and justified. Although the global impact of World War II will be explored later in this work, a word is in order here about its impact on Europe. First, it was the most cruel and devastating war in the history of Europe—whether measured in lives lost, the geographical extent of the fighting, or the cities reduced to ashes. Twenty million Russians were killed, six million Poles, three million German fighting men and immense numbers of German civilians, nearly three hundred thousand Englishmen and over two hundred thousand Frenchmen.

Whole towns and villages were destroyed. Lidice in Czechoslovakia and Oradour su Glane in France were systematically raised by the Germans, while other cities struck by Allied bombers became virtual ghost towns. Suffering the same fate were many of Europe's architectural monuments, her historic archives and irreplaceable records. Matching these material losses was a psychological devastation brought on by the Nazi terror, by saturation bombing and by the holocaust of the death camps. Many wondered whether Europe had a future at all. Writing in 1947, Winston Churchill asked "What is Europe now? A rubble heap, a charnal house, a breeding ground of pestilence and hate."

The result of all this was to further the undermining of Europe's global hegemony that had been started by World War I. Europe was simply too tired, and too devastated to hold on to its far-flung empires. Within two decades after the war, European empires around the world had all but disappeared. For Europe these were decades of decline, both politically and militarily.*

Into this vacuum, caused by Europe's demise stepped two new powers, the Soviet Union and the United States. Conflicting ideological and political aims of these two powers led to a breakdown of their wartime cooperation and a division of Europe between the new superpowers. Because of the diverging interests of these countries, no peace treaty ending the war with Germany has ever been signed.

---

*The bases for European material recovery was laid in 1947 when the United States government implemented the "Marshall Plan" for the rebuilding and restoration of the European economy.

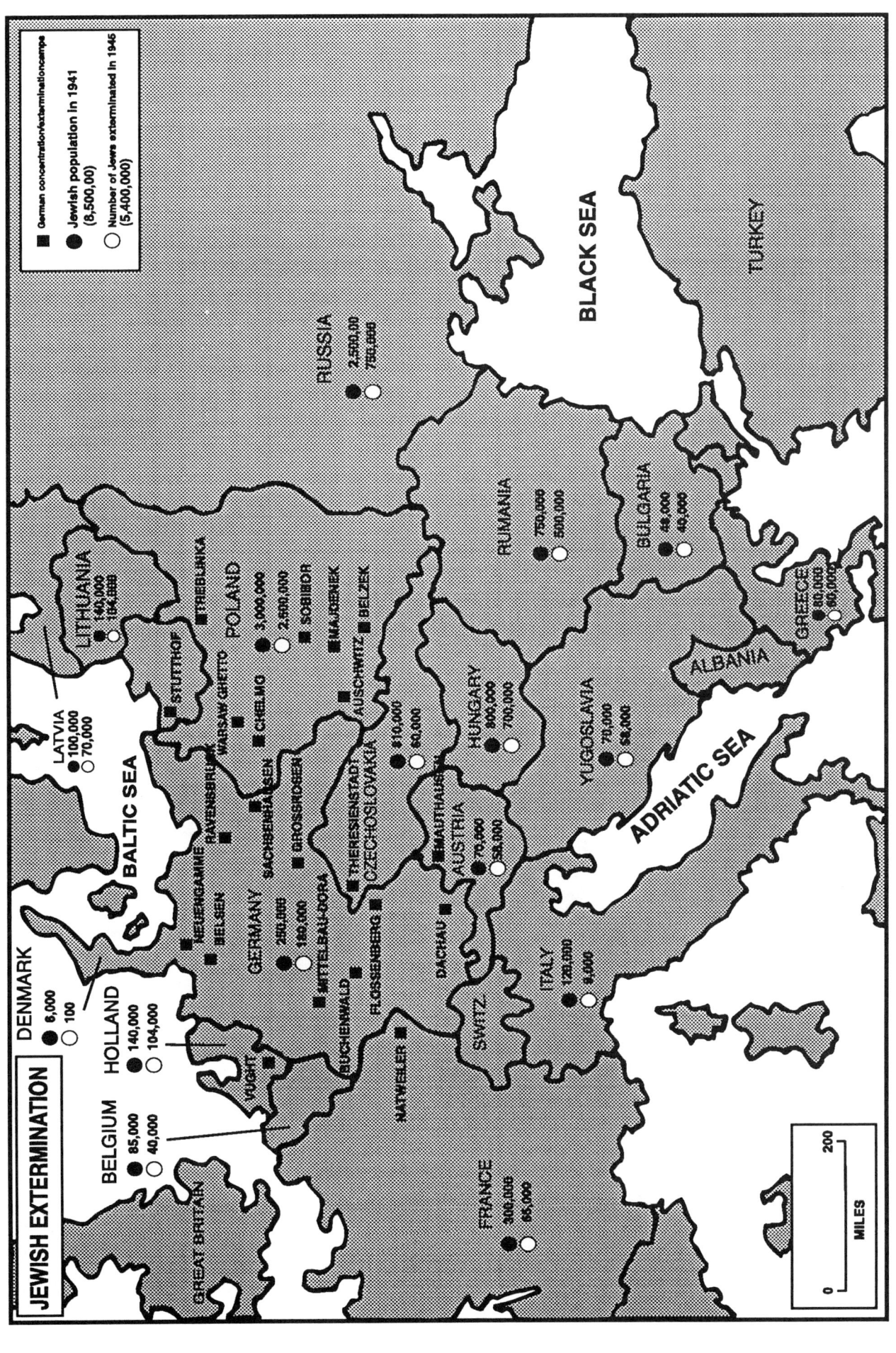

Chapter XIII
The Rise of Japanese Militarism

❖ ❖ ❖

The war in Asia, which was merged with the fighting in Europe on December 11, 1941, predated the European conflict by eight years. The Japanese invasion of Manchuria in 1931, the opening shots of the Asian war, can, in fact, be traced back even further, to Japan's nineteenth century modernization. With the Meiji Restoration (restoration of the emperor) in 1868, Japan launched a massive program of modernization and industrialization modeled along the lines of western Europe. The goal was to make Japan powerful enough militarily to compete on equal terms with western imperialist powers. This program was so successful that Japan not only survived the crush of nineteenth century European imperialism, which literally carved up the world, but proceeded to create her own empire, the only non-European nation to do so. Japan's victory over China in 1894–95 brought her Formosa, and her defeat of Russia in 1904–05 gave her control over previously-held Russian territory in South Manchuria, and ultimately led to Japanese annexation of Korea in 1910. During World War I, Japan seized Germany's South Sea Islands—the Carolinas, the Marshalls, and the Marianna Islands. The Paris Peace Conference following the war gave Japan mandate rights over these islands. All of these acquisitions further fed a growing belief by the Japanese military that it had a divine mission to extend its control over Asia and to safeguard Japanese economic well-being.

But there were obstacles to continued Japanese expansion—namely, the lack of raw materials to support an industrialized economy and external markets to absorb her industrial output and to furnish the revenue for the purchase of the needed raw materials. Thus, although Japanese expansion and economic development in the late 19th and early 20th centuries had been impressive, it was exceedingly vulnerable, and as the 20th century progressed, it became a fixed idea in Japan that the country was in great economic peril.

That well-being was severely threatened by the Great Depression which began in the United States in 1929 but soon became a worldwide phenomenon. The resulting economic slump eroded markets for Japanese manufactured goods and slowed the flow of the needed raw materials into the country. Coinciding with the economic downturn was the appearance of the so-called Tanaka Memorial—a purported memorandum from the Japanese Minister of War, Tanaka, to the throne. The document, which the Japanese government claimed was a forgery, outlined a scenario for Japanese conquests in Asia, beginning with the seizure of north China. This area contained the raw materials and the markets necessary for Japanese economic well-being.

Whether the Tanaka Memorial was indeed a fraud or not may be debated. What is not open for debate, however, is the increasing interest which Japan, particularly the army, gave to Manchuria. Located north of the Great Wall, Manchuria was not part of Old China, although it was the home of the Manchu tribe that had penetrated the Great Wall and overthrown the Ming dynasty in 1664. The Manchus then ruled China for the next 247 years until they were overthrown in 1911 by republican forces in China. A war-lord by the name of Chang Tso-lin managed to take control of most of Manchuria during the Civil War which followed the Manchu demise. In essence he governed the area as a Japanese puppet and Japanese economic interests made considerable headway in the area. Chang Tso-lin died in 1928 when the train he was traveling in was blown up. He was succeeded by his son, Chang Hsueh-liang, who gradually reversed his father's policies and finally accepted Chinese suzerainty over Manchuria.

103

The Japanese interpreted this act as hostile to their interests, and the military prepared for a wholesale invasion of Manchuria.

On the night of September 18, 1931, an explosion occurred in the marshaling yards of the Japanese owned South Manchurian Railroad just outside of Mukden.* The Japanese alleged that the blast was aimed at a Japanese troop train. In fact, the Japanese staged the incident themselves in order to give the Kwantung army, which was protecting Japanese Imperial interests in Manchuria, an excuse to take over the country.

The Nationalist government of Chiang Kai-shek, which was embroiled in a civil war with the Communist forces of Mao Tse-tung, offered little resistance. Chiang took his case to the League of Nations, but got little support. When the League finally did condemn Japanese aggression in 1932, Japan simply walked out, and the League was powerless to do anything to force Japan to abandon its conquests. By February, 1932, Japan was in control of the three provinces that made up Manchuria, and she proclaimed a separate nation by the name of Manchukuo (land of the Manchu) under Japanese protection. To head this puppet state, the Japanese installed Henry Pu Yi, the infant who had been the last Manchu ruler of China at the time the Republic had been established.**

The conquest of Manchuria was launched by the Kwantung Army without the knowledge or approval of the civilian government. When the Cabinet and the Army General Staff in Tokyo intervened and ordered the Kwantung Army to limit the expanse of hostilities, the Army leaders simply ignored it and continued their conquest of Manchuria. Such action was supported by several secret societies within the military in Japan itself, and is evidence of the growing military influence within the country. From now on, civilian officials who did not support army interests soon lost their jobs and often their lives.

In 1932, military officers killed the Finance Minister as well as the President of Mitsui, and on May 15, nine Navy and Army officers shot and killed the Prime Minister, Tsuyaski Inukai. None of the assassins, who surrendered to authorities, received the death penalty; indeed, almost all were free in a few years. Popular opinion, it was clear, increasingly looked upon the military as Japan's champion and savior from the crippling depression. Civilian officials who did not recognize that fact were forcibly removed.

Above both the army and civilian government loomed the figure of the Emperor, Hirohito. Theoretically all decisions in Japan needed his approval, but according to Japanese tradition, once the Cabinet and military leaders reached agreement, the Emperor could not withhold his approval. He was to remain above politics and to transcend party feuds. Still, the Emperor possessed considerable moral power and influence, and a stronger ruler might have used them to restore internal peace in Japan. But Hirohito was a studious man with strong intellectual interests, particularly in marine biology, and he chose to reign, not rule. As a result, the military continued apace, unchecked.

Phase two of Japanese expansion began in 1937, sparked by an incident at the Marco Polo Bridge, fifteen miles southwest of Peking. Japanese troops had been stationed in the Peking area ever since they had assisted American and European troops in putting down the anti-foreign Boxer Rebellion in 1900. The Boxer Protocol in the following year allowed foreign powers to occupy key points near Peking. On July 5, 1937, a new threat arose to the Japanese presence here, as well as in North China, when Chiang Kai-shek's government (Kuomintang) and Mao's Communists signed a formal agreement to unite and to drive the Japanese out of Peking and North China.

Two days later, on the night of July 7, a skirmish took place between Japanese troops stationed near the Marco Polo Bridge and a large Chinese unit. The fighting was brief and the Japanese suffered only one casualty—one man missing. As a truce was being arranged, however, additional shots were fired into the Japanese companies, leading to another scuffle. Eventually, peace was restored to the area, and Japan canceled orders to transfer more troops to North China. However, Chiang Kai-shek's refusal

---

*The Japanese controlled previously Russian held territory in this area as a result of their victory in the Russo-Japanese War. They also owned the railroad and had the right to station troops along it.

**Henry Pu Yi died only in 1968. His life is the subject of the 1988 academy award nominated motion picture, "The Last Emperor."

to sanction terms worked out between Chinese and Japanese commanders led to another incident on the night of July 25 at a railway station some fifty miles south of Peking. This skirmish soon turned into a major conflict, Japanese planes bombed Chinese barracks in the nearby town, and her troops soon occupied the town itself.

This event forced the hand of the Japanese Premier, Prince Fumimaro Konoye, who announced to the Japanese Diet (Parliament) that the government must protect Japanese property and lives. This was tantamount to a declaration of war on China (although none was declared), a war that Japanese military leaders believed would be over within three months. At dawn on July 28, Japanese planes bombed three Chinese cities and ground troops attacked Chinese troops all over the Peking area.

The fighting spread from Peking south to Shanghai. Japanese planes bombed the city, ships shelled it, and Japanese troops attacked it by land. By December, Shanghai was in Japanese hands and Chinese troops were retreating up the Yangtze River Valley toward the capital of Nanking, pursued by nearly 100,000 Japanese troops. On December 13, the Japanese captured Nanking.

The fall of Nanking was accompanied by a particularly savage and barbaric attack on its citizens, despite orders to the contrary from the Japanese commander. Chinese civilians, men, women and children were shot, bayoneted, used for hand-grenade practice or doused with gasoline and set afire. The Japanese troops perpetrated a massacre that has virtually no parallel in recent history. Expert witnesses at the International Military Tribunal of the Far East held in Tokyo in 1946 to try Japanese war criminals, estimated that some 250,000 non-combatants were slaughtered in cold blood. Many experts now believe the number to be over 350,000, an extraordinary figure for a city with a population of only 650,000 many of whom had already fled.

Although most foreigners in the city were spared, an American gunboat, the *Panay*, stationed in the Yangtze in order to protect American lives and property, was sunk by Japanese planes, despite the fact that it was clearly marked as an American vessel. Two Americans died and forty-eight were injured in the attack. The United States government was outraged but the Japanese quickly apologized, agreed to indemnity payments, and the crisis soon passed away.

Before Nanking fell, Chiang Kai-shek moved his capital 400 miles up the Yangtze to Hankow, a major industrial city. Although the Japanese were slowed a bit in the spring of 1938, they still captured Hankow in October. But Chiang again was one step ahead of the Japanese, moving his government 500 miles farther west up the Yangtze to the city of Chunking. This time the Chinese moved whole factories with them to the city, located high on the cliffs overlooking the Yangtze, well removed from Japanese land threats.

It was now obvious that Japan's timetable was falling behind. It had been a year since the incident at the Marco Polo bridge and no end to the fighting was in sight. She now had over a million men on the Chinese mainland, but they were conquering territory, not people, as the Chinese "sold space in order to buy time." And buy time they did, as no large-scale fighting took place for the next *six* years.

Despite this stalemate, it should be recognized that the Japanese army which confronted the Chinese was a very capable military force. By the 1930s, it had become largely autonomous, *i.e.*, it was isolated from the rest of society and from the government as well, and it believed it had a divine right to control the destiny of the country. This outlook was, in essence, a revival of the *samurai* mentality that theoretically had been ended at the time of the Meiji Restoration. The *samurai* had been a military caste who guided themselves by a code known as *Bushido*, the way of the warrior. Japanese officers in the 1930's considered themselves modern-day *samurai*, committed to this same code of conduct.

Bushido guided the life of the soldier on every point. Its gloomy, pessimistic message was that the fate of every soldier was to die. Just as the cherry blossom fell at the height of its beauty, so too should a soldier fall at the peak of his manhood. Naturally, he was to kill as many of the enemy as possible, but ultimately his fate too was to die. *Bushido* taught endurance, submission to authority, the carrying out of impossible orders, and savage disdain for the underdog. It also stressed that a soldier should never surrender—surrender meant disgrace. Instead of shaming and discrediting his country and family, the warrior was to commit *hara-kiri*, (literally, self-slaughter) in an extremely painful manner. Perhaps this harshness and gloom of *Bushido* was best reflected in the Japanese military uniform—a drab, colorless outfit with little or no glitter.

Such was the life of the Japanese soldier. As a follower of *bushido,* he was dedicated, obedient, and ready to die for his emperor. The enemy held no fear for him nor did the conditions under which he had to fight; whether in the jungle, the desert, or the mountains. He fought to the bitter end, preferring death to surrender. In short, there was no better fighting machine in World War II than the Japanese combat soldier, as American G.I.'s were later to find out.

One result of the China war was a further deterioration in relations with the United States. When the Japanese invaded Manchuria, the United States responded with the so-called Stimson Doctrine, which asserted that we would refuse to recognize such conquests brought about by military means. With the country preoccupied by the crippling depression, no one really cared what was happening in North China, and the government would take no concrete action to halt Japanese aggression. After Japan consolidated its 1931 takeover of Manchuria, the American-Japanese situation remained stable for several years.

In the Sino-Japanese war that broke out in 1937, the United States favored China but refused to render much important aid. President Roosevelt did agree to arms sales to China, bending the Neutrality Act, which forbade sales of arms to belligerents by defining China as a non-belligerent, since no official declaration of war had been given by the Japanese. The sinking of the *Panay* in December, 1937, stunned the American public, but the United States was reluctant to consider retaliating. The Japanese apology and payment of reparations to families of those killed caused a temporary truce to return to U.S.-Japanese relations.

As Japanese expansionists tightened their control of domestic policies in 1938, Japanese foreign policy turned in a new direction. Prime Minister Konoye began talking about Japan creating a "New Order" in Asia, by which he meant the integration of Manchukuo, Inner Mongolia, and Korea into the Japanese Empire, with later colonial holdings to be added in Southeast Asia and in the Pacific Islands. Japan anticipated strong resistance from the United States as she pursued these aims. Again, however, American foreign policy was constrained by internal economic problems. A new major recession hit the U.S. in 1937–38, further deflecting Americans from thoughts of foreign entanglements. By 1939, President Roosevelt decided that America's isolationist policy must end, and he set out to persuade Congress and the American public to prepare for the possibility of granting aid to embattled countries and ultimately for the possibility of war. As the war in Asia escalated, Japan was more and more edging into conflict with America's concept of world order, and Roosevelt wanted to put a halt to it. He did manage to extend a token $25 million loan to China, but could do little else. Congressional leadership in the United States still remained in the hands of isolationists who opposed any efforts by the President to assist aggressed countries in either Europe or Asia.

Japanese-Soviet relations also declined in the 1930's. Relations between the two countries had never been really good. Japan had always looked upon Russia as a perpetual threat to its existence. In 1904–05 Japan defeated Russia in a war that most Japanese saw as the first of many to come between the two countries. Following the 1917 Russian Revolution, Japan took part in Allied intervention in the new Soviet state by occupying part of eastern Siberia. In 1925, Japanese troops were persuaded to withdraw, but Japanese-Soviet relations remained strained.

After the establishment of Manchukuo in 1932, relations between the two countries deteriorated even further. Japan now stationed a large part of her army there, and border clashes with Soviets occurred. In the summer of 1938, Japanese troops battled with Soviet forces for possession of a barren hill on the Soviet-Manchurian border. Two months later, another border squabble occurred. In both incidents, Soviet forces gave the Japanese a severe drubbing. These defeats had several important effects on Japan. In the first place, Japan reevaluated her weaponry and her military tactics. Secondly, she moved closer to a formal alliance with Italy and Germany.* And finally, Japan began to look to the south for future expansion rather than to the north toward Soviet territory. It was this new orientation of Japanese expansionist interests that was ultimately to lead to mortal conflict with the United States.

---

*The Tri-Partite Agreement among these three powers was signed in September, 1940.

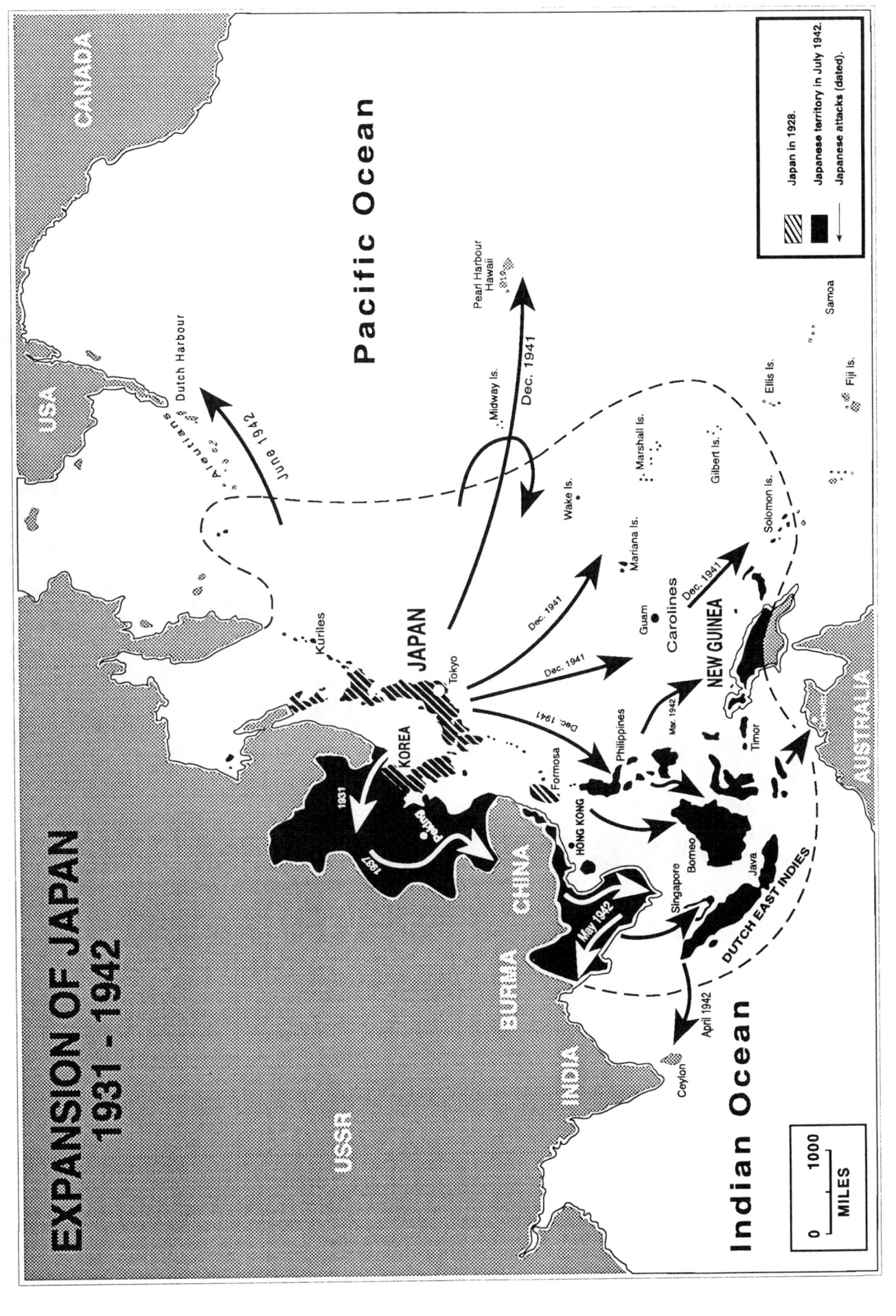

U.S. NAVY

Chapter XIV

Pearl Harbor

❖ ❖ ❖

Military defeats at the hands of the Russians to the north were not the only factors causing a shift in Japan's future expansionist goals. To the south lay abundant natural resources—crude oil, rubber, tin, tungsten and bauxite. But even more significantly, most of these areas—French Indochina, Burma, Indonesia (Dutch East Indies) were the possessions of European powers locked—after May, 1940—in a deadly struggle for survival with Nazi Germany. Within two months France and Holland were defeated and the British—their troops snatched from the continent at the beginning of June, 1940—seemed on the verge of extinction. Dutch, British, and French colonies in Asia were ripe for the taking.

In September, 1940, the Japanese pressured the Vichy French government, the proto-fascist regime that now controlled French colonies, to allow Japanese troops to be stationed in Indochina (later to be called Vietnam). Japan claimed that it needed a military presence in Indochina to cover the southern flank of China. The Vichy government accepted the Japanese ultimatum and granted operational bases, airbases and the port of Haiphong to the Japanese.

In July 1941, Japan demanded the right to send troops into southern Indochina. Again, the Vichy government knuckled under, and Japanese soldiers went ashore at Cam Ranh Bay and occupied Saigon and Da Nang. These facilities were essential for any future operations in Southeast Asia. President Roosevelt reacted to the Japanese troop movements by announcing a complete embargo on all oil shipments to Japan. Earlier, in December, 1940, he had embargoed shipments of other vital materials such as scrap iron to Japan. In addition, all trade with Japan was cut off and all Japanese assets in the United States were frozen. Great Britain and the Netherlands soon followed the lead of the United States.

Roosevelt and Secretary of State Cordel Hull made it clear that the embargoes would be lifted only if: 1. Japan got out of Indochina; 2. Japan got out of China; and 3. Japan renounced the Tri-Partite Pact with Germany and Italy. These were demands to which Japan would not consent. To back down from her newly won possessions would mean to lose face, and in the samurai mentality that would be equivalent to the disgrace of surrender. The American Ambassador to Japan, Joseph C. Grew, wrote Roosevelt that the Japanese, "... would never abandon their invasion of China." Grew also urged that the president meet with the Japanese Prime Minister, Fumimoro Konoye, which Roosevelt was willing to do. Hull, however, torpedoed the proposal. He simply did not believe that Japan would ever abandon her plans for conquering Asia, thus a "summit" would be meaningless.

The effects of the American actions, particularly the oil embargo, were immediate for Japan. She had no domestic supply of oil, although she had stored enough to last for two years if carefully rationed. Denying her the opportunity of replenishing it would be a severe blow to her expansionist plans, indeed to her very survival. Japanese leaders also feared that being deprived of U.S. dollars would lead to Japanese economic bankruptcy within two years.

Negotiations between the United States and Japan for an Asian peace settlement now assumed urgent proportions. Admiral Kichisaburo Nomura, Japanese Ambassador to the United States, initially carried out the bulk of these negotiations. He was hampered, however, by several factors over which he had no control. In the first place, the Japanese government was not really bent on peace but in fact was preparing for war. Nomura and special envoy, Saburo Kurusu, an able diplomat who joined Nomura in September, 1941, had to communicate "uncompromising" proposals to the Americans, proposals that were hardly acceptable.* Indeed, the negotiations were bogus—which Nomura and Kurusu knew—since Japan was willing to make no concessions whatsoever to the United States.

The second factor undermining the efforts of the Japanese diplomats was the fact American cryptographers, under the leadership of William Friedman, had broken Japan's diplomatic code known as "Purple" and from the Summer, 1940, they could intercept the secret cable traffic between Tokyo and its overseas embassies. The code name for these intercepts was Magic and they gave the American Secretary of State a true picture of Japanese intentions before he ever met with Nomura and Kurusu. No matter how sincere the Japanese representatives might be in relaying proposals from Tokyo, Hull knew that their government was not truly interested in peace, except on their own terms. Thus, when the Japanese cabinet on September 5 made the decision to prepare for war, U.S. officials knew about it, although not about the nature of the battle plans that were kept secret from Nomura and Kurusu.

Still, Konoye continued to favor the negotiations and they continued. However, when an attempt was made on Konoye's life he resigned; the new Japanese Prime Minister was General Hideki Tojo, who had been Konoye's Minister of War. Tojo's new government numbered seven generals and admirals among its fourteen members. Known as the "Razor Brain," Tojo was a rigid disciplinarian who demanded absolute obedience. Deeply devoted to the emperor, who was strongly opposed to abandoning diplomacy, Tojo continued the discussions with the United States, even though the General Staff felt that they were now at a dead end. Although Chief of Staff General Sugiyama believed that the negotiations should continue in order to give Japan a military advantage, he did agree to setting a deadline of November 30 for reaching an agreement with the United States. After that, the plans for war with the United States would inexorably go into effect.

A more flexible approach by Secretary of State Hull and some recognition by the United States of Japanese interests in Asia might yet have prevented a military confrontation. Certainly Japan's seizure of Manchuria, the invasion of China, and her move to the south through Indochina, had been aggressive acts. But they had been, in the minds of the Japanese, the result of the Great Depression and Japan's necessity for finding new resources and markets to maintain her economic prowess. The United States, rich in resources, free from fear of attack, simply could not understand Japan's perceptions of her own needs. Thus, the unyielding Hull and the American government, generally ignorant of the Orient and the workings of the Oriental mindset, took a no-compromise stand on maintaining the status quo in Asia and on the territorial integrity of China. The result was to drive the Japanese into a corner with no way to save face and no way out except surrender or war.

The basic plan to which Japan adhered in the 1930s, in case of war with the United States, was to let the Americans make the initial move. It was generally known that in case of war, the Americans would send their fleet westward to engage the Japanese fleet in the western Pacific. As this fleet sortied across the Pacific, the Japanese planned to harass it with submarine and air attacks. By the time the American fleet arrived in Japanese waters—somewhere in the area of Iwo Jima and Saipan—it would be so weakened that it could be defeated easily by the still-powerful Japanese fleet. Japanese expansion into the Philippines, the Dutch East Indies, and Malaya could then proceed, unhampered by United States military action.

In the middle of 1939, Admiral Isoroku Yamamoto became Commander-in-Chief of Japan's Combined Fleet, the highest operational command in Japan, a position which also made him one of the men responsible for planning naval operations. Yamamoto had studied at Harvard as a young man and later had served as the Japanese naval attache in Washington. As a result, he had become duly impressed with the immense potential military strength of the United States. Japan could not, in his mind, survive a protracted conflict with such a powerful country. If, for some reason, the American fleet was not destroyed following its marathon voyage across the Pacific, the war could well drag on, in which case Japan's doom was certain.

---

*Kurusu's wife was an American, Alice Jay, born of British parents in New York City.

Although hardly a firebrand, Yamamoto soon developed a much bolder and, in his mind, more certain plan for dealing with the United States Pacific fleet if war should come between the two countries—something, incidentally, which Yamamoto did not favor. His proposal was to launch a seaborne air attack on the American fleet at its home port in Hawaii and destroy it before it could sail. Japanese expansion in Asia could then proceed without any United States military opposition. The American government, with no way to stop Japanese actions, would then be forced to sign a separate treaty with her recognizing Japan's creation of a Greater East Asia Co-Prosperity Sphere. Above all, a lengthy conflict with the United States, which Japan could not win, would be avoided.

There were nine basic elements in the plan, as it was worked out by the Japanese. The first element, naturally, was surprise. Yamamoto's scheme depended, above all else, on a naval task force sailing across the Pacific within range of Pearl Harbor without being detected. The second element of the plan was the designation of the United States' aircraft carriers as the main objective of the attack. This would deprive the United States fleet of its long-range striking arm. The third element of the plan was to secure Japanese control of the air by destroying land-based American planes, preferably on the ground. These targets dictated the fourth element, which was to utilize all types of bombing—torpedo, dive, and high level bombing, but with the priority on torpedo bombing. This presented the Japanese with a major problem because of the shallowness of Pearl Harbor's waters, which averaged about 45 feet in depth. The British, who had pioneered the development of air-dropped torpedoes, calculated that a depth of 75 feet was necessary; otherwise the torpedoes would hit the bottom and explode. It wasn't until October, 1941, that the Japanese solved this problem by stabilizing the torpedoes with special fins to slow their descent into the water.

The remaining elements of the plan called for the use of every available carrier, the employment of fighter planes to escort and protect the attacking planes at Pearl Harbor, the use of a daylight attack, the utilization of refueling at sea, and the necessity to keep all planning in absolute secrecy. Some problems did occur, such as a shortage of heavy bombs (this was solved by converting armor-piercing shells) and a shortage of aircrew. But, by the end of October, all of these problems had been overcome and the fleet was poised to sail.

When President Roosevelt decided in 1940 to move the United States Pacific fleet from California to a more westerly anchorage in order to act as a deterrent to Japanese aggressive action, there were few choices other than Pearl Harbor. Located about 3000 miles from the mainland, Pearl Harbor was far from an ideal base. Its distance made for logistical problems. In addition it had to be entered through a narrow channel, two miles long and a quarter mile wide. Any ship sunk here could stop the fleet's passage into or out of its mooring place. The harbor itself was also restricted in size and because it was so shallow it could barely accommodate large vessels. A congested harbor meant that maneuvering was difficult and in order to provide more space, the torpedo nets around the ships were usually left down. Most all of the base could be seen from the surrounding hills, thus allowing enemy spies to relay accurate information about Pearl Harbor's defenses. Yamamoto knew, for example, that there were no barrage balloons (to stop low-flying planes) at Pearl and that there was no torpedo netting around the ships. Admiral Richardson, Commander of the Pacific fleet in 1940, had indeed opposed stationing it in Hawaii, recommending its return to the safer haven of California. But for diplomatic reasons, Roosevelt decided against his advice.

Of course, once the fleet was moved to Pearl Harbor, it became a possible target should war with Japan ever become a reality. Captain Richmond Kelly Turner, Chief of War Plans in the Office of Naval Operations, drafted a letter to Secretary of War Henry L. Stimson in January, 1941, which read in part:

The security of the U.S. Pacific Fleet while in Pearl Harbor has been under renewed study by the Navy Department and forces afloat for the past several weeks....If war eventuates with Japan, it is believed easily possible that hostilities would be initiated by a surprise attack upon the Fleet or the Naval Base at Pearl Harbor.

In my opinion, the inherent possibilities of a major disaster to the fleet or naval base warrant taking every step, as rapidly as can be done, that will increase the joint readiness of the Army and Navy to withstand a raid of the character mentioned above.

Also in January, 1941, Grew, the American Ambassador to Japan, wrote in his diary:

There is a lot of talk around town to the effect that the Japanese, in case of a break with the U.S., are planning to go all out in a surprise mass attack on Pearl Harbor. I rather guess the boys in Hawaii are not precisely sleeping.

The Peruvian Ambassador to Japan heard rumors about a Japanese sneak attack on Pearl Harbor and relayed his information to Washington via Grew.

Yet no one took undue alarm at such warnings. For one thing, the United States never really took the Japanese very seriously. They were, in fact, often depicted as funny little men with thick glasses, buckteeth and bowlegs, who were considered inferior to Americans. Certainly the inferior Japanese would not be foolhardy enough to attack Pearl Harbor and risk the wrath of the mighty U.S. Pacific fleet. Racism got in the way of military judgment. *Time* Magazine reported in August, 1941, that the U.S. Navy was fairly well-off with its own defenses. Admiral Husband E. Kimmel, appointed commander of the Pacific Fleet in January, 1941, was aware of a possible surprise attack on Pearl Harbor but felt such an attack more likely after war had already broken out and the fleet had sortied out of Pearl in search of the enemy. He did ask for more interceptor aircraft, anti-aircraft guns, and additional radar equipment, as well as more anti-submarine forces, in order to protect Pearl. But he largely discounted the danger of a Japanese air attack.

American forces at Pearl were also lulled into a sense of security by the general belief that the Japanese would strike somewhere in Southeast Asia—either Malaya, the Dutch East Indies, or the Philippines. The biggest danger to Pearl Harbor in the mind of Lt. General Walter C. Short, the United States Army Commander at Pearl Harbor, was not an air attack but sabotage from Japanese agents in Hawaii. Thus, neither the Navy nor the Army commander at Pearl greatly feared the possibility of a sneak Japanese attack, and American blindness to the danger continued until the very morning of the attack itself.

As noted earlier, from the summer of 1940, U.S. Intelligence had been reading Japan's diplomatic messages, and knew by Fall, 1941, that Japan was preparing for war in the event that negotiations with the United States failed to produce an agreement. But the Japanese naval codes had not been broken. Hence Washington did not know of the orders Yamamoto sent to his fleet or the messages radioed to the Pearl Harbor task force. By late November, however, Yamamoto had imposed radio silence on his Pearl Harbor Strike Force (*Kido Butai*), which sailed from remote Uitokappu Bay in the frozen Kurile Islands at 6 A.M. on November 26. With no radio signals coming from Japanese carriers, American intelligence officers had no idea where they were located. Since Japanese ships often kept radio silence while in port, many American officials assumed that's where the Japanese carriers were. No one had an inkling they were sliding through the cold waters of the North Pacific towards Pearl Harbor.

On November 27, Admiral Stark sent a "war warning" message to the Pacific admirals. Magic intercepts had revealed that war was imminent. But, Stark added, the evidence indicated "an amphibious expedition against either the Philippines, Thai or Kra Peninsula or possibly Borneo," No mention was made of Hawaii. On December 6, American officials received a report from the British Admiralty that a Japanese fleet of 35 transports, eight cruisers, and twenty destroyers was moving directly toward the Malay Peninsula. When Navy Secretary Frank Knox wondered whether they were going "to hit us," he was told by Turner that they were going to the hit the British. "They are not ready for us yet," said Turner.

Early on December 7, Magic revealed that the Japanese were presenting an ultimatum to the American government and were under orders to destroy their code machines immediately. Shortly after noon,

Washington time, the message was sent to American commanders in San Francisco, the Panama Canal and the Philippines. But atmospheric conditions prevented its transmission to Hawaii. Instead, the message was sent by commercial telegraph (Western Union) to Pearl Harbor. It arrived too late.

There were also two other last-minute warnings to Pearl, which were discounted. Shortly before 4 A.M. on December 7 (Hawaii time), a U.S. minesweeper patrolling the entrance to Pearl Harbor reported seeing a periscope of a submerged submarine, but subsequent searching failed to produce further sightings and no message was sent to headquarters. Three hours later a destroyer, the *Ward*, spotted another periscope. This time the American ship opened fire, scoring a direct hit on the conning tower. The *Ward* proceeded to drop depth-charges and then notified headquarters of the attack. Officers there thought the sighting was probably false; but if not, they believed that the *Ward* and other destroyers in the vicinity could handle the situation. Actually, the sub that was sunk was a midget sub, from a Japanese force of 27 submarines, five carrying midget subs, all intended to distract U.S. attention from the air attack and cause what damage they could. The Japanese also hoped that, if the air attack should not succeed, the submarines would deal the knockout blow if and when the American fleet came out of the harbor.

The second warning was more clear cut and imminent. A mobile radar unit on the island of Oahu, operated by two Army privates, picked up mysterious bleeps on its screen. Since the units were relatively new and their operators still not fully trained on them, their sightings were discounted. Also, since a flight of American B-17s from the mainland was due that morning, the operators were simply told not to "worry about it," that they were probably the expected flight of American planes. The planes, of course, were not American, but the first wave of the Japanese attack force.

They had taken off from carriers in the Japanese Strike Force which, under the Command of Admiral Chuichi Nagumo, had steamed undetected to a point 230 miles due north of Oahu. Just before dawn, with the sky still dark, fighter planes, high-level torpedo bombers and dive bombers, roared into the sky—the first wave of 183 planes led by Commander Mistsuo Fuchida preceded the second wave of 180 planes by less than an hour. Guided by Hawaiian radio stations, which they picked up on their plane radios, they flew down the island's west coast until Pearl Harbor was clearly visible. Fuchida carefully counted all the ships at anchor below. Then he flashed his fateful message to his fleet and to Tokyo—*Tora, tora, tora*—Tiger, tiger, tiger. This signified that the attack was a complete surprise. It was 7:49 A.M. in Hawaii.

Among the first targets of the Japanese were the American planes, lined-up wingtip to wingtip on the runways in order to protect against Short's perceived threat of sabotage. They were "sitting ducks" for the Japanese pilots. Only 30 United States Army Air Force fighters managed to get into the air while not a single navy plane made it. As a result, of the 394 American aircraft on Oahu, 188 were destroyed and 159 others damaged.

As Japanese planes swooped low across the Bay, nearly everyone thought they were just stunting naval pilots acting up as they sometimes did. Suddenly, explosions erupted aboard a number of ships at once, and loudspeakers blared "Air Raid! No Drill!" Japanese surprise was complete. Only about one-fourth of the fleet's 780 anti-aircraft guns were manned, and of the army's 31 anti-aircraft batteries, only 4 were in position and these had no ready ammunition.

Within the space of two hours, the Japanese sank or seriously damaged 18 ships of war, including all eight United States battleships. However, only two of the big ships—the *Arizona* and the *Oklahoma*—could not be repaired or refloated. In all, the United States lost 2,403 killed (nearly half of them trapped inside the *Arizona*) and 1178 wounded.* Japanese losses were exceedingly light: 29 planes and pilots were lost, along with five midget submarines and one large sub (this part of the Japanese attack was a complete failure) and their crews. Admiral Nagumo was pleased, stating that "....the results we anticipated have been achieved." Naval supremacy in the Pacific had now passed into the hands of the Japanese.

---

*The *Arizona* is still today a commissioned ship in the U.S. Navy. Each morning the American flag is raised on the monument built over the ship's superstructure.

Yet, Japanese success was not complete. In the first place, there were no aircraft carriers, the backbone of the U.S. fleet, in Pearl Harbor at the time of the attack. The three carriers operating out of Pearl had been top priority in Yamamoto's plan, but on December 7, none were in port. The *Lexington* was on its way to deliver dive bombers to Midway Island; the *Enterprise* was west of Oahu on its way back from taking planes to Wake Island; the *Saratoga*, the third of the carriers was well out of harm's way. It had just completed a routine refitting at the Puget Sound Naval Yard in Bremerton, Washington, and on the morning of December 7 was nearing San Diego. Thus, the long-range arm of the U.S. Pacific fleet remained intact.

Secondly, the Japanese pilots, in their concern to hit American shipping and aircraft, failed to hit fuel storage facilities at Pearl as well as the dry-docks necessary for repairing damaged ships. Some Japanese pilots wanted to launch a second attack on Pearl Harbor in order to hit the dockyards and fuel tanks, but Admiral Nagumo demurred. With the American carriers still at large and their locations unknown, he feared the risk too great. He had already undergone considerable risk and his ships had come through without a scratch. He could not bring himself to tempt fate a second time, and he decided to turn back.

The major mistake the Japanese made, however, was to underestimate the impact of the Pearl Harbor attack on American public opinion. For most, Pearl Harbor became a deep emotional experience that welded together the American people. No more did Americans ask whose fight it was or question what they should do about it. The U.S. would very likely have entered World War II, even without Pearl Harbor. But that attack ensured that the entire nation would stand as one until final victory was achieved. The next day, December 8, the President addressed a joint session of Congress and announced that a state of war now existed between the United States and the Empire of Japan. It was a short speech, fewer that 500 words, and was broadcast around the country and heard by a record radio audience of 60 million Americans. The only negative vote against the war declaration came from Jeannette Rankin, a Republican member of the House of Representatives. Rankin was a pacifist who had also voted against U.S. entry into World War I. The United States was joined almost immediately by Great Britain. Three days later, Italy and Germany made the conflict truly a world war, declaring war on the United States in support of Japan. One more word is in order here about the Pearl Harbor attack. A rather widely circulated myth, one that is still with us, soon arose, claiming that Roosevelt knew well in advance about the Pearl harbor attack but did nothing to stop or prevent it. It was, in this view, his way of pulling an isolationist United States into a conflict which he saw as necessary. The implausibility of this "legend" lies in the fact that it: 1. would have required the American President to somehow hypnotize Yamamoto into planning to attack Pearl Harbor; 2. would have forced Roosevelt to confide in his Hawaiian Commanders and persuade them to allow the enemy to proceed unhindered. This view also suggests that Roosevelt, in order to get the U.S. into the war, created a situation whereby the U.S. was nearly deprived of the means with which to fight. That would be tantamount to a boxer entering the ring with both hands tied behind his back. Finally, it is this author's suggestion that such a "myth" has racial overtones to it, in that it demeans the brilliance and daring of the Japanese plan. The only way that the Japanese could possibly succeed in their plan was if the United States let them. Perhaps that is the crowning implausibility of the myth that Roosevelt "set up" Pearl Harbor.

THE JAPANESE ATTACK ON PEARL HARBOR, DECEMBER 7, 1941

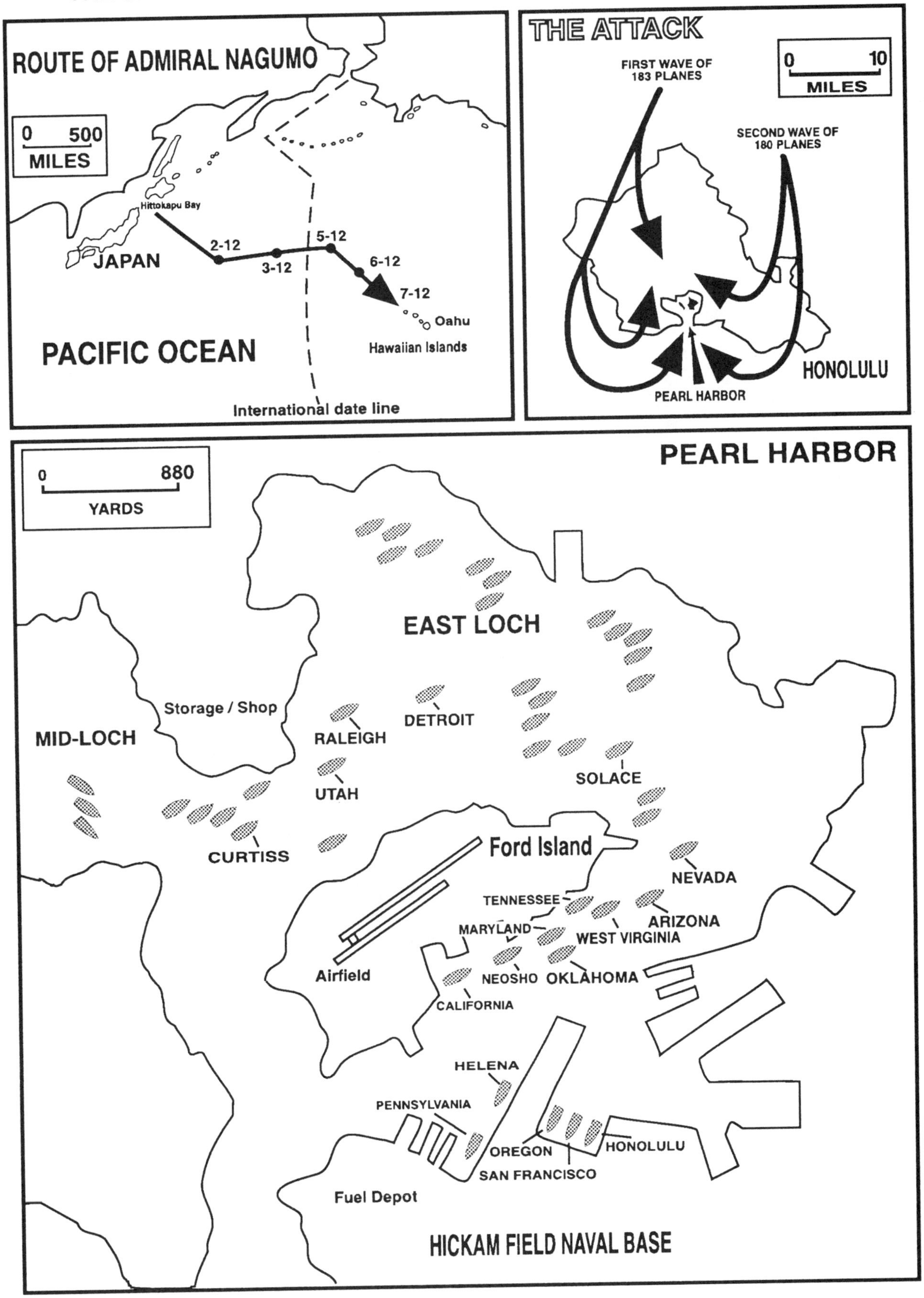

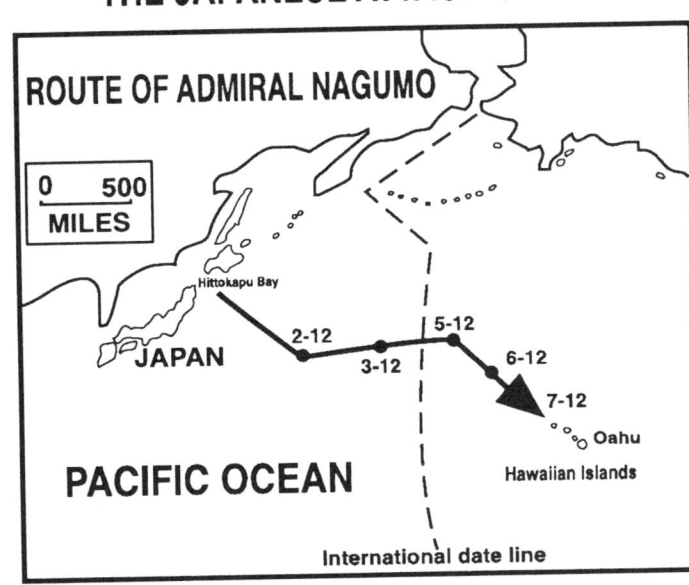
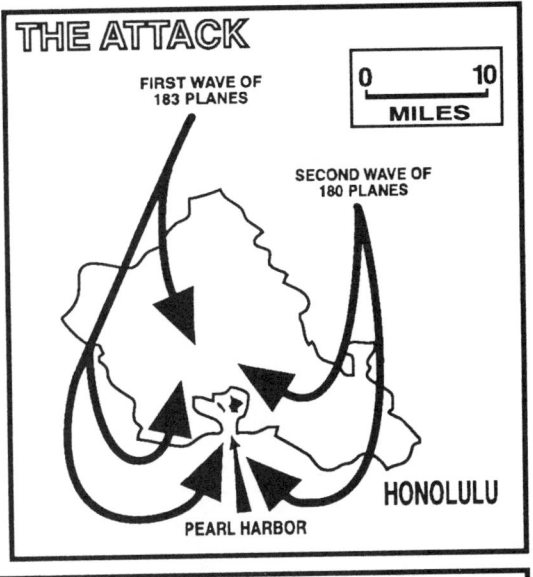

Chapter XV

Japan's 100 Days of Glory

❖   ❖   ❖

Japan's attack on Pearl Harbor was in fact only a tactical maneuver designed to facilitate a two-phase program for expansion in Asia. Phase One of the plan called for the occupation of Hong Kong, Wake Island, and Guam, and the landing of troops in the Philippines and Malaya. Phase Two would bring about the conquest of Singapore, the Dutch East Indies, and Burma. These territories would provide the raw materials that Japan lacked, create a defensive barrier against any future onslaughts from the United States, and protect Japan from any British counteroffensive emanating from India. Inexorably, Japan realized these objectives. In the five months following Pearl Harbor, she achieved a series of unremitting successes as she rolled up the colonial territories of the Western powers in Asia.

The first Japanese victory in the Pacific came at the American held island of Guam. Located in the Mariana Islands, Guam was not really prepared for war. It was defended only by a token force of some 400 Marines and navy men, plus a small force of native troops. Equipped primarily with weapons of World War I vintage, they could hardly hold off a force of over 5,000 Japanese marines and infantrymen, who landed shortly after midnight on December 10. By dawn, it was all over, and the American commander surrendered the only United States territory in this part of the Pacific.

Several thousand miles to the East, about 2300 miles west of Hawaii, lay another American possession, Wake Island. As war approached in 1941, the United States decided to turn the three islet atoll into an airbase designed to block Japanese expansion into the southwest Pacific. At the time of the attack on Pearl Harbor, there were 1200 civilian construction workers on the island, laboring to convert it into a military base. There were also some 400 plus marines, 75 Army and Navy personnel, and a squadron of 12 U.S. Marine fighter planes (Grumman Wildcats that were slower and less maneuverable than Japanese Zeroes). The Marines also had six 5-inch guns and about a dozen antiaircraft guns.

The first attack on Wake came just before noon on the same day that Pearl Harbor was bombed. Planes operating from Kwajalein Atoll, 650 miles to the South, evaded American air defenders by coming in under the clouds of a rain squall, to bomb and strafe Wake's airstrip. Seven American planes were destroyed on the ground and one was damaged.

On December 11, a Japanese invasion force appeared off Wake. Despite heavy shelling, the defenders held their fire until the Japanese closed the range. When the Americans did open up, they damaged a Japanese cruiser, which limped away and sank a Japanese destroyer. During the rest of the day, the Marine gunners hit two more destroyers, a troop transport, and a cruiser. The surviving Marine planes also bombed Japanese ships, sinking one destroyer, which blew up with no survivors. The Japanese invasion fleet, battered by the resistance at Wake, sailed back to Kwajalein, minus about 500 men and two destroyers.

Jubilant American defenders knew, however, that the Japanese would be back. Wake was simply too valuable an outpost to be left in United States' possession. Air raids became an everyday event and on December 23, another Japanese invasion force, which this time included two aircraft carriers used in the Pearl Harbor raid, landed nearly 2000 tough Japanese marines. Their numerical superiority was too great for the defenders. After putting up a stiff, savage defense, Base Commander Winifield Scott

Cunningham, and Marine Commander Major James Devereux, surrendered. Over 100 men died defending Wake Island, which the Japanese now renamed Bird Island.

The next victim of the Japanese was the British Crown colony of Hong Kong. A trade and political center, Hong Kong was a small off-shore island of China. It had never been seriously prepared by the British for a military defense. It was surrounded on all sides by the Japanese Army (in China) and Navy. It was too far from other British possessions, namely Singapore, for help. And finally, its water supply, which came from the mainland, was highly vulnerable. Thus, the British realized that there was no chance Hong Kong could withstand a Japanese attack.

Still, Hong Kong's defenders managed to hold out for thirteen days, before surrendering on Christmas Day, 1941. Her loss was a blow to British pride, but its strategic value was not really that significant. One serious result of its fall, however, was the loss of several Far Eastern experts in the British Army. For some time the British, particularly in India, were short of people to interrogate prisoners and read captured documents. All in all, nearly 12,000 British and Commonwealth troops were captured in Hong Kong. The Japanese lost about 3,000 killed, wounded, and missing in the attack.

On the same day that they attacked Pearl Harbor, the Japanese made a similar raid on Clark Field, the main United States air base in the Philippines. An island group off Southeast Asia, the Philippines had passed from Spain into the possession of the United States following the latter's victory in the Spanish-American War of 1898. Always uneasy about its participation in 19th century imperialism, the United States was grooming the Philippines for independence and had already set such a timetable before Japanese aggression in Asia began. The United States did have a weak garrison of soldiers in the Philippines, mainly the 31st Infantry Regiment and the 4th U.S. Marine Regiment, which had arrived from Shanghai in November, 1941. There was also one division of the regular Philippine Army which was in fighting shape. In all, the Americans could rely on 25,000 to 30,000 regulars as well as 100,000 Philippine reservists, who were poorly trained and equipped. The Commander of the combined U.S. and Philippine Army forces was General Douglas MacArthur, a former Chief of Staff of the American army who had been loaned to the Philippines to organize that country's future armies.* At the time of the Japanese attack, he had completed six years of a ten-year plan for accomplishing this task.

Because of the time difference between Hawaii and the Philippines, American officials in Manila received word of the Japanese attack on Pearl Harbor just after 3:00 A.M. on December 8. Major General Lewis H. Brereton, MacArthur's Air Commander, wanted to prepare an immediate attack against Japanese targets on the island of Formosa, a request that MacArthur denied. Brereton did order his planes into the air, hoping to avoid having them caught on the ground as they had at Pearl Harbor. The Japanese attacking force on Formosa, however, was fogged in and no morning raid came. Around noon the fighters protecting Clark were recalled for refueling—the bombers were already back on the ground. Unfortunately, the fog over Formosa had lifted about 30 minutes earlier and a fleet of Japanese war planes—108 Mitsubishi bombers and 84 Zeroes—were roaring toward the Philippines. By this time most of the American flyers were at lunch.

As at Pearl Harbor, the Japanese pilots could hardly believe their eyes. The American planes were bunched up together, almost wingtip to wingtip. When the bombs began to fall at around 12:30 P.M., the American pilots ran to their planes but only four of them got off the ground. In the next hour, the Japanese obliterated Clark Field to the point that it was unrecognizable. All the hangers were destroyed as were the operations office, the field's headquarters, and the fighter control shack. All of the B-17 bombers, with the exception of one that was airborne, were destroyed on the ground. Fifty-three P-40 fighter planes and some 30 other planes were destroyed, while 80 servicemen were killed and 150 wounded. In one hour of fighting, MacArthur had lost one-half of his airforce.

---

*MacArthur's father had been the first military governor in the American rule of the island.

In the week that followed the big raid on Clark Field, small Japanese forces landed on Luzon, the Philippine's northern-most island. These were simply diversionary forces. The main Japanese attack came at dawn on December 22, when 43,000 troops under the command of Lieutenant General Masaharu Homma landed on the beaches of Lingayen Gulf, 120 miles north of Manila. A small force also came ashore at Lamon Bay, 70 miles southeast of Manila. Originally, MacArthur had intended to fight for all of the Philippines, but the swift movement of the Japanese forces caused him to revive an old contingency plan, which was to pull back all his forces on Luzon into the Bataan Peninsula. Shaped like a miniature Florida, Bataan was twenty-five miles long and twenty miles wide at the neck. Down its spine, jungle-clad volcanoes rose to nearly 5,000 feet There were just two roads into the peninsula, one dirt and the other cobblestoned. There were also dense jungles, precipitous cliffs and treacherous ravines.

Moving into Bataan meant leaving Manila to the Japanese without a fight but it was believed that American and Filipino forces on the island of Corregidor at the entrance to Manila Bay would deny the Japanese the use of Manila harbor.* MacArthur surmised that the strategic withdrawal would delay the Japanese Pacific and relieve the Philippine defenders.

On January 9, 1942, the battle for the Bataan Peninsula began. For over two weeks Homma's forces battered the American and Filipino lines. With complete control of the air, the Japanese broke through and MacArthur ordered a withdrawal to a new defensive line halfway down the peninsula. New Japanese amphibious landings behind the line were contained and by mid-February, Homma's forces were so bogged down that he called off the offensive. With more than 7,000 dead and wounded and more than 10,000 troops down with malaria and other tropical diseases, Homma asked Tokyo for reinforcements. The unexpectedly determined resistance had checked the Japanese advance.

General MacArthur continually bombarded Washington with requests for carrier raids against the Japanese, for transports bringing reinforcements, for freighters with supplies, for aircraft (he begged for "just three planes") even for submarines carrying cargoes of ammunition. Washington responded with encouraging messages. But neither supplies nor reinforcements arrived. By February, there was no more talk about convoys headed toward the Philippines. Tired of looking to the skies for planes or to the ocean for supply ships, American infantrymen wrote "caustic doggerels which became epitaphs for their brave stand." The most famous stanza went:

> *We're the battling bastards of Bataan:*
> *No mama, no papa, no Uncle Sam,*
> *No aunts, no uncles, no nephews, no nieces,*
> *No rifles, no planes, or artillery pieces,*
> *And nobody gives a damn.*

On February 22, Roosevelt sent a telegram to MacArthur ordering him to leave the Philippines and go to Australia to organize the war from there. MacArthur had been prepared to stay to the end, to be taken prisoner or to die. But he could not refuse an order from his Commander-in-Chief. On March 10, he summoned Major General Jonathan Wainwright, one of the corps commanders on Bataan, to his fortress headquarters on Corregidor. He told Wainwright of his departure order and assigned him to command the forces on Luzon. The next night, MacArthur, his wife and son, and some of his staff departed from Corregidor onboard a PT boat skippered by Lieutenant John Bulkeley. After a perilous journey through waters infested with Japanese ships they arrived on Mindanao, the southernmost of the Philippine islands, 500 miles to the south. From there MacArthur's party flew in a B-17 to Darwin, Australia. Shortly after his arrival, MacArthur appeared before news reporters and concluded his short statement to them with the now famous words, "I came through and I shall return."

---

*The fortress of Corregidor was built in the seventeenth century by the Spanish. It was interlaced with tunnels and provided with large mortars whose shells could reach the mainland.

By the end of March, Homma's forces were reinforced with over 20,000 troops, new field guns and bombers. On April 2, they struck and by the next morning, the stalemate on Bataan came to an end, as the front crumbled. Some 2000 persons managed to escape by boat or barge to Corregidor. A final U.S.-Filipino counterattack was called off and on April 9, Major General Edward King Jr., the American Commander on Bataan, surrendered his remaining 76,000 men to the Japanese. Utilizing Corregidor's Malinta Tunnel, an elaborate network of underground passages reinforced with concrete, Wainwright continued to hold out. The island's coastal guns and mortars were supplemented by 14-inch and 6-inch guns and delivered formidable blows against the Japanese.

Still, the final outcome was never in doubt. For nearly a month, the American and Filipino troops on Corregidor were bombarded by Japanese artillery. The terror of the shelling compounded the hunger and fatigue of the isolated garrison. On May 2, Corregidor's last big gun emplacement was hit and destroyed. Three days later Homma's forces landed on Corregidor, and on May 6, Wainwright surrendered not just Corregidor but all forces in the Philippines, much to the dismay of General MacArthur. Most American and Filipinos complied with the surrender order although some disappeared into the hills and jungles where they carried out guerilla activities against the Japanese until MacArthur and the Americans returned two and one-half years later.

A terrible fate still lay ahead for the surviving garrisons of Bataan and Corregidor. Those from Corregidor were not fed for a week and they were hauled on freighters to Manila where they were driven through the streets, before being shipped by train to an improvised prison camp.

Bataan's survivors suffered an even tougher ordeal. The 76,000 prisoners were far more in number than the Japanese expected, and far worse in health—most were sick and starving. The Japanese lacked the trucks and trains to transport the prisoners and so most of them were forced to travel the 65 miles to the Prisoner-of-War Camp—Camp O'Donnel—by foot. The Japanese soldiers, who regarded surrender as anathema and looked down upon those who did surrender, were cruel in the extreme. Stragglers were shot, clubbed, or bayonetted and some were even buried alive. Over 300 Filipino soldiers were beheaded. The so-called Bataan Death March claimed between 7,000 and 10,000 American and Filipino troops. Some of the survivors managed to escape into the jungles during the long march and joined the growing Filipino resistance. In all, more Americans and Filipinos died on the march than on the battlefields of Bataan.

Such Japanese actions in the Philippines were not systematic nor sanctioned by General Homma, whose orders for humane treatment of the captives were thwarted on the spot by his subordinates. Still, it was Homma who was ultimately held responsible for the atrocities, and after the war he was tried, convicted, and executed as one of Japan's war criminals.

Whereas the Philippines were the center of American influence in the Pacific, British interests centered on Malaya and its impressive island naval base of Singapore, at the southern-most tip of the peninsula. Known as the "Pearl of the Orient," it set astride the Straits of Malaca, controlling passage from the Pacific into the Indian Ocean. Since it lay at the southern end of 200 miles of jungle, Singapore was considered by the British to be impregnable to a land attack. In their mind the only danger to it lay in a naval attack.* Consequently all the big guns, the most modern artillery available, pointed seawards to protect the great naval fortress from such an eventuality. Fixed in concrete they could not be turned to fire on an enemy who came over land.

On the same day that Japan attacked Pearl Harbor, her 25th Army, commanded by Lieut. General Tomayuki Yamashita, landed at Kota Bharu in Malaya.** Although they put up a stubborn defense, the British defenders soon pulled back and within 24 hours Kota Bharu and the air base, still intact, were in Japanese hands. From this point, Yamashita proposed to advance down the peninsula, with the

---

*Singapore was regarded as one of the four greatest sea fortresses in the world. The other three were Pearl Harbor, Malta, and Gibraltar.

**The Japanese attack on Malaya occurred approximately one hour before Japanese planes began bombing Pearl Harbor.

main attack along its west coast, and a secondary drive along the east coast. Difficult jungle terrain would be bypassed by sea, and the two forces would eventually converge for the assault on Singapore. Although the British troops in Malaya outnumbered the Japanese, they were indeed a rather motley crew, made up of Australians, British, Indians, and native Malayans. Few were trained or equipped for jungle fighting, and they were short of tanks, artillery, spare parts and air support. Malaya was only fourth on the list of British military priorities, behind Great Britain itself, the Middle East, and Russia.

Japanese soldiers, on the other hand, were well-trained and equipped for jungle fighting. They had lightweight weapons and clothing and could exist on a few handfuls of rice and dried fish. The jungle did not seem to hold the same fear for the Japanese as it did for the British troops. In addition, the Japanese had tanks, which the British lacked. Many also had bicycles, and when their tires burst under the hot sun or were punctured, the Japanese simply rode on the rims. To the retreating British the resulting clamor sounded like tanks and added to their fear.

An indication of just how ill-prepared British forces really were came even before Kota Bharu fell. At 4:30 A.M. on December 8, Japanese Navy bombers raided Singapore. The lights of the city remained on during the entire attack because no one knew how to turn them off. Warning sirens never went off (until after the Japanese had left), and civilian defense offices were empty. Much of this ineptness resulted from British racism. Similar to the Americans prior to the Pearl Harbor attack, the British looked down on Orientals. They believed that the Japanese could not fight well because of poor vision and that poor balance, caused by being carried on their mothers' backs as babies, prevented them from being good pilots. The Japanese soon laid these myths to rest.

At sunset of December 8, the British dispatched a six ship taskforce from Singapore to seek out and destroy the Japanese invasion forces along the Malayan coast. The task force consisted of four destroyers and two newcomers to the Pacific, the battle cruiser *Repulse* and the battleship *Prince of Wales*.* On the ninth, Japanese air patrols spotted the task force and Admiral Sir Tom Phillips turned his ships back toward Singapore. However, a report of another Japanese landing along the coast caused him to turn once again in order to attack. Land-based Japanese torpedo planes now located the task force (known as Z force) and attacked. Lacking air support, the British lost the *Repulse* and the *Prince of Wales* within an hour of each other. About two-thirds of the crews were rescued by the destroyers, but British naval power in Malaya was now virtually destroyed.

On land the Japanese rushed ahead. By mid-January, the Japanese controlled two-thirds of Malaya. The British land commander in Malaya, Lieut. General A.E. Percival, was ordered to pull back to Jahore, Malaya's southernmost state, separated from Singapore by a shallow, one-mile channel of water. Here, the British fought tenaciously, but when one end of their defensive line was breached, they were forced to cross the Straits of Jahore and retreat into Singapore itself. On February 8, 1942, the Japanese attacked across the straits. By this time Singapore was in ruins, being bombed now around the clock. The island's water supply was running out, as was the British will to resist. On Sunday, February 15, General Percival met General Yamashita at the Ford Motor Company assembly plant, and surrendered to the Japanese, the greatest military defeat ever suffered by the British.** Over 80,000 British and Commonwealth troops were captured by the Japanese, doomed to hard years of captivity similar to those depicted on screen in the movie, "Bridge over the River Kawi." Many did not survive at the hands of an enemy, who looked down upon those who surrendered.*** Indeed, there were many stories of Japanese atrocities in Malaya. Two hundred Australian and Indian troops

---

*The *Prince of Wales* was a new ship, the pride and joy of the Royal Navy. Churchill had used it the previous August to cross the Atlantic and meet with President Roosevelt off Newfoundland.

**From this time on, Yamashita was known as the Tiger of Malaya. After the war he was tried and executed as a Japanese war criminal.

***The Japanese claimed that not one Japanese soldier was captured in the Malayan fighting.

were decapitated; 300 patients and staff at a military hospital were bayonetted. Accustomed to being brutalized by their own superiors, Japanese infantrymen did not hesitate to "pass it on" to the enemy.

The British had lost Hong Kong and Malaya to the Japanese. It was now Burma's turn. An isolated, mountainous country, Burma had been a British possession since the late 19th century. It had separated from India in 1937 and the British had paid little attention to her defenses since that time. The Japanese goals in Burma were to cut the "Burma Road," which began in Lashio and extended to Chungking in China; and to create a buffer zone to guard against a possible British offensive from India. The Japanese probably also considered the possibility of using Burma to launch an attack on India, but this was not the main motivation behind the invasion.

The Burma campaign began on December 23, 1941, with a Japanese bombing of Burma's capital, the port city of Rangoon.* This was followed by continuous bombing attacks for the next week. The land attack, which began in early January, 1942, entered Rangoon in March—an important acquisition because of its harbor, oil refineries, and commodities, which had been left intact, as many Burmese workers had fled in panic. The Japanese then moved up the Irrawaddy River, pushing back the British forces (Indian and Burmese soldiers were under British Commanders) and Chinese troops who had entered Burma to help protect the "Burma Road." They took Lashio, then Mandalay. So intimidated were the British that they decided to evacuate Burma and take refuge in India, a decision carried out with great difficulty and high losses. The monsoon season finally put an end to the fighting, but the main supply route to China was cut and Japanese troops were now poised at the border of India.**

The other great Asian empire to fall to the Japanese in the first 100 days of the war was that belonging to the Dutch in the East Indian Islands. This area was particularly attractive to the Japanese because it contained oil, which Japan lacked. The Japanese plan was to move through the numerous islands, Timor, Borneo, the Celebes, and Sumatra, the second largest of the Dutch East Indies and the location of perhaps the best oil wells in Asia. When all of these objectives had been taken, the island of Java, another oil producing island and the headquarters of American-British-Dutch operations in southeastern Asia, would be invaded.

Nearly 100,000 Dutch soldiers were in the East Indies, but lacked up-to-date equipment, and they quickly surrendered, almost without fighting. A combined Allied fleet—British, American, Dutch, and Australian—under the command of Rear Admiral Karel Doorman, did try to forestall the invasion of Java. On February 27, the Battle of the Java Sea began, when the Allied forces encountered two Japanese convoys. For three days the battle raged. In the end, only one Japanese destroyer was sunk while the Allied force lost two cruisers and three destroyers.*** The Japanese invasion of Java went ahead as planned. On March 9, in Batavia, the Dutch formally surrendered the East Indies to the Japanese, ending three centuries of Dutch control of the island Archipelago.

In April, 1942, a Japanese naval force, commanded by Admiral Nagumo, forayed into the Indian Ocean, attacking the British fleet in harbor at Colombo, Ceylon (today Sri Lanka) with carrier aircraft. The British Admiral, Sir James Somerville, was alerted to Nagumo's presence, since the Allies had by this time broken the Japanese naval code (see Chapter 16). Thus, there were no British ships at Colombo when the attackers appeared. The Japanese did later sink two British cruisers, which approached the Japanese aircraft carriers, and some merchant shipping. On April 9, they also sank a British aircraft carrier, but then withdrew from the Indian Ocean, never to reappear again. Their losses were only five bombers and six fighters. But they had failed to destroy the British Indian Ocean fleet.

---

*In January, 1942, the warehouses in Rangoon contained over 100,000 tons of goods intended for Chungking.

**The new supply route to China was an air route from India over the world's highest mountains, the Himalayas, into China. This became known as flying the "hump."

***This was the first combat for the Dutch Navy in 150 years.

With the conquests of the Philippines, Malaya and Singapore, Hong Kong, Burma, and the Dutch East Indies, the amazing succession of Japanese conquests came to an end. In the area now controlled by the Japanese lay 80 percent of the world's rubber, 54 percent of its tin, 19 percent of the tungsten, as well as large supplies of oil, iron ore, and manganese. But before the Japanese could even begin to organize these assets, indeed even before their amazing series of victories had come to an end, the tide of battle began to turn.

Chapter XVI
The Turning Points

❖   ❖   ❖

Beginning in April, 1942, a series of American actions in the Pacific first began to stem the Japanese victory tide, then stopped it. This chapter will examine those events.

The first of the American actions was more symbolic than it was effectual. Its origin lay in an earlier desire expressed by President Roosevelt to bomb Japan in order to gain revenge for the sneak attack on Pearl Harbor. Although the distances involved in such an attack seemed prohibitive, a member of Fleet Admiral Ernest J. King's staff raised the possibility of launching U.S. Army bombers from an aircraft carrier.

By March, 1942, twenty four American air crews were training in modified twin-engined B-25 bombers for just such a raid. Their commander was Lieutenant James H. Doolittle, the first man to fly across the United States in twelve hours. Sixteen crews were selected from those undergoing training and on April 1, 1942, they boarded the aircraft carrier *Hornet* and set sail across the Pacific.

The attack's scenario called for the *Hornet* to sail to a point about 500 miles from Japan before launching her aircraft. Thirteen planes would bomb Tokyo (each carried four bombs) and one each would hit the Japanese cities of Nagoya, Kobe, and Osaka. The planes would not return to the carrier but would overfly Japan and make for small fields in friendly parts of China.

Early on April 18, while the *Hornet* and its accompanying ships were still more than 700 miles from Japan, two enemy patrol ships were detected, one of which began sending a message in the clear that enemy aircraft carriers had been sighted 700 miles from Japan.* Both patrol boats were sunk, but rather than steam closer to Japan and risk the loss of the carriers, the order was given to launch the Doolittle raiders at the extreme range of over 700 miles.

Japanese headquarters in Tokyo received the patrol boat's message and was aware that an aerial attack was imminent but believed it wouldn't come for another day because of the 700 mile distance of the American forces. Japan was unaware that twin engine bombers were on board the American carriers with sufficient range to fly the 700 miles.

Just as Doolittle's planes reached Tokyo an air raid drill was just coming to an end, and many Japanese believed the attack to be just a realistic conclusion to the air raid drill. The planes were over their targets for only about six minutes, and the bombs they dropped did not do great damage to the Japanese ability to wage war. In fact, as far as physical damage was concerned, the raid was probably a failure. But it was a decided shock to the people of Japan who had been led to believe that their homeland was inviolate to attack. It also caused the Japanese high command to move additional air defense units to the home islands, units needed elsewhere, to protect against any future attacks.

The impact on American morale was also significant. For a country which had experienced an unending series of military defeats in the Pacific, including the recent Bataan Death March, it was reassuring to know America could go over to the attack. And the raid seemed to be a sign that the United States was set to begin to roll back the Japanese gains in Asia.

---

*On April 13, a task force including the aircraft carrier *Enterprise* had joined the *Hornet*.

None of Doolittle's planes were shot down over Japan. One B-25 flew on to Vladivostok in the Soviet Union where the crew and plane were interned by the Russians, who had a valid non-Aggression Pact with Japan. The other fifteen planes came down in Japanese-occupied China. The premature take-off had made it impossible for them to reach friendly bases in China. Three men were killed either in crash landing or in bailing out of the planes, and eight were captured. These eight were brought to Tokyo to stand trial. The trial lasted only one-half day and no English translations or interpreters were provided by the Japanese. Three of the eight were sentenced to death, and another of the prisoners died in captivity. Those of the attack force who survived, including Doolittle, worked their ways to friendly Chinese lines, and were eventually returned to the United States. When Doolittle finally returned to the United States, he was awarded the Congressional Medal of Honor, the highest honor accorded by the United States government.

The second major turning point in the Pacific War followed soon upon the heels of the first. Indeed, Doolittle's raid caused the Japanese to accelerate their plans in the Pacific, which included neutralizing Australia and destroying the remainder of the United States Pacific fleet. Pursuit of these goals led to the Battle of the Coral Sea, where American planes and ships inflicted the first real wound of the war on Japan.

The Coral Sea lies off the northeast coast of Australia. It is often described as one of the world's most beautiful bodies of water and is buffeted by warm, summer-like breezes year round. Japanese plans in the area called for a three-prong attack. One Japanese force would seize the island of Tulagi in the Solomons for a seaplane base. Another Japanese force of 12 troop transports under the protection of the new light carrier *Shoho* and four cruisers, would advance south from the Japanese bastion at Rabaul, and land troops near Port Moresby in New Guinea. This would put Japanese forces within easy striking distance of Australia and threaten American supply lines to that continent.

A third Japanese force consisting of two heavy cruisers, six destroyers, and two aircraft carriers *Shokaku* and *Zuikaku*, both veterans of the raid on Pearl Harbor, would provide protection for the Tulagi attack and then move into position to do the same for the landing at Port Moresby. Japanese leaders did not really anticipate any American resistance to their plans. Their intelligence services indicated that the United States had only three carriers left and that they were with the force that had recently launched the Doolittle raid.

The United States was aware of the Japanese plans, however, well before the operations ever got underway. American codebreakers had cracked enough of Japan's operational code, JN-25, to reveal most of the Japanese plan. Radio traffic analyses of Japanese fleet movements provided the rest. By the end of April, Chester A. Nimitz, Commander-in-Chief of the Pacific Fleet, had the basic details of the Japanese plans in his possession.

Nimitz decided to attempt to stem the Japanese move into the Coral Sea. Even though he could not match the stronger Japanese force, he hoped that surprise and clever placement of his ships could stop the Japanese forces. He placed Rear Admiral Frank J. Fletcher, already in the area on board the aircraft carrier *Yorktown*, in command of the American Task Force 17. Fletcher was to join up with Task Force 11, built around the aircraft carrier *Lexington*.* These two forces were then to merge with a force of four cruisers coming up from Australia. All in all, Fletcher's total force would be equal to about half that of the Japanese.

On May 3, the Japanese occupied Tulagi. Fletcher decided to hit back at the Tulagi force. Shielded from Japanese search planes by frequent rain squalls, his ships avoided detection and on May 4, American planes hit Tulagi. The attacks did little damage; four Japanese landing craft were sunk and one destroyer damaged.** The attack force lost three planes.

---

* The Japanese incorrectly believed that a submarine had sunk the *Lexington* in January, 1942.

**American pilots experienced problems with accuracy when their windows and gunsights fogged over as the planes dropped from higher and colder air into the lower, warmer atmosphere.

The Japanese, however, were shocked by the attack. They now knew that at least one American aircraft carrier was in the area, and they began their search. On May 7, the day after the American surrender at Corregidor was completed, Japanese planes located and hit the American tanker *Neosho* and her escort destroyer, *Sims*. The *Sims* sank almost immediately while the *Neosho* drifted helplessly for four days before the American destroyer *Henley* found her, took aboard the survivors, and then sank her with torpedoes.

On the same day, planes from the *Yorktown* and *Lexington* accidentally stumbled upon the *Shoho* and four heavy cruisers. At 10:50 A.M. 93 American planes began their attack. The *Shoho* was caught by surprise and by 11:25 it was all over. She sank with all but three of her airplanes and more than 600 of her 900 man crew, the first Japanese ship larger than a destroyer sunk by American forces in the war.

On May 8, planes from the Japanese force attacked the American ships, and planes from the *Yorktown* and the *Enterprise* went after the *Shokaku* and the *Zuikaku* which ducked into a dense rain squall and escaped. The *Shokaku* avoided attacks by the torpedo planes, but dive bombers made direct hits, starting fires. When her crew brought the fires under control, the *Shokaku* headed for home.

Almost simultaneously, Japanese planes attacked the American carriers, both of which were hit. The *Lexington* was particularly hard hit and by late afternoon on May 8, the captain gave the order to abandon ship. Amazingly, even though 216 men died as a result of the bombing attack, 2735 other men (including the captain and his dog, "wags") went over the side and were rescued without one drowning. At 10:00 P.M. the destroyer *Phelps* finished off the *Lexington's* burning hulk. The *Yorktown*, although losing 37 men, was able to bring her fires under control and to still operate at a respectable 24 knots of speed.

The sinking of the *Lexington* was a tactical victory for the Japanese, but strategically the United States came out ahead. Most of *Lexington's* crew survived to man new American carriers, while the *Yorktown* was repaired in time to be an important factor in the Battle of Midway. The damaged *Shokaku* reached Japan on May 17, where experts decided repairs would take three months. Four days later the *Zaikaku* reached home port, undamaged, but with her air group in tatters. Since there were no replacement groups that could be transferred to her, the *Zaikaku* had to draw new pilots fresh out of training and integrate them into the remaining squadrons, a process requiring two-to-three months. Japanese carrier strength was thus reduced by one-third, perhaps tipping the scales in America's favor at the Battle of Midway in the following month.

Equally as important to the Americans, however, was the fact that the Japanese transports headed for Port Moresby turned back, and for the first time in the war, a Japanese invasion had been thwarted. Of course, the resulting boast to American morale was significant. Newspapers headlined, "Japanese Repulsed in Great Pacific Battle," and coming on the heels of Doolittle's raid, made the Japanese juggernaut no longer seem so invincible and finally, the Coral Sea conflict was the first naval battle in history in which the opposing fleets never saw each other. It was, in fact, the world's first battle between aircraft carriers, as planes from each side attacked the other. As such, the battle set a precedent for forthcoming naval battles in the Pacific, a format in which the United States was to prove far superior to the Japanese.

Fighting in the Coral Sea further enhanced Admiral Yamamoto's belief that Japanese security in its conquered areas of the Pacific could only be safeguarded with the complete destruction of the American Pacific fleet. The task begun at Pearl Harbor had to be completed, and in particular, the backbone of the fleet, the aircraft carriers, had to be brought into decisive battle and crushed. However weakened by the strike at Pearl Harbor, the American Pacific fleet was still a menace to Japan and thus had to be annihilated.

To accomplish this, Yamamoto developed a rather complex scheme to lure out the American fleet, so that it could be destroyed. The target he selected as the bait was the American base on Midway Island, some 1,000 miles from Pearl Harbor. But Midway was only a means to an end. It was to be the bait that would lure the United States into battle. So close was Midway to Pearl Harbor and indeed to the United States mainland, reasoned Yamamoto, that an attack there would draw out the American fleet from Pearl Harbor, which Japan then could destroy. Yamamoto also provided for a diversionary attack on the American held Aleutian Islands, extending down off the coast of Alaska. This would serve to divide the ships of the American fleet and make easier its total destruction.

Yamamoto's plan called for one battle group to carry out the attack on the Aleutians. A second force, the First Carrier Striking Force, commanded by Vice Admiral Nagumo who had also commanded the Pearl Harbor attack, would smash Midway itself, so that Japanese troops could land on the island. Then when the Americans steamed out of Pearl Harbor, Yamamoto's main force, several hundred miles away from Midway, would join the warships already there and together they would blow the American Pacific fleet out of the water.

Japanese numerical superiority was overwhelming. Yamamoto's armada included eight aircraft carriers to three for the Americans, 20 cruisers to 8; and 60 destroyers to 14. Against eleven Japanese battleships, the Americans had none; the 6 battleships that had survived the Pearl Harbor attack were still too damaged to use. The Americans did have a 19–15 superiority in submarines but these were not to be decisive vessels in the Midway fighting. Finally, on Midway itself the Americans had only about 100 planes to confront the nearly 700 aircraft available to the Japanese. Since Yamamoto did not believe any American aircraft carriers were in the vicinity of Midway, he assumed that the Japanese aircraft superiority would remain, even when the American carriers did appear.

What Yamamoto and the Japanese did not realize was that United States naval intelligence had, as in the case of the Coral Sea, learned about the Japanese attack. By mid-May it was clear that a major Japanese offensive in the Pacific was planned against a target referred to as AF. Lieutenant Commander Joseph Rochefort, Chief of the 14th naval District's Combat Intelligence unit, was convinced that AF was Midway. To test his thesis, he sent out a bogus message in a code which the U.S. believed (rightfully so) that the Japanese had broken. The message reported the breakdown of the water distillation plant on Midway. Two days later, a Japanese message, intercepted by the United States, reported that island AF was short of fresh water. It was clear that Midway was to be the primary Japanese target.

With the knowledge of the planned Japanese attack, Nimitz ordered the aircraft carriers *Hornet* and *Enterprise* back to Pearl Harbor as fast as they could. They arrived on May 26 and were followed the next day by the *Yorktown*, trailing a 10 mile oil slick from her Coral Sea battle damages. The estimate was that the ship would need 90 days to be put back into fighting shape; Nimitz gave the repair facilities 72 hours to get the job done.

Preparations to face the Japanese onslaught also began on Midway Island itself. Bunkers were built, tunnels dug, mines laid and new anti-aircraft batteries were installed. What few planes the navy could spare were also sent to Midway. Thirty Catalina Flying Boats were provided to fly patrols up to 700 miles around the island. But Nimitz made it clear that Midway could expect no assistance from the United States carriers, which were lying in hiding for the Japanese Carrier Striking Force.

On May 28, the *Hornet* and *Enterprise* and Task Force 16 left Pearl Harbor and steamed towards Midway. Two days later, Task Force 17, with the *Yorktown*, hastily followed. Fourteen hundred workmen had accomplished 3 months' work in two days. Command of Task Force 16 had almost literally fallen into the hands of Rear Admiral Raymond Spruance, when Vice Admiral William (Bill) Halsey fell ill and had to be hospitalized. Spruance had no experience with aircraft carriers, but he was known as a brilliant tactician and Nimitz respected his intellect. In command of Task Force 17 and in tactical charge of both forces was Rear Admiral Jack Fletcher. The two forces rendezvoused on June 2, some 300 miles northeast of Midway Island.

On June 3, the Japanese attacked in the Aleutians, bombing the United States base at Dutch Harbor. They ultimately occupied the islands of Attu and Kiska. On June 4, Nagumo's First Carrier Force launched its air strike against Midway. An American patrol craft spotted the Japanese carriers and reported that planes were heading for Midway. This alerted the American carriers hiding northeast of Midway. American fighter planes circling above Midway managed to shoot down three of the

Japanese bombers, but succumbed to the faster Japanese Zeros flying escort. But despite an intense bombing attack, Midway's runways and anti-aircraft batteries were still intact when the Japanese departed. The Japanese decided a second attack was necessary. Nagumo was particularly worried because his own fleet had been under attack by planes from Midway, and although they did not score a single hit, Nagumo realized these aircraft had to be destroyed before Midway could be invaded.

He thus ordered his torpedo planes, which had been kept back to deal with any American ships which might appear, rearmed with bombs in order to attack facilities on Midway.

On board the *Enterprise*, Admiral Spruance, now aware of the Japanese fleet, launched all of his aircraft from the *Enterprise* and *Hornet* at the maximum range of some 170 miles from the Japanese fleet. He hoped to gain the element of surprise. Not all of the planes found the enemy. Among those that did, the losses were high. Only one man from Torpedo Squadron 8 from the *Hornet* survived that group's attack on the Japanese carriers.* Ten of the fourteen planes from Torpedo Squadron 6 of the *Enterprise* were shot down, as were ten of the twelve planes from Torpedo Squadron 3 of the *Yorktown*. A few managed to launch their torpedoes, but they scored no hits. All in all, only 54 of 200 American carrier planes remained after the initial attack.

Nagumo recalled his fighter protection after the torpedo plane attack had been repulsed in order to refuel them. He also began to replace the bombs on his aircraft with torpedoes in order to attack the American ships that had launched the attack. Just as he was readying to do so, American dive bombers appeared over his fleet. None of the Japanese fighters that had just begun taking off had sufficient altitude to deal with the attackers. Within five minutes the attack was over and the whole nature of World War II in the Pacific was changed. The Japanese aircraft carriers, *Akagi*, *Soryu*, and *Kaga* were mortally damaged and sinking.

The last of Nagumo's four carriers, the *Hiryu*, was still very much alive, however, and its dive bombers and fighters took off seeking revenge. One of the pilots cleverly followed the returning American planes directly back to the *Yorktown*. Eight Japanese planes reached the *Yorktown* and three bomb hits left the ship dead in the water. A second Japanese attack left two torpedo hits on the *Yorktown*, and the ship listing dangerously in the water. The order was given to abandon the ship.

Meanwhile, American planes searched for the *Hiryu* and at about 3:30 P.M. spotted her. Four bombs hit the big flat-top and started massive fires. For seven hours, her crew struggled to save her, but just before midnight an explosion blew out her insides, and her captain ordered the ship abandoned. With his four largest aircraft carriers destroyed, Yamamoto canceled the Midway operation. That same day a Japanese submarine torpedoed the *Yorktown* under tow, and the next morning that gallant ship finally sank.

Yamamoto's failed plan had cost the Japanese four aircraft carriers, one cruiser, 322 planes and 3500 men, including at least 100 first-line and irreplaceable pilots. The numerically smaller American force lost one aircraft carrier, one destroyer (sunk by a Japanese submarine), 150 planes, and 307 lives.

The Japanese people were not told about the Midway defeat. The wounded were brought back to Japan and were kept in isolation wards and not allowed to communicate with the outside world. Indeed, when the war ended, papers relating to the Midway disaster were destroyed, and it was only in the 1950s when survivors began to publish their memoirs that the Japanese people learned the true toll of the Midway disaster.

The Japanese Navy never recovered from this battle, and would never return to the offensive. In fact, the only Japanese offensive after this time was to be in China. Basically, from this time forward, it was the Americans who were on the offense and the Japanese the ones forced to react to American attacks. Thus, the Battle of Midway was the decisive turning point in the Pacific War.

---

*The man was Ensign George Gay who clung to a raft and watched the Battle of Midway from the water.

Chapter XVII
America on the Offensive

❖   ❖   ❖

In March, 1942, before any of the pivotal events discussed in the previous chapter had occurred, at a time when things indeed looked bleak for the United States, President Roosevelt made an important command decision. He divided the Pacific front against Japan between two commanders: General Douglas MacArthur and Admiral Chester Nimitz.

MacArthur was to exercise control over Australia, the Philippines, the Solomon islands, and most of the Dutch East Indies. The rest of the Pacific fell to Nimitz. All amphibious operations, however, were to be under Nimitz' direction, a decision that was difficult to stand by and often ran counter to logical reasoning. MacArthur opposed the division, writing:

Of all the faulty decisions of the war, perhaps the most inexpressible one was the failure to unify the command in the Pacific....It resulted in divided effort, the waste of diffusion and duplication of force, and undue extension of war with added casualties and cost.

MacArthur's initial problem, however, was defending Australia, where he was put in command of all Allied troops. Although he found scant resources for stopping the Japanese sweep towards that country, he decided nonetheless that the best way to protect it was to throw as much weight as he could into New Guinea, the island just to the north of Australia, where the Japanese had established footholds early in 1942. He felt it particularly imperative that the Japanese be kept on the far side of the rugged Owen Stanley Mountains which bisected the island.

At the Battle of the Coral Sea, discussed in the previous chapter, the Japanese attempt to bypass the Owen Stanleys and land troops at Port Moresby had been thwarted. Nevertheless, on July 21, 1942, they did land troops at Buna on the northern coast of that part of New Guinea known as Papua. The ultimate objective of the landing was Port Moresby, which lay beyond the Owen Stanley range in southern Papua. The pathway they followed was the so-called Kokoda trail, a narrow, shoulder-wide footpath running along precipitous slopes for nearly 100 miles.

The Japanese pushed along this treacherous route until by mid-September, they were only thirty miles from Port Moresby. But Australian reinforcements, and Japanese shortage of supplies caused the offensive to falter. Many of the Japanese were ill with malaria and dysentery, and their rations were exhausted. No reinforcements were available to the Japanese commander, and Imperial General Headquarters ordered him to withdraw back to Buna and hold on there until reinforcements could be made available.* The fighting in Papua was some of the "nastiest" of the whole war. As Australian troops drove the Japanese back to the Buna coast in November, they found human skeletons and evidence of cannibalism. Meanwhile, American units landed near Buna and joined the fight. By January, 1943, the Japanese had been cleared from the Buna area. Thus, six months after the beginning of their overland drive to Moresby and about one year after securing their footing on the northern coast, the Japanese in New Guinea were back to where they had started. General MacArthur proclaimed that the Allies had

---
*Most Japanese reinforcements were earmarked for Guadalcanal, where American troops had landed in August.

won "a striking victory" in Papua. But in two months of savage fighting, the Allies lost 3,095 killed and 5,451 wounded—a higher total than the better known Guadalcanal campaign.

While the fighting in New Guinea was in full swing, the United States undertook its first amphibious operation in the Pacific. Thus far, in the months since Pearl Harbor, the Japanese had appeared to be unstoppable. The American victory at Midway was not yet recognized as the turning point it was, although it was generally acknowledged that the Japanese navy had experienced a major, serious defeat. But the Japanese army, as of the summer of 1942, had tasted no defeat at all. In August, 1942, the United States army set out to change that.

In May, 1942, the Japanese seized the island of Tulagi in the Solomon Islands and then a month later crossed over to the island of Guadalcanal, where they started to build an airfield. An air base on Guadalcanal would be a serious matter for the Allies. Planes from the island would be within striking range of other Allied-held islands while Japanese shipping operating from Tulagi would threaten the main shipping routes from the United States to Australia. Guadalcanal and Tulagi, therefore, had to be retaken before they became operational.

Technically, the area concerned lay in the jurisdiction of General MacArthur, but since he and Admiral Nimitz disagreed on the best way to meet the Japanese threat, the demarcation line was moved westward one degree so that both Guadalcanal and Tulagi now lay in Nimitz' sphere, and he was given the directive to seize the two islands.

The assaults on Tulagi and Guadalcanal came at dawn on August 7 and caught the Japanese completely by surprise. Their troops on Tulagi held out for only 31 hours, but the American invaders received a taste of what they would often experience in the Pacific War. The Japanese holed up in deep caves in the hills back of the shore, forcing the Americans to clear them one by one. And rather than surrender, the Tulagi defenders made last-ditch suicide charges across open fields. The fighting was also ferocious on two neighboring islets—Gavutu and Tanambogo, which were linked together by a causeway. The capture of these three islands cost the U.S. Marines, 144 dead. Over 700 Japanese troops were killed; 23 were captured, of whom only 3 actually surrendered. Guadalcanal was Japan's southernmost outpost, lying just ten degrees below the Equator. It was 92 miles long and 33 miles wide, and appeared to be a tropical paradise. Yet, its green forested mountains contained malaria-carrying mosquitoes; crocodiles, giant lizards, poisonous snakes and spiders. Indeed, it was more of a paradise lost than a true paradise.

The Marine landing on Guadalcanal—under the command of Major General Alexander Vandegrift—was unopposed. Japanese construction workers laboring on the airfield simply fled back into the jungle, along with the sailors who had brought them over from Tulagi. The marines seized the airfield the next day, after a brief skirmish with a small Japanese force. The field was basically intact and nearly ready for use. However, the Marines were soon to discover that there was a big difference between seizing the airfield and holding on to it.

On the night of August 8–9, the United States Navy suffered a major setback when Japanese ships attacked an American force of six cruisers and six destroyers patrolling off Savo Island at the western entrance to Guadalcanal. In 40 minutes the battle was over. Two Allied cruisers were sunk and another two so badly damaged that they were later abandoned. A fifth cruiser was put out of action and one of the destroyers heavily damaged. Over one thousand Australian and American sailors were killed, a loss greater than the total number of marines who were to die on Guadalcanal. The Japanese emerged from the Battle of Savo Island basically unhurt.

Allied naval efforts were hampered by the fact that Vice-Admiral Jack Fletcher, commander of Task Force 61, had decided to remove the three American aircraft carriers from the Guadalcanal waters. Fletcher was concerned about their safety in hostile waters. But not only was the American navy deprived of its air arm, the marines on shore now stood alone. With the carriers gone, Japanese planes raided marine emplacements regularly, while Japanese ships shelled the marines' bridgehead. Marine supplies were also cut off when the transports, only partially unloaded, were forced to withdraw because of lack of air cover. Not only was food in short supply but still on board the ships were such items as ammunition, shovels, axes, saws, and virtually all of the marines' heavy equipment.

Yet the marines fought on and the labor battalions worked on to ready the airfield to receive American planes. Within two weeks, the airfield was completed and named Henderson Field, in honor of Major Lofton R. Henderson, a marine dive-bomber squadron leader who had died in air combat during the Battle of Midway. On August 20—13 days after the marines had landed—a flight of dive bombers landed on Guadalcanal, followed by a flight of Wildcats.

The arrival of the aircraft was timely because the Japanese had landed about 1,000 men on the island as part of an effort to retake it. After heavy fighting the invasion force was defeated, but another Japanese troop convoy was spotted 100 miles west of Guadalcanal. Dive bombers from Henderson managed to sink one transport and damage a cruiser. B-17 bombers from Allied bases in the New Hebrides joined the fray and sank a Japanese destroyer. The rest of the Japanese warships and transports took off without carrying out their mission.

American supplies now began to arrive on Guadalcanal but so too did more Japanese soldiers, brought to the island at night by fast destroyers and barges. Most of the barges were sunk by planes from Henderson Field, but the destroyers deposited 6000 men on the island. The destroyer runs were made through the channel dividing the Solomons to the south from those to the north. The marines dubbed the channel "The Slot," and the nightly runs, usually accompanied by shelling of marine positions on Guadalcanal, were call the "Tokyo Express."

The Japanese troops launched a three-pronged attack on Henderson Field, hoping to capture it. They would then land additional support units from Rabaul, the main Japanese bastion on the island of New Britain. Japanese troops did manage to penetrate to within 1000 yards of the airfield where they were stopped along a low, grassy ridge, which came to be known as Bloody Ridge to the Americans.

In October, a full division of Japanese troops (from the Japanese Seventeenth Army) was sent into Guadalcanal against the marines, who had been reinforced as well. Again, the Japanese effort could not penetrate American defenses at Bloody Ridge and from this point forward, the Japanese concentrated on defending the western end of the island against stronger and stronger American attacks.

Japanese efforts to win control of the waters around Guadalcanal were also thwarted. From late October to early November, a series of naval engagements were fought at various points around Guadalcanal. A one day battle off the Santa Cruz Islands cost the Japanese 100 airplanes and heavy damage to two aircraft carriers and a cruiser. The United States, however, lost the aircraft carrier *Hornet* and a destroyer, both of which were sunk, and 74 carrier planes were also lost. The aircraft carrier *Enterprise* and the new battleship *South Dakota* were damaged.

In mid-November three days of battles took place near Cape Esperance on Guadalcanal. This time the Americans lost two light cruisers and seven destroyers, and suffered damage to seven other ships. Japanese losses totaled 13 ships sunk—including two battleships, a heavy cruiser, three destroyers and seven transports. Nearly 6000 Japanese troops intended as reinforcements for Guadalcanal were killed.

Another encounter on November 30 cost the Americans one cruiser sunk, while the Japanese lost only one destroyer. Yet the Japanese withdrew and from this point on did not contest American presence in the waters near Guadalcanal; supplies and fresh fighting men now poured in to reinforce the Americans. On December 9, General Vandegrift and his First Marine Division left Guadalcanal for a rest in Australia; the entire unit was awarded a Presidential Unit Citation for its success.

In early February, 1943, American forces approached the last of the major Japanese forces on Guadalcanal. But in a daring escape plan, carried out over three successive nights, the Japanese evacuated 13,000 survivors from the island, utilizing their fast-moving destroyers. Twenty five thousand others were left behind, dead. American losses totaled 1592, of whom 1,042 were United States Marines. In addition, the Japanese had lost many thousands of tons of shipping, and although their navy had sunk about as many American ships as they themselves had lost, Japanese losses were irreplaceable.

In March, 1943, Japanese forces suffered a further set back, this time in the Bismarck Sea, between Rabaul and New Guinea. Sixteen Japanese ships, eight transports and eight escorting destroyers, left Rabaul, intending to resupply and reinforce Japanese forces on New Guinea. Nearly 7,000 Japanese soldiers, their equipment and supplies were packed into the transports. In the afternoon, a plane from the American Fifth Air Force spotted the Japanese convoy. For the next two days American and Australian planes attacked the convoy, sinking one transport and damaging two others. On the third day, as the convoy streamed through the Vitiaz Strait between New Guinea and New Britain, the Fifth Air Force, commanded by General George Kenney, struck again, this time utilizing a new technique of "skip bombing," which Kenney himself had proposed. First developed by the British, this type of attack utilized light bombers coming in low across the water and dropping 500-pound bombs which would bounce across the water, hitting the enemy ship at, or below, the waterline. Canons mounted in the nose of the American planes neutralized deck guns on the ships, and delay fuses allowed the planes time to pull away and avoid the explosions.

At the end of the third day, all eight of the Japanese transports had been sunk and four of the destroyers. Kenney's airmen also shot down 61 Japanese aircraft, losing only four American planes. American planes and P.T. boats came in and shot up the survivors, although over 2,000 managed to make it back to Rabaul. From this point on, the Japanese were no longer able to adequately supply or reinforce their troops in New Guinea. Some troops and supplies were brought in at night by submarines and barges operating along the coastline.

One month following the Battle of the Bismarck Sea, the United States scored another success. Intercepting a message that Admiral Yamamoto, Commander-in-Chief of Japan's navy, would be flying to the Japanese occupied-island of Bougainville on April 18, and knowing that Yamamoto was always punctual, Admiral Nimitz authorized a plan for American planes from Guadalcanal to ambush and shoot down Yamamoto's plane.* On the morning of the 18th, 16 P-38 fighter planes spotted two Japanese bombers, escorted by 6 "Zero" Fighter planes. In the ensuing "dog fight" the two bombers were shot down. The one carrying Yamamoto plunged into the jungle, where Japanese troops later found the charred body of the man who had masterminded the attack on Pearl Harbor and Midway Island.

Throughout the spring and summer of 1943, Allied forces continued their operations in the South Pacific, with the intention of isolating the Japanese stronghold at Rabaul. On June 30 American troops invaded the island of New Georgia and its neighboring islands in the central Solomons, southeast of Rabaul. Planned as a quick operation by one division, the battle for New Georgia lasted over one month and ultimately necessitated the use of nearly 4 divisions.

On August 15, American troops landed on Vella Lavella, another in the Solomon chain. Only a few hundred Japanese occupied the island and they were quickly subdued. By September an airfield there was operational. Rabaul and Japanese supply lines were now within easy bombing range. In November, 1943, American troops struck again, this time at Bouganville, the last of the big islands in the Solomons on the road to Rabaul. One hundred twenty five miles long, with narrow beaches bordered by vast swamps, and with a tangled, mountainous interior dominated by two active volcanoes, Bougainville was not to be an easy undertaking. Indeed, it wasn't until April, 1944, that it was secured at the cost of 7000 Japanese dead and more than 1000 Americans killed. The noose was drawn tighter on Rabaul in December, 1943, when General MacArthur's 112th Cavalry Regiment landed on the southwest corner of the island of New Britain, only 270 miles from Rabaul, which was located on the island's northeastern tip. On December 26, the 1st Marine Division, veterans of Guadalcanal, attacked Cape Gloucester, on the island's western tip. It took three weeks of hard fighting in monsoon rains to secure Cape Gloucester.

Allied bombers and fighters could now hit Rabaul regularly. But since there were still some 135,000 Japanese troops, well dug in at Rabaul and because several hundred miles of jungle separated them

---

*Final approval for the plan had to come from President Roosevelt.

from the nearest American troops at Cape Gloucester, it was decided that Rabaul itself need not be taken. It had been reduced to impotence and could safely be bypassed.

In November, 1943, Admiral Nimitz began his drive across the central Pacific in the Gilbert Islands, some 2,000 miles southwest of Pearl Harbor. His targets were two atolls, Makin and Tarawa, seized by the Japanese from the British shortly after Pearl Harbor. Makin was the first target, and although it held only 300 trained Japanese troops and 400 civilian laborers, it took 6500 American troops (marine and army) four days to capture the island. American losses were 66, although more that 600 men died when a Japanese submarine torpedoed the Escort Carrier, *Liscome Bay*, standing offshore from the Atoll.

Tarawa proved to be even more of a problem for the Americans. It was heavily fortified and held by nearly 5,000 Japanese troops. Of the Atoll's 47 islands, the Americans' chief target was Betio, Tarawa's largest island and one that contained an airstrip. For nearly three hours American ships and planes poured over 3,000 tons of shells and bombs on Betio, blanketing the island in flames. But the Japanese had simply retreated into bombproof shelters and holes in the ground, and when the shelling stopped they came out and manned their posts.

The initial assault waves immediately ran into difficulty. They had to surmount a four foot high sea wall, constructed of coral and coconut logs, behind which were gun emplacements and trenches. The first marines to come ashore were cut down by rifle and machine gun fire. Still, by noon on the first day, 5,000 marines were ashore and over one-half of the Japanese defenders dead. But, the Japanese fanatically fought on. By the third day, American planes were landing on the airstrip and the island was declared secured, although stray survivors continued to be rounded up for days afterwards. Only 17 Japanese troops (of the nearly 5,000) surrendered at Tarawa Atoll. The rest died, either in last ditch "banzai" charges or at their own hand. American losses were 1,027 marines and 29 naval officers and men killed and 2,292 wounded; a figure that many Americans found hard to accept for a chunk of coral in the far off Pacific.

Yet Makin and Tarawa were the first halting steps across the Pacific towards Tokyo. And the lessons of amphibious warfare learned here were to save many lives in future Pacific battles: such things as better coordination of sea and air bombardment; new shells and techniques to destroy fortified enemy positions; and better equipped armored craft for getting troops ashore.

Soon after the victory in the Gilberts, American planes were bombing the Marshall islands, and on February 1, 1944, American troops attacked Kwajalein Atoll in the central Marshalls, where a Japanese bomber strip was under construction. Although it took a week to secure the island, the cost in American lives was only 373 dead. On February 17, the Americans invaded Eniwetok Atoll, 380 miles from Kwajalein in the western Marshalls. On the same day, American carrier planes also attacked Truk, 770 miles to the west of Eniwetok in the Carolina Islands, the home base of the combined Japanese fleet. In two days and one night of raids, the Americans destroyed nearly 200 Japanese planes (mostly on the ground) and sank 41 ships.

Benefiting from captured Japanese documents that revealed Japanese strength on Eniwetok and Parry island, just across the channel from Eniwetok, American troops captured the two islands. The 800 Japanese troops on Eniwetok operating from underground bunkers with connecting tunnels and trenches, held out for two and a half days, while 3 days of shelling and one day of ground fighting overwhelmed Parry Island. Within a few weeks U.S. Naval parties occupied about 30 other small islands and atolls in the Marshalls. At the end of February, 1944 troops commanded by General MacArthur invaded the Admiralty Islands, 200 miles off the northern coast of New Guinea. The Admiralties offered a superb harbor for American ships as well as Japanese built airfields, which could be utilized by American aircraft. Although there were more Japanese troops on Manus, the largest of the Admiralty Islands, than on the smaller Los Negros island, the Americans predominated. Because of the Japanese desire to die rather than surrender, casualty figures in the attack were overwhelmingly in favor of the Americans: 326 dead Americans to 3,280 Japanese lives.

MacArthur's next step towards his ultimate objective of the Philippines was Hollandia, near the northwest end of New Guinea. Its capture would make it possible to seize points farther west along New Guinea's coast and key islands off the coast. These, in turn, would serve as stepping stones to the Philippines. The operation began on April 22 and caught the 11,000 Japanese defenders by complete surprise. The great majority of the Japanese troops were service troops and were quickly overrun by the 52,000 American invaders. A week later MacArthur landed troops in the Sarmi area of New Guinea, over 100 miles further west. Mafin Bay fell to the Americans, but only after heavy fighting, lasting from May until September. Wakde Island, a tiny enclave just off the New Guinea coast, which contained an excellent airfield, was also captured, but again only after heavy fighting.

MacArthur then moved west, against Biak, a small, but strategically located island in the mouth of Geelvink Bay, New Guinea's largest bay. Biak contained three Japanese airfields, defended by over 10,000 men. The invasion began on May 27, but it took nearly two months for organized Japanese resistance to be overcome. Indeed, sporadic Japanese attacks continued on until the end of August. Biak's capture brought a practical end to the New Guinea campaign.

On September 15, MacArthur landed troops, unopposed, on Morotai, in the Moluccas, islands lying between New Guinea and the Philippines. Standing on the beach following the landing, MacArthur reportedly turned his gaze towards the Philippines, and said, "They are waiting for me there. It's been a long time."

His original plan was to hit the southernmost island in the Philippines, Mindanao. But while MacArthur was heading for Morotai under radio silence, his Chief-of-Staff, Lt. General Richard Sutherland, approved a change of plans. Because navy pilots bombing the Philippines had reported the central area wide open, the new invasion target would be Leyte.

Chapter XVIII

America on the Offensive II: 1944–45

❖ ❖ ❖

While MacArthur was preparing to return to the Philippines, Admiral Nimitz was rushing ahead across the central Pacific in an effort to isolate Japan from her possessions to the south. In March, 1944, Nimitz was ordered by the Joint Chiefs of Staff to occupy the Mariana Islands by June 15, 1944.*

The Marianas were a chain of volcanic islands discovered in 1521 by Ferdinand Magellan, who named them the Islands of the Laten Sails. In the Seventeenth Century, the Spanish changed their name to the Mariana Islands, after Mariana of Austria, widow of Philip IV of Spain. During the Spanish-American War, the United States seized the biggest of the islands, Guam, and in 1899 Spain sold the rest of the islands to Germany. During World War I, Japan—which was fighting on the Allied side against Germany—seized the islands and was given a mandate over them when the war ended. In the 1930s the Japanese began to fortify their possessions, particularly the island of Saipan.**

Some fourteen miles long and five miles wide, Saipan contained towns, sugar plantations, and a large civilian population. During the early years of World War II it served mainly as a supply base and a staging area. The garrison was a token force and did little other than build a few pill boxes. The Japanese commander, Admiral Nagumo, who had commanded the Pearl Harbor attack force, apparently did not expect an imminent American invasion. Yet, the island was Nimitz' first target in the Marianas.

Despite difficulties, which included the landing of men at the wrong beaches, 20,000 United States Marines under the command of Lieutenant General Holland "Howlin' Mad" Smith, made it ashore on the first day, June 15, 1944. Although their preparations had not been extensive, the Japanese resisted bitterly. The Marines suffered over 2,000 casualties that first day and were able to secure only half of the beachhead. They were well enough entrenched, however, to repulse two suicidal counter attacks launched by the Japanese army commander, Lieutenant General Yoshitsugu Saito. The besieged Marines were quickly reinforced on June 16 by two regiments of the United States Army's 27th Division.

While the fighting raged on Saipan, the Japanese Mobile Fleet under the command of Vice Admiral Ozawa steamed toward the American fleet, stationed west of the island, hoping to destroy it and isolate the American beachhead. Included in the Japanese force was virtually every remaining ship in the Japanese navy—nine carriers (with 430 planes aboard), 5 battleships, 13 cruisers and 28 destroyers. The American force—Task Force 58 commanded by Admiral Marc A. Mitscher—had seven battleships, 21 cruisers, a number of destroyers, and 15 carriers with 891 combat planes on board. Altogether, the United States Fifth Fleet, operating in the area, had more than 500 ships at its disposal. In addition to being outnumbered, the Japanese attack force was weakened by the inexperience of its pilots, many of whom had little training and virtually no combat experience.

Admiral Raymond Spruance, commander of the U.S. Fifth Fleet, was alerted to the Japanese force by two of his submarines operating in the Philippine Sea, and he sent Mitscher's Task Force 58 to

---

*The Marianas and the Carolinas Islands had been named as the last defensive line at a Japanese Imperial Conference.

**The Japanese buildup here helped to give rise to postwar rumors that Amelia Earhart's last flight was a spy mission on the Japanese and ended when her plane crashed on Saipan. She and her navigator were supposedly imprisoned and later either died or were executed by the Japanese.

confront them. When their reconnaissance planes spotted the Americans on June 18, the Japanese launched several raids against Mitscher's ships. The result for the bold but inexperienced Japanese pilots was disastrous. The new American F6F Hellcat fighters could outclimb and outdive the Japanese Zero and not only were they heavily armed, but their pilots were protected by heavy armor plating and a thick bulletproof windshield, none of which the Japanese had. The American planes shot down over 240 Japanese planes on that first day in what has become known as the "Marianas Turkey Shoot," since, to many American pilots, it was like "shooting turkeys in a barrel." Two days later, on June 20, Mitscher launched his planes, at extreme range, against the Japanese fleet, already crippled by American submarines, which had sunk two of their carriers. This strike eliminated another Japanese aircraft carrier, 65 more Japanese planes and damaged a number of other Japanese ships. Many of the American planes ran out of fuel on the way back to their carriers, although the majority of their pilots were later rescued. In an attempt to aid the returning pilots, arriving in the pitch black of night, Mitscher turned on the lights of his aircraft carriers to guide his planes.* Altogether in the two-day battle, the Americans lost 130 planes and 76 pilots. The Japanese, however, who began the battle with 435 carrier planes, now had only 35 in flying condition. In addition, the battle cost the Japanese three aircraft carriers. "The Marianas Turkey Shoot" or the Battle of the Philippine Sea (the battle's official name), in effect destroyed Japanese naval airpower.

On Saipan, despite some rather bitter disputes between the Marines and the Army, the Americans continued their relentless advance.** On July 9, the island was secured at a cost of over 16,000 Americans killed and wounded. The Japanese lost 29,000 dead, including both Admiral Nagumo and General Saito, who committed suicide. One other victim of Saipan was Prime Minister Tojo, who resigned along with his entire cabinet.

Saipan's fall was followed on July 24 by an invasion of Tinian, only 3 and one-half miles to the south, which fell within a week. One hundred miles further south was the third major island in the Marianas, the former American possession of Guam. A rugged island, nearly 30 miles long, Guam was invaded on July 20. The fighting raged for two more weeks, and even after the island was declared secure, small Japanese units fought on for several months.

By August, 1944, the main Mariana Islands were in the possession of the United States, which now had airbases only 1300 miles southeast of Tokyo, within range of the new B-29 Superfortress bombers.*** Almost daily raids, beginning in the Fall of 1944 and lasting until the end of the war, now struck Japan. Over 800,000 Japanese civilians were to die as incendiary bombs set fire to the residential areas of Japan's major cities. American attention now turned to the Philippines, 1500 miles to the west, but there was still one potential obstacle to that goal, the Palau islands in the western Carolinas, some 500 miles east of the Philippine island of Mindanao. Admiral Nimitz thought the islands too great a threat to the Philippine invasion to be ignored, although not everyone agreed with him. On September 1, American Marines landed on Pelelieu Island, site of the largest airbase in the Palau group. Marine Commander, Major General William Rupertus, thought the island could be secured in two or three days. Instead the fighting dragged on for a month. According to historian John Toland, "Pelelieu was defended with such determination that it took a statistical average of 1589 rounds of heavy and light ammunition to kill each Japanese soldier." American casualties on the island were quite high, with over

---

*This was a violation of standard operating procedure, as ships generally ran blacked-out at night in order to guard against submarine attack.

**The Army Commander, Major General Ralph Smith, was relieved of his command, sent to Hawaii, and later was transferred to Europe.

***With bases in the Marianas the difficult bombing raids on Japanese possessions from bases in China and India began to wind down. Until March, 1945, however, raids from China continued against Formosa, Manchuria, and Nagasaki. From India, American bombers hit Japanese targets in Southeast Asia—Burma, Thailand, Indochina, and Singapore. The engineers who built the air bases, roads, the hospitals, the harbors, and the barracks for the advancing Americans, were known as Seabees, from the initials for Construction Battalions. They were essential to the U.S. march across the Pacific.

1200 Marines and 700 Army troops dying in the bloody combat. The 1000 Japanese soldiers and civilians perished. This fierce battle, which Admiral Halsey felt was unnecessary, went largely unnoticed in the United States, although it was one of the bloodiest in the Pacific War.

While the Palaus were under siege, an American naval armada set sail for Leyte, the initial target in MacArthur's return to the Philippines—the ships carried over 165,000 troops of MacArthur's Sixth Army. This was to be the greatest operation in the Pacific, bringing together for the first time the forces of Nimitz and MacArthur. American troops went ashore on October 20 at 10 A.M., while General MacArthur watched the operation from the Cruiser Nashville. Then about 2 o'clock in the afternoon, he climbed into a barge with officers and newsmen, picked up Sergio Osmena, the president of the Philippines and General Carlos Romulo from a nearby transport, and proceeded to go ashore. Despite fighting close-by, marked by the rattle of rifle and machine gun fire, MacArthur stepped before a microphone on the beach and broadcast a two minute speech:

> *People of the Philippines, I have returned....The hour of your redemption is here....As the battle rolls forward to bring you within the zone of operations rise and strike....For future generation of your sons and daughters, strike! In the name of your sacred dead, strike! Let no heart be faint. Let every arm be steeled.*

All in all, the landing went well as the Sixth American Army met only small rear-guard resistance from the Japanese. The bulk of the Japanese forces had retreated inland to escape the preinvasion naval and air bombardment.

MacArthur's return to the Philippines led to the war's last great naval battle, and the biggest naval battle of all time. Following the fall of the Marianas, Japan's Imperial General Headquarters had issued a defense plan designed to muster all Japanese forces for a single battle. Known as *Sho-Go* (Victory Operation), the plan divided Japan's Pacific holdings into four defense areas, each with its own specific plan for dealing with an Allied attack. The plan for the Philippines was known as *Sho-1*, but it was not to go into effect until the northernmost island of Luzon, considered to be the most important by the Japanese, was invaded. When the Allied force appeared at Leyte Gulf, however, the Japanese changed their minds and decided to fight the climactic battle there.

Assuming that the American invasion fleet would be screened by a carrier force, the Japanese planned to decoy the American carriers away from the main fleet. Then their surface fleet, led by the battleships, could steam in and destroy the American transports and their remaining escort vessels. For decoys the Japanese chose their aircraft carriers, even though their naval air arm had been virtually depleted in the "Marianas Turkey Shoot" (There were only 116 Planes on the Japanese carriers). The role of Admiral Ozawa's carriers was to sail south and lure the American aircraft carriers to follow them to the north, away from Leyte. The main Japanese force, divided into two strike groups, would attack as soon as the American transports were deprived of their protective escorts. The Japanese gambled on the attack going off free from American air attacks once the carriers were decoyed away, since the American transports were beyond American land-based aircraft.*

The Japanese plan began well. Admiral Bull Halsey, Commander of the protecting fleet, fell for the Japanese ruse and gave chase to the Japanese aircraft carriers, which turned north away from the Philippines. However, the Japanese Center Force, which included two super battleships, the *Yamato* and the *Musashi*, both of which had 18-inch guns, was spotted by American submarines. The second of the Japanese attack fleets, the Southern Force, was observed by reconnaissance planes from George Kenney's Fifth Airforce. On the 24th, carrier planes from the American 3rd Fleet, which was still within range, repeatedly struck at the Center Force. The day-long attacks sank the *Musashi*, crippled the cruiser *Myoko*, and damaged the *Yamato* and two other battleships. Halsey, however, believed that the damage had

---

*This was the first time in the Pacific war that forces under MacArthur's command had exceeded land-based air cover.

been even greater and that the Northern Force was now the biggest threat, he turned his ships and their search planes back to the north in pursuit of the Japanese decoy fleet.

The Japanese Southern Force, the second arm of the Japanese pincers, approached Surigao Strait, the southern entrance to Leyte Gulf, in the early morning hours of October 25. American search planes and coastwatchers stationed in the island groups kept the Americans well informed of this Force's progress. As the Japanese ships steamed single file through Surigao Strait, retreating to the west, American (and Australian) P.T. boats and destroyers ambushed them, unleashing salvos of torpedoes. One Japanese battleship was sunk and another, was damaged. The American naval commander then carried out the classical naval maneuver of crossing the enemy's "T." This involved the American fleet cutting in front of the Japanese column in a single-file formation, which allowed every American ship in the battle line to fire broadside at the Japanese, who could return fire only with their forward guns. All but one of the Japanese ships was crippled or sunk. No American ship was lost.* The southern pincer of the planned Japanese attack on Leyte Gulf was destroyed.

Halsey's pursuit of the Northern decoy force, however, now opened the way for the Center Force, which he believed to be destroyed, to steam through the now unguarded San Bernardino Strait. As the Japanese neared Leyte they encountered a group of American escort carriers providing air cover and anti-submarine patrol for the Leyte landing.** This was Taffy-3, commanded by Rear Admiral Clifton A.F. Sprague. The carriers were protected by three destroyers and four destroyers' escorts, whose guns, however, could hardly dent the armor of the bigger Japanese ships. A rain squall, which provided a temporary refuge for the outmanned and outgunned Americans, was only a temporary lull, and the fierce battle soon resumed. Many of the American planes and ships fought until all their ammunition, bombs, and torpedoes were depleted. Repeated pleas for assistance finally caused Halsey to detach his fast battleships to race south to assist Taffy-3.

The bravery and daring of Taffy-3 caused the fighting in Leyte Gulf to take an unexpected turn. The hits scored by American ships and planes and the confusion they sowed among the Japanese, caused them to retire the way they had come, back through the San Bernardino Strait. Taffy-3 had outfought the overwhelmingly superior enemy force and had saved the American transports and MacArthur's beachhead on Leyte Island. There were many acts of heroism in the battle, but none more so than that of the U.S. destroyer *Johnston*, commanded by Commander Ernest E. Evans, a Cherokee Indian from Oklahoma. Continually pressing the attack, even after all of his torpedoes were gone, Evans at the end had only one 5-inch gun operable. Yet he continued to fight, even though his upper clothing was sucked off by the explosion of Japanese shells, and he lost two fingers from his left hand. Finally, the *Johnston* went down with the loss of 186 men out of a crew of 327. Evans went down with his ship, and was later posthumously awarded the Medal of Honor, the nation's highest military award.

Halsey's Task Force 34, dispatched to aid Taffy-3, arrived too late to stop the Japanese from exiting the San Bernardino Strait. Yet the Battle of Leyte Gulf was a great American victory that knocked the Japanese navy out of the war for good. It cost them four carriers, three battleships, six heavy cruisers, four light cruisers, nine destroyers, and perhaps 10,000 lives. The desperate plight of the Japanese was made clear on the final day of the battle when a new Japanese weapon, the *Kamikaze*, or suicide planes, made their debut.*** Eleven volunteers stationed on Luzon, attempted to crashdive their planes on the American ships, particularly the aircraft carriers. They did manage to sink one American escort carrier

---

*Included in the American force were three battleships that had been damaged at Pearl Harbor and two (the *California* and the *West Virginia*) which had been sunk at Pearl Harbor but refloated.

**Sometimes called "jeep" or "baby" aircraft carriers, these were actually former merchant ships with short flight decks. They carried only about 28 planes each, and their speed was only about half that of a Japanese battleship.

***The term *Kamikaze* means "divine wind" and was derived from a great typhoon that destroyed or dispersed a huge Mongol invasion fleet, under Kublai Khan in 1281. The Japanese people considered this storm as evidence of heavenly protection and credited the Empire's salvation to the *Kamikaze*—the Divine Wind.

and damage four others. But this was just the beginning. The closer the Americans got to Japan, the greater became the human sacrifices of the Japanese and the higher the losses of American men and ships.

On land, American forces continued to press forward, although somewhat slowed by the weather. The 35 inches or so of rain that fell on the Leyte valley particularly hindered the repair and development of airfields captured on Leyte. Thus, for some weeks, MacArthur's forces had to fight without control of the air. The Japanese were able to bomb American port facilities, shipping in Leyte Gulf, and the beachhead itself. The toughest battle on Leyte was for Breakneck Ridge at the northern end of the island. Fighting from elaborate trench systems, foxholes and firing pits, the Japanese were a formidable foe to overcome. The fighting was often hand-to-hand in nearly monsoon rains, which made trails impassable and caused roads to disintegrate. By Christmas Day, the remaining Japanese forces on Leyte were isolated, and although it took a few more weeks to wipe out pockets of resistance, the fighting on the island was over by the end of 1944. Nearly 60,000 Japanese soldiers had died in its defense. United State's losses were 3500 killed and 12,000 wounded.

On January 9, 1945, American troops landed at Lingayen Gulf, on the main Philippine Island of Luzon. The forces of General Tomoyuki Yamashita, the conqueror of Singapore, bitterly resisted but with little hope for victory. Japanese supplies and reinforcements were having great difficulty even reaching the Philippines—over one half the ships carrying reinforcements and supplies had been sunk. In addition, Japanese airpower was down to 200 planes. Yamashita's plan was to delay and harass the American forces, not to engage them in a major, decisive battle. This strategy forced the Americans to flush out the Japanese from caves, tunnels, and hidden pillboxes lining the major roadways, an undertaking that delayed but did not halt the American advance. MacArthur landed troops just north of the Bataan peninsula on January 29 and on January 31, American forces put ashore south of Manila. Now a pincers movement, from north and south, was applied to the Philippines' capital.

General Yamashita wanted Manila declared an open city—he considered it too flat and flammable to be defended, but the local commander, Admiral Iwabachi, chose to fight for the city. The first American forces rolled into Manila on February 3, 1945. These were elements of the 1st Cavalry Division, commanded by Major General Vernon D. Mudge, which had been formed into flying columns to speed to Manila in an attempt to rescue Allied P.O.W.'s and civilian internees. The cavalrymen quickly freed most of the internees at the San Tomas University, which the Japanese had converted into a prison camp. Subsequent fighting to wrest the city from the Japanese did not come with the same speed or ease, however. Engaged in their first urban fighting of the Pacific War, the Americans had to fight house to house, and it wasn't until March 4, 1945, that the city was declared officially cleared. Japanese survivors, under General Yamashita, retreated to the mountains to the north where they continued to resist until Japan officially surrendered in September, 1945.

While the fighting for Manila was in progress, American airborne troops landed on the island of Corregidor on February 16. Until that island—which blocked the entrance to Manila Bay—could be recaptured, American ships could not freely enter that body of water nor reach Manila. The airborne drop was followed some two hours later by a seaborne landing. It took about 10 days and 1200 casualties to clear the island of Japanese troops, who were hiding in the network of tunnels originally built by the Americans.

At the same time, MacArthur prepared to launch an operation to recapture all the bypassed islands in the southern Philippines. Aided by Filipino guerrillas, who had already seized control of some islands from the Japanese, the Americans in most cases proceeded quickly and efficiently. The bloodiest and largest of all the operations was the battle for Mindanao, launched on April 17. It took the Americans over two months to clear the island, and another six weeks to mop-up Japanese stragglers. The U.S. lost 820 men killed in the operation and another 3000 wounded. Japanese losses were an astounding 13,000 men killed.

MacArthur's policies of hitting the enemy at weak spots, utilizing the terrain wherever possible, and never exceeding his land-based air cover (except at Leyte), and utilizing friendly natives, worked to great success in the Philippines. Japanese dead in the fighting in the Philippines totaled over 192,000 compared to only 7,933 for the Americans invaders. The campaign in the Philippines ended the war for MacArthur—at least he did no more fighting. Instead he now busied himself with planning for the expected Allied invasion of Japan itself, which was expected to take place around December 1, 1945.

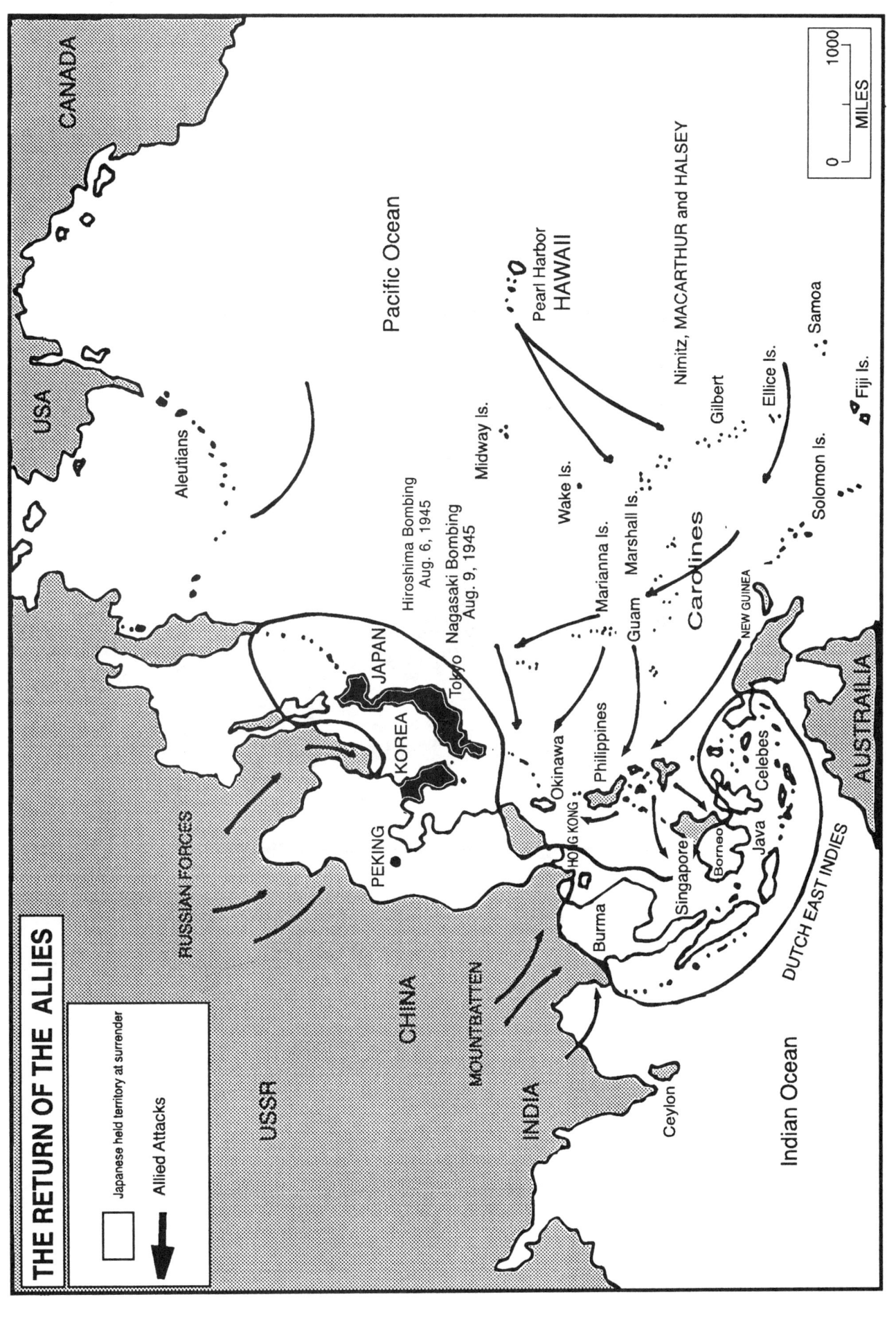

U.S. MARINE CORPS

Chapter XIX

The Fall of Japan

❖ ❖ ❖

American victory in the Philippines caused Japan's inner defensive ring to collapse, although Japan itself was still far from defeat. To hasten that end, Allied planners decided in early October, 1944 to invade two more Japanese-held islands before launching the anticipated attack on mainland Japan. The two selected were Iwo Jima (Sulphur Island) and Okinawa.

Located in the Bonin islands, Iwo Jima was a main bastion of Japanese air defense. Japanese fighters based here harassed American bombers flying from the Marianas to Tokyo and Japan's other industrial centers. Another consideration behind the decision to invade Iwo was the 2800 mile roundtrip which American B-29 bombers had to fly between the Marianas and Japan. This was too far for fighters (even the P-51 Mustang) to fly protective cover for the bombers. Iwo Jima had two airfields (a third was under construction) which would provide bases for fighters close enough to Japan that they could escort the bombers. Light bombers operating from Iwo could also raid the Japanese mainland. Finally, since Iwo Jima was traditionally Japanese territory, populated by Japanese nationals, it was hoped that American occupation of the island would serve to weaken Japanese morale.

Iwo is a small island about 750 nautical miles south of Tokyo. At its longest point, it is five miles long and two and a half miles at its widest point. At the southwest tip of the island there is an extinct volcano, Mount Suribachi. The sand in the southwest is of a dry, volcanic nature with very little vegetation and no real ground cover except for the side of Mount Suribachi. Indeed most of the island's surface is covered with a choking, fine volcanic sand and ash. The island's northwestern side is rocky, with many caves and canyons providing good defensive positions.

By the beginning of 1945, the Japanese Commander, Lieutenant General Tadamichi Kuribayashi had constructed an impressive defensive fortress on Iwo, including an underground network of caves, bunkers, medical facilities and control centers, all connected by some 16 miles of tunnels.* Above ground were concealed concrete bunkers and mortar pits.

Pre-invasion bombardment by the U.S. weakened, but failed to destroy, the Japanese defenses. Most of the beach blockhouses and pillboxes were destroyed but hundreds of guns and mortars were untouched. Still, Major General Harry Schmidt, the American commander of the invasion force, predicted that the island would be taken in ten days.

February 19 was D-Day for the operation, code-named Operation Detachment. After a thunderous naval and air bombardment, the first four waves of marines went ashore. What they ultimately encountered was the closest thing to hell they had ever seen. The Japanese defenders were deeply entrenched and bunkers and caves had to be taken hole by hole. On February 23, a marine patrol reached the summit of Mt. Suribachi and soon afterwards hoisted an American flag. The photograph of the flag's raising was to become the most famous picture of World War II. Yet the campaign for Iwo Jima had barely begun. Securing the island would take far longer than Schmidt envisioned. In fact, the island was not declared secure until March 26. Iwo Jima turned out to be the most costly battle in U.S. Marine Corps history, with the number of dead marines totaling over 6,000. Japanese dead numbered approximately

---

*Kuribayashi knew a great deal about the U.S., having taken his cavalry training in Texas. As a military attache to Canada, he often visited the U.S. He was a sometime poet and had written two songs popular in Japan.

145

20,000. When the Marines were replaced by United States Army troops in early April, 1945, nearly 3,000 Japanese still remained alive underground on Iwo. Most of them were persuaded to surrender, although the last two members of the island's garrison didn't give up until 1951, six years after the war's end.

Iwo's value to the Americans was almost immediate. American fighters and bombers began to operate from the island's runways almost immediately. Search and rescue operations for downed airmen were launched from Iwo, and its long runways (one of its airfields had a 10,000 foot runway, the longest in the Pacific) provided emergency landing facilities for bombers damaged in raids over Japan. By the time the war ended, it is estimated that a total of nearly 25,000 airmen were rescued when over 2250 B-29s made emergency landings at Iwo.

The final American amphibious operation of World War II was against the island of Okinawa, only 350 sea miles from Kyushu, Japan's southern most home island. Part of the Ryukyu island group, Okinawa had four airbases and was considered an ideal bomber base, along with Le Shima, one of its satellite islands. Additionally, it had good harbor facilities and would be a natural staging base for any invasion of Japan proper. Admiral Perry had called Okinawa, "The very door of the Japanese Empire," when he landed there in 1853.

Japan had occupied the island in 1879 and had given it status as an integral part of the homeland. Its geography made it a formidable objective. About sixty miles long, it squeezes at the waist to a width of only two miles. North of the waist are mountains; the south is composed of rugged hills. Its coastline is jagged, "suggesting," according to one author, "a rampant Oriental dragon."

Defense of the island was led by Lieutenant General Mitsuri Ushyima. With over 100,000 men at his disposal, as well as more weaponry than previously available for defending Pacific islands, Ushyima was determined to make the Americans pay dearly for the island of Okinawa. Rather than contest the invasion on the beaches, he concentrated his defensive forces in the southern part of the island, utilizing ridges and cliffs, stretching the width of the island, as natural barriers. Ushyima planned to resist the Americans ridge by ridge as they advanced, using caves and tombs of Okinawan dead for gun emplacements and an underground labyrinth of tunnels to hide troops.

The American landing on April 1, 1945 (Easter Sunday) went remarkably well, with the main assault force of four divisions under the command of General Simon Bolivar Buckner, going ashore on the west coast. Expecting harsh resistance, the Americans instead encountered virtually none. By the end of the first day, 60,000 troops were safely ashore with the loss of only 28 lives. As the Americans moved southward, however, they began to meet more concerted Japanese resistance, and by April 5 it was obvious that the real fighting was just beginning and that it was going to last a long time.

Okinawa turned out to be the bloodiest fight of the Pacific War. Total American casualties were nearly 50,000, with 7,613 Americans killed. Included in that number was General Buckner, the highest ranking officer killed in the Pacific, and Ernie Pyle, perhaps the best of WWII war correspondent who was fatally wounded by a Japanese sniper on the satellite island of Le Shima. Additionally, Japanese kamikaze attacks killed over 3,000 navy personnel. Ten major kamikaze attacks were sent against Okinawa and sank 29 Allied ships while damaging nearly 100 others. Japanese losses on Okinawa were approximately 110,000 killed and nearly 11,000 taken prisoner. Included in this number was General Ushyima who committed *hara kiri* on June 22, the same day the Allies declared Okinawa secure—83 days after it had been invaded. Also, 1465 Kamikaze fliers died in raids on and around Okinawa. Japanese naval losses at Okinawa included their last great battleship, *Yamato*, sunk by American aircraft before it could carry out a final suicide attack against American forces on the island.

The terrible cost of the Okinawan campaign provoked criticism from the American press at the time and subsequently from American military analysts. General MacArthur was also critical of the operation, failing to understand why American commanders insisted on driving the Japanese off the island, particularly once we had gained our major objectives of the airfields and the harbor facilities. His strategy would have been to isolate the Japanese on the southern part of the island then let them wither on the vine, cut off from outside supplies.

Okinawa turned out to be our last amphibious operation of the Pacific War although it was still believed that an invasion of Japan would have to be carried out. Plans for such operations were worked out by the end of May, 1945. There were to be two invasions: "Olympic" which called for an invasion of Kyushu on November 1, 1945; and "Coronet," an invasion of the main island of Honshu on March 1, 1946. After the fanatical Japanese resistance on Iwo Jima and Okinawa, American losses were expected to be high. One forecast was for 100,000 casualties just getting ashore and perhaps one million overall. Japanese losses as they fought to the death for their country were incalculable. To help ameliorate such fantastic casualty estimates the United States undertook three major initiatives.

The first was an effort to get the Soviet Union into the war against Japan. Reluctant to abandon its non-aggression Pact with the Japanese until Germany had been defeated, the Soviet Union resisted American attempts to involve her in the Pacific War, but at the Yalta Conference in February, 1945, the Soviets finally agreed to enter the conflict within three months after the surrender of Nazi Germany. In return, the Soviet Union would receive the Southern half of the island of Sakhalin, the Kurile Islands, dominance of Darien and Port Arthur on the Manchurian Liaotung Peninsula and control of the Chinese Eastern Railway and the South Manchurian Railway. American hopes were that the Soviets could confront the still undefeated Japanese Kwantung Army in Manchuria.

The second American action was to carry out a series of fire-bombing raids on Japan. The American Air Commander in the Pacific, Major General Curtis E. Le May, thought he could end the war without an invasion of Japan. Air power and strategic bombing alone, he believed, could force a Japanese surrender. The new wrinkle that Le May introduced was to send American B-29s over Japan at low altitude (5000–7,000 feet) at night, carrying only incendiary bombs. The first such raid came on March 9, 1945 against Tokyo. The result was horrendous for the Japanese. The wood and bamboo construction of Japanese buildings caused a raging fire that wiped out nearly 16 square miles of the main section of the city. Casualties in Tokyo were greater than London, Berlin, or Dresden had ever suffered. They were even greater than those to be felt by Hiroshima and Nagasaki whose ordeals were yet to come. Such raids rolled on through May and June and Japanese civilian losses and hardships mounted. Food supplies fell dangerously short and much of what was available could not be distributed because of the destruction of the railways and the breakdown of commercial organization in Japan. Many Japanese fled the cities to the countryside and in some cases even turned against the military. Yet both civilian and military morale remained amazingly high. There were no food riots in the cities and although the majority of Japanese detested the war, they still endured the worst the Allies could throw against them. When Germany surrendered in May, the Japanese Supreme War Council met and approved a decision to carry on the war. LeMay's fire-bombing raids devastated Japanese cities, but the country still seemed far from surrendering in the Summer of 1945.

Finally, and most importantly, the United States pushed ahead with a project to drop atomic bombs on the cities of Japan. Actually, the bomb had been evolving for over six years. The atom first had been split in 1939 and scientists soon realized that it was theoretically possible to produce a weapon of unbelievable power, one that could alter the course of history. The possibilities were spelled out for President Roosevelt in a letter from Albert Einstein:

> *Sir:*
> *Some recent work by E. Fermi and L. Szilard, which has been communicated to me in manuscript, leads me to expect that the element uranium may be turned into a new and important source of energy in the near future. Certain aspects of the situation which has arisen seem to call for watchfulness and if necessary, quick action on the part of the Administration....It may become possible to set up a nuclear chain reaction in a large mass of uranium, by which vast amounts of power and large quantities of new radium-like elements would be generated....It is conceivable—though much less certain—that extremely powerful bombs of a new type may thus be constructed....*

Two years later, following the Japanese attack on Pearl Harbor, the United States launched a program to build such a bomb. The Manhattan Project as the program came to be called was headed by General Leslie Groves, a 46 year-old West Point engineer. Research and production were centered at three places: Hanford, Washington; Oak Ridge, Tennessee; and Los Alamos, New Mexico. The weapon itself was to be designed at Los Alamos under the supervision of Julius Robert Oppenheimer.

The next phase of the program was to work out procedures for delivering the bomb once it was perfected. A newly created 509th Composite Group, commanded by 29 year-old Colonel Paul Tibbets, was established at Wendover Field in the Utah desert at the end of September, 1944. Under Tibbet's direction, training flights took place in which each aircraft dropped one large mock bomb from an altitude of more that 30,000 feet. The targets were white circles on the desert floor. In May, 1945, the 509th embarked for the island of Tinian in the Marianas, the launching site for the atomic bombs raids on Japan.

On July 16, an experimental plutonium bomb was exploded in the desert of New Mexico. The next day, President Truman, in Potsdam Germany for a major allied conference, was told about it. At the close of the conference Allied powers issued a declaration, the so-called Potsdam Declaration, demanding Japan's complete surrender and threatening her with complete destruction unless she did so, although American possession of the bomb was not mentioned. The declaration left unclear the future status of the emperor. And it was this that Japanese leaders in Tokyo most wanted clarified. Without such clarification, they decided to withhold response to the Allied demand, although the Japanese word used to express this view literally meant "to treat with contempt" or "ignore." President Truman interpreted this to mean unequivocal rejection, and he allowed plans for utilizing the bomb to go forward. On July 26, the last parts of the atomic bomb—a uranium bomb nicknamed little boy—were delivered to the island of Tinian by the cruiser *USS Indianapolis*. Other components had been flow in earlier.

The question of dropping the bomb on Japan had come up for the first time at a May 31, 1945 meeting of the Interim Committee, a committee created to advise President Truman about future use of the new weapon. One suggestion was for a non-military demonstration explosion that would so impress Japanese leaders that they would surrender. When no one could offer a satisfactory answer to the question of how to make such a demonstration convincing enough that the Japanese would end the war, the idea of a demonstration was ruled out. Ultimately, the Committee decided to recommend to President Truman that the bomb be dropped on Japan without any prior warning. The only mention of a target was that it be a military installation of some type.

Another committee, composed of scientists and military strategists, had already been established to evaluate and determine potential targets. Initially, four cities were singled out. The first was the city of Kokura on the island of Kyushu and the site of one of Japan's largest munitions plants. Hiroshima on the main island of Honshu was selected because it was the site of several war plants and an assembly spot for Japanese naval convoys. Nigatu, a port on the Sea of Japan, made the list as did Kyoto, which had once been Japan's capital and was the site not only of war plants but also of several universities and religious shrines. Secretary of War, Henry L. Stimson, quickly struck Kyoto from the list because of its historic and venerated place in Japanese life and society. The port of Nagasaki ultimately replaced Kyoto as the fourth potential target. On July 23, Truman approved the use of the atomic bomb against Japan as soon as visual bombing was possible after August 3, 1945.

On August 1, Tibbets sent the order for the first atomic attack in history to LeMay's headquarters on Guam. It called for seven B-29s to be used in the attack. One would be at Iwo Jima as a standby aircraft to take over the bomb and the mission if the lead plane ran into mechanical problems. Three would leave the island of Tinian far ahead of the bomb-carrying plane, one to each of the three possible targets—the primary and the two secondary ones—to check on the weather conditions. The bomb-carrying aircraft would be accompanied by two observer planes. On August 2, two important details were added to Tibbets' document: the date for the strike was set for August 6; and the targets selected were: Primary—Hiroshima; Secondary—Kokura; Tertiary—Nagasaki.

At 2:45 A.M. on August 6, Tibbets' plane, the *Enola Gay* (named for his mother) took off from the island of Tinian. At 3:00 A.M. William Parsons, the bomb's ordinance specialist began to insert the detonating charge. Having watched four B-29s crash just after takeoffs in one evening, Parsons had been worried about what might happen to the island of Tinian if the bomb should detonate as a result of the *Enola Gay* going down on takeoff. Parsons and his assistant completed the job at 3:20 A.M.

Precisely at 8:15 A.M. on August 6, 1945 the *Enola Gay* released the world's first atomic bomb from an altitude of 31,000 feet; 1890 feet above the ground an electrical impulse detonated the uranium-cored bomb. The temperature at the center of the resulting fireball reached 50 million degree centigrade. Fires were started a mile away from the target center and skin was burned two miles away. Of the estimated 320,000 people in the city on that day, some 80,000 were killed instantly or seriously wounded. Later estimates raised the death count to 140,000 as a direct result of the bomb.

Two days later, August 8, the Soviet Union abrogated its non-aggression pact with Japan and declared that from August 9, the Soviet Union would consider itself in a state of war with Japan. On that day 1.6 million Soviet troops attacked the 600,000 man Kwantung Army in Manchuria. Earlier that same morning, a B-29 named Bock's Car, with Major Charles Sweeny at the controls, lifted off the island of Tinian. On board was a plutonium bomb—Fat Man—destined to be dropped on Kokura. However, clouds and smoke from a recently bombed city nearby obscured the target. Since the aiming point had to be fully visible, Sweeny declared, "no drop." Three passes over Kokura found no improvement so Sweeny diverted to the secondary target, Nagasaki. Although visibility was limited there as well, Sweeny was able to release the bomb which detonated at a height of 1500 feet above the city. Although casualty estimates for Nagasaki vary, they probably reached about 70,000, with nearly everyone within a 1000 yard "circle of death" around Ground Zero dying almost immediately. To the list of horrors suffered by the people of Hiroshima and Nagasaki was added one that few people at the time knew much about, latent radiation poisoning. Decades later, people were still succumbing to the effects of radiation sickness.

Much debate has taken place over the years about the American decision to use the atomic bomb against Japan. Many still believe that a demonstration of the weapon should have been staged. Some feel that conventional bombing would have sufficed to end the conflict, without the use of nuclear bombs (although casualties from conventional air attacks were in some cases higher than those from the atomic bombs). Admiral Nimitz continued to believe that American naval supremacy alone would have sufficed to defeat Japan. Latter-day revisionist historians have argued that the real reason the U.S. used the bomb was not to force Japan's surrender but rather to blackmail the Soviet Union into moderating its policies in Europe. Whether or not this motive lurked in the minds of Truman and his advisors we don't know, but there is little or no historical evidence to suggest that it did.

It is this author's contention that the American use of the bomb must be viewed in the context of the time when it occurred. The closer our forces came to Japan, the greater the number of American casualties—as demonstrated on Iwo Jima and Okinawa. The horrendous predictions of the casualties to be incurred in an invasion of the Japanese mainland, an unescapable necessity in the minds of most American officials, seemed too great to contemplate. That fact, coupled with the way the Japanese had begun the war at Pearl Harbor, as well as a general hatred of the Japanese, rooted in large degree in racism, made the use of the bomb almost a foregone conclusion. To have possessed a weapon which could end the war, and then not to have used it, would have appeared traitorous to many Americans.

Dropping of the second bomb on Nagasaki is somewhat more difficult to understand, let alone to defend, than the use of the first one on Hiroshima. Rationale for the decision to use the second bomb on Nagasaki was a desire to make the Japanese believe we had the weapon in mass-production. Somewhat more patience on the Allied part to allow the Japanese more time to respond to the Hiroshima bombing might have curtailed the need to use "Fat Boy." In fact, on the very day that the bomb was dropped on Nagasaki, the Supreme War Council, which had overall responsibility for directing Japan's military activities, was debating accepting the Potsdam Declaration.

Although the combination of the two atomic bombs and the Soviet Union's entrance into the war left Japan with virtually no choice but to surrender, hardline militarists continued to oppose such action despite the suffering and hopelessness which surrounded them. It took the unprecedented intervention of Emperor Hirohito, the day after Nagasaki, to break the deadlock. He personally requested the Council to accept the Potsdam Declaration with the provision that the position of emperor be retained. On this basis, on August 10, the Japanese government accepted the Declaration. Some Americans, including Secretary of State James Byrnes, opposed retention of the Emperor. Others realized how revered the emperor was to the Japanese people and urged the granting of this concession. On August 11, the United States decided to compromise, allowing the Emperor to remain but making his authority dependent on an Allied Supreme Commander.

Japanese military leaders still did not want to surrender and it again took Hirohito's intervention to sway the War Council. The Emperor urged them to accept surrender and he recorded a message to that effect for broadcast to the Japanese people. Militant Japanese officers made one last effort to block the surrender. They broke into the palace grounds hoping to destroy the recording and coerce Hirohito into continuing the war. But the coup failed and on August 15, 1945, the Emperor's recorded message was broadcast at noon to the Japanese people. Never before had the Emperor talked personally to them; it was the first time they had ever heard his voice.

Officially, the conflict did not cease until September 2, 1945—V-J (Victory over Japan) Day—when the Japanese signed the surrender document on board the U.S. battleship, *Missouri* in Tokyo Bay. The American flag raised over the Missouri that day had been the one flying above the Capitol building in Washington, D.C. on the day the Japanese had bombed Pearl Harbor. A second American flag with only 34 stars was on a nearby bulkhead. It was the one flown on Commodore Perry's flagship when it entered Tokyo Bay in 1854.

General MacArthur presided over the ceremonies. After the Japanese delegation was on board, MacArthur faced the Japanese.

> *It is my earnest hope, indeed the hope of all mankind, that from this solemn occasion a better world shall emerge out of the blood and carnage of the past....*

Japanese Foreign Minister, Mamoru Shigemitsu, signed first for Japan followed by General Yoshyijiro Umezu, the Army Chief of Staff. MacArthur signed for the Allies, using three pens to write his name—a few letters with each one. The first pen he gave to an emaciated General Wainwright, his successor in the Philippines, who had been flown from a Japanese Prisoner of War camp to Tokyo to witness Japan's surrender. General Percival, the British Commander who had surrendered Singapore and Malaya to the Japanese received the second pen. The third pen MacArthur kept for his wife and son.

Admiral Nimitz signed for the United States while representatives of the other Allied nations, England, France, the Netherlands and the Soviet Union, signed for their respective countries. MacArthur closed the ceremonies with these words:

> *Let us pray that peace be now restored to the world and that God will preserve it always. These proceedings are closed.*

As MacArthur concluded his remarks a massed flight of 1900 B-29s and carrier planes flew overhead just as the sun broke through for the first time. Thus ended the greatest tragedy in human history. It had claimed at least 50 million lives. Over 30 million people had been displaced from their homes in Europe alone. One source has estimated that the total direct and indirect costs of the war at around four trillion dollars.

As in Germany, another international tribunal was convened in Japan to try war criminals. Twenty eight leaders faced charges; seven of them received death sentences, including former Japanese Prime Minister Tojo. Eighteen others received prison sentences. There were other trials in various parts of Japan's former empire. In Manila, for example, the Tiger of Malaya, General Yamashita, was sentenced to death.

CHAPTER EXERCISES

Name: _____

Section: _____

Chapter III
The German Invasion of Poland and the Phony War

❖ ❖ ❖

Identification Questions: Identify and tell the significance of the following:

blitzkrieg

Phony War

Winter War

Graf Spee

Essay: Answer the following essay:

Discuss the Phony War and the exceptions to it.

Name: _____

Section: _____

Chapter IV
Blitzkrieg on the Western Front

❖   ❖   ❖

Identification Questions: Identify and tell the significance of the following:

Case Yellow

Rotterdam

Ardennes Forest

Eben Emael

Gamelin

Dunkirk

Marshal Petain

Quisling

Essay: Answer the following essay:

Write an essay in which you explain why you believe that Germany was able to defeat France so easily.

Name: _____

Section: _____

Chapter V
The Battle of Britain
❖ ❖ ❖

Identification Questions: Identify and tell the significance of the following:

Operation Sea Lion

Battle of Britain

radar

Sir Hugh Dowding

Hermann Goering

blitz

Essay: Answer the following essay:

Write an essay in which you discuss why the British won the Battle of Britain.

Name: _____

Section: _____

Chapter VI
The German Invasion of the Soviet Union

❖   ❖   ❖

Identification Questions: Identify and tell the significance of the following:

Richard Sorge

Operation Barbarossa

Siege of Leningrad

Stalingrad

"General Winter" and "Colonel Mud"

General Vlasov

General von Paulus

Operation Citadel

Essay: Answer the following essay question:

Discuss Operation Barbarossa. How do you account for its initial successes and its ultimate failure?

Name: _____

Section: _____

Chapter VIII
The Italian Campaign

❖ ❖ ❖

Identification Questions: Identify and tell the significance of the following:

Casablanca Conference

Operation Husky

Peter Badoglio

"soft underbelly"

Gustav Line

Monte Cassino

Gothic Line

Anzio

Mark Clark

Essay: Answer the following essay:

What was the German defensive strategy in Italy? How effective was it?

Name: _____

Section: _____

Chapter IX
The Second Front

❖   ❖   ❖

Identification Questions: Identify and tell the significance of the following:

COHQ

Dieppe

COSSAC

SHAEF

Normandy

von Rundstedt

Rommel

Atlantic Wall

Fortitude

Omaha Beach

Utah Beach

Essay: Answer the following essay:

Discuss the Allied invasion of continental Europe in June, 1944. Why do you think it was so successful?

Name: _____

Section: _____

Chapter X
Victory in Europe

❖   ❖   ❖

Identification Questions: Identify and tell the significance of the following:

Operation Bagration

Liublin Committee

Hedgerows

Operation Cobra

Falaise Pocket

Operation Anvil

General von Choltitz

Essay: Answer the following essay:

Discuss Operation Market Garden. Did it succeed? Why or why not?

Name: _____

Section: _____

Chapter XI
Disintegration

❖ ❖ ❖

Identification Questions: Identify and tell the significance of the following:

Battle of the Bulge

Bastogne

V-Weapons

Fortress Redoubt

Admiral Karl Doenitz

The Bunker

Essay: Answer the following essay:

How did the Battle of the Bulge shorten the war in Europe?

Name: _____

Section: _____

Chapter XII
The War in Europe: Conclusion

❖ ❖ ❖

Identification Questions: Identify and tell the significance of the following:

Enigma Machine

Dresden

Grossraum

Wannsee Conference

Extermination Camps

Nuremburg Trials

Essay: Answer the following essay:

Discuss why you believe the Allies won the war in Europe.

Name: _____

Section: _____

Chapter XIII
The Rise of Japanese Militarism

❖   ❖   ❖

Identification Questions: Identify and tell the significance of the following:

Meiji Restoration

Russo-Japanese War

Tanaka Memorial

Henry Pu Yi

Hirohito

Panay

samurai

bushido

Manchukuo

Tri-Partite Agreement

Essay: Answer the following essay.

Discuss the events leading to the rise of the military in Japan.

Name: _____

Section: _____

Chapter XIV
Pearl Harbor

❖ ❖ ❖

Identification Questions: Identify and tell the significance of the following:

Indochina

Cordell Hull

Nomura

Kurusu

"Magic"

Tojo

Admiral Yamamoto

Admiral Kimmel

General Short

Tora, tora, tora

U.S.S. Arizona

Admiral Nagumo

Essay: Answer the following essay question:

Discuss the Japanese attack on Pearl Harbor. What were it goals? What were its successes? Its failures?

Name: _____

Section: _____

Chapter XV
Japan's 100 Days of Glory

❖ ❖ ❖

Identification Questions: Identify and tell the significance of the following:

Wake Island

Hong Kong

Guam

Bataan

Corregidor

General Homma

General Wainwright

Bataan Death March

Singapore

General Yamashita

Repulse

Prince of Wales

Battle of the Java Sea

Essay: Answer the following essay.

Discuss Japanese expansion in the first 3 months following the attack on Pearl Harbor.

Name: _____

Section: _____

Chapter XVI
The Turning Points
❖   ❖   ❖

Identification Questions: Identify and tell the significance of the following:

Hornet

James Doolittle

Battle of the Coral Sea

Aleutian Islands

Battle of Midway Island

Essay: Answer the following essay:

Discuss the major turning points in the Pacific War.

Name: _____

Section: _____

Chapter XVII
America On the Offensive

❖ ❖ ❖

Identification Questions: Identify and tell the significance of the following:

General MacArthur

Admiral Nimitz

Guadalcanal

Rabaul

Battle of the Bismarck Sea

Tarawa

Essay: Answer the following essay:

How was command in the Pacific divided? What were the strategies of the respective commanders. Give examples.

Name: _____

Section: _____

Chapter XVIII
America On the Offensive II

❖ ❖ ❖

Identification Questions: Identify and tell the significance of the following:

"The Great Marianas Turkey Shoot"

Pelelieu Islands

Battle of Leyte Gulf

Kamikaze planes

Essay: Answer the following essay:

Discuss the U.S. invasion of the Philippines. Why was it so successful?